JEWISH ALLEGORY IN EIGHTEENTH-CENTURY CHRISTIAN IMAGINATION

BIBLE AND ITS RECEPTION

Robert Paul Seesengood, General Editor

Editorial Board:
Lisa Bowens
Stephen R. Burge
Siobhan Dowling Long
J. Cheryl Exum
Michael Rosenberg

Number 7

JEWISH ALLEGORY IN EIGHTEENTH-CENTURY CHRISTIAN IMAGINATION

Rebecca K. Esterson

Atlanta

Copyright © 2023 by Rebecca K. Esterson

All rights reserved. No part of this work may be reproduced or transmitted in any form or by any means, electronic or mechanical, including photocopying and recording, or by means of any information storage or retrieval system, except as may be expressly permitted by the 1976 Copyright Act or in writing from the publisher. Requests for permission should be addressed in writing to the Rights and Permissions Office, SBL Press, 825 Houston Mill Road, Atlanta, GA 30329 USA.

Library of Congress Control Number: 2023946504

For Raphael, ben Aharon

Contents

Preface...ix

Acknowledgments... xiii

Abbreviations..xv

Introduction 1

1. Enlightened Contradictions: An English Context............................21

2. Allegory and Conversion: Johan Kemper's Christian Kabbalah 47

3. Unmasking Plurality: Moses Mendelssohn on
   Language and Religion 71

4. Kant and Swedenborg: Anti-Judaism and
   Interpretation at the Borders of Metaphysics 97

5. Poetry and Prejudice: William Blake's Allegoric God.....................131

Conclusion 157

Bibliography...165

Ancient Sources Index..179

Modern Authors Index..181

Subject Index...182

PREFACE

White man, hear me! History, as nearly no one seems to know, is not merely something to read. And it does not refer merely, or even principally, to the past. On the contrary, the great force of history comes from the fact that we carry it within us, are unconsciously controlled by it in many ways, and history is literally *present* in all that we do. It could scarcely be otherwise, since it is to history that we owe our frames of reference, our identities, and our aspirations. And it is with great pain and terror that one begins to realize this. In great pain and terror one begins to assess the history which has placed one where one is, and formed one's point of view. In great pain and terror because, thereafter, one enters into battle with that historical creation, Oneself, and attempts to recreate oneself according to a principle more humane and more liberating.

James Baldwin, "The White Man's Guilt"[1]

My journey with this material began as a series of revelations regarding my own tradition as I encountered the history of Christian Hebraism in graduate school. I was raised and continue to identify as a Swedenborgian Christian. Through an immersive religious education from kindergarten through high school, I was absorbed in a world that understood the Bible to have essentially two kinds of meaning: an internal sense and an external sense. In my world, each of the characters in the Bible as well as the places, numbers, colors, building measurements, and materials had second meanings. I knew each of these things as part of an interconnected and dynamic spiritual world that reflected the cosmos as well as dimensions and characteristics of my own soul. I was Esau and Jacob. I was Mary and Martha. I was Israel and Egypt. Reading this way was, and continues to be, a method of interpreting my whole self in the light of the narratives and poetry of sacred texts. I did not know growing up that Christians and Jews have read the Bible in similar ways since ancient times, believing instead that this

---

1. James Baldwin, "The White Man's Guilt," *Ebony Magazine*, August 1965, 47.

spiritual sense of scripture was realized only in recent history. Nor did I understand that Swedenborg's troubling framing of this approach, which relied on his characterization of the Jews as limited to the external sense of scripture, had its roots in the exegetical formulas of the church fathers. Learning the political and social origins of this idea and then tracing it through the works of medieval and Reformation theologians helped me to identify and confront a troubling thread in my spiritual lineage. I found myself drawn to the work of those in other denominations, such as the Evangelical Lutheran Church of North America, who are also wresting with this heritage and inspire notions of interreligious exchange grounded in moral integrity and honesty about the whole truth of our traditions.[2]

It was sometime around 5:00 a.m. in Jerusalem during the holiday of Shavuot, having been invited to an all-night study session blessed by the teaching of Dr. Avivah Zornberg, that the full weight of the tragedy of my inherited way of thinking about Jewish exegesis hit me. How could I have been so ignorant regarding the skillful weaving and layering of rabbinic methods, the "murmuring deep" of Jewish textuality? Where did the idea of Jewish externality come from, and how could it have survived so long given its patent falsity? These questions motivated my subsequent preoccupation with the history of Christian discourses about Jews, Judaism, and the Old Testament and continue to be a driving force in my teaching and research. My discomfort and curiosity about this history has only intensified since these early epiphanies.

It was during my journey with this material that I began to notice curious instances of ideas about Jewish allegory that appeared in the eighteenth century in precisely Swedenborg's time period. As soon as I had mastered the ancient sources of Swedenborg's characterization of Jews as literalists, I was confronted with confounding instances from his contemporaries that seemed to present the opposite, celebrating Christian literalism and characterizing Jews as allegorists. I am not the first to notice these instances. David Ruderman's *Connecting the Covenants: Judaism and the Search for Christian Identity in Eighteenth-Century England* helped shape my thoughts about this puzzling trend. The absence of a sustained study of the phenomenon spurred my reading of diverse sources from this period, which I eventually organized around the five chapters presented here.

---

2. See, for instance "A Declaration of the Evangelical Lutheran Church in America to the Jewish Community," April 18, 1994, https://tinyurl.com/SBLPress6706c1.

PREFACE   xi

The final stages of writing this book came amid a global pandemic and a national racial reckoning. As they did for so many others, these events triggered a period of personal introspection. As a result, the reality of my *self* as a historical creation seems more urgently connected to my academic study of history. For all these reasons this book is undeniably personal, even though it has been written according to the conventions of our academic forebearers, who believed history could be removed from the biases of its narrators. I am also aware that by uncovering and presenting the anti-Jewish perspectives of my subjects I risk giving them a voice. I am grateful to colleagues and friends who have engaged me in wrestling with the urgent methodological questions raised by these issues and who have helped me discern a path forward that walks the line between describing the past and evaluating it. That this history comes to you from a second-naïveté Swedenborgian may be ironic or it may be irrelevant. My hope is that it contributes a perspective that understands the weight of the discourses of the past on constructions of religious identity today.

ACKNOWLEDGMENTS

Early inspiration for this project sprang in part from my mentorship with the faculty in the Department of Religion at Boston University, including Deeana Klepper, Michael Zank, and Diana Lobel. I will be forever grateful for their driving questions and guidance as I engaged the varied and troubled histories of Jewish-Christian relations.

More recent stages of this project are indebted to collegial discussion partners and draft readers, including Jim Lawrence, Devin Zuber, Kathryn Barush, Sam Shonkoff, and Marcy Latta. The faculty of the Graduate Theological Union, and particularly those at the Center for Swedenborgian Studies and the Center for Jewish Studies, have been invaluable in supporting a climate of intellectual curiosity and integrity regarding the ways we investigate and communicate historical data. I am grateful to be able to do my work in such a climate.

The library staff at the Graduate Theological Union have been especially valuable in helping me access primary source material during a global pandemic when more usual avenues of access were barred. I am grateful to Colyn Wohlmut, Beth Kumar, Kathy Farrell and the rest of the GTU library staff for going out of their way to ensure my research could continue unimpeded.

Finally, I am grateful to my life partner, who is also my study partner. Rafi Esterson navigated all the impossibilities of pandemic parenting with me as I struggled to structure a sabbatical book project in apocalyptic conditions. Rafi has also been my *chevruta*, sitting at my side, head bowed over primary texts, puzzling over intertextual allusions and translation conundrums. This could not have happened without you.

Abbreviations

b.	Babylonian Talmud
Dial.	Justin Martyr, *Dialogus cum Tryphone*
Gen. Rab.	Genesis Rabbah
HTR	*Harvard Theological Review*
JBRec	*Journal of the Bible and Its Reception*
JECS	*Journal of Early Christian Studies*
JQR	*Jewish Quarterly Review*
JR	*Journal of Religion*
JSQ	*Jewish Studies Quarterly*
Sanh.	Sanhedrin

INTRODUCTION

This book explores the surprising rhetorical connection made between Jews and biblical allegory by key figures of the eighteenth century. It is surprising because from the time of the church fathers in the early centuries of the Common Era, there had been an established rhetorical connection in Christian exegetical discourses between Jews and the literal sense of scripture. This is not a book about what allegory is in any essential or universal sense, nor is it a book about what Judaism is or how Jews fundamentally read and interpret scripture. Rather, it is a book about how the eighteenth-century ambivalence toward biblical allegory merged with an existing ambivalence toward Jews and Judaism to produce novel conceptions regarding the allegories of the Jews. It will consider how this construct functioned in an age fixated on reason and mathematical certainty, despite the perplexing contradictions on display where it appeared. The success of the trope of Jewish allegory was due to its value in addressing anxieties about the Bible, Christianity, science, and reason that materialized in this age.[1]

The eighteenth century witnessed attacks on the accuracy and reasonableness of biblical religion from a variety of disciplines and discourses, including textual criticism, the sciences of physics and natural history, and the growing freethought of deists who challenged traditional sources of religious authority in unprecedented ways. As they had done so often in the past, many Christian scholars responded by looking to Jewish sources and Hebrew study for answers and tools that could be applied to interpretive challenges. However, we find in the early modern period a twist in the plot. While Christian theologians had long made discursive associations between Jews and the literal sense of the Bible, now they linked Jews and allegory. In this era, Christianity would be heralded for its understanding of history, grammar, and literalism while Judaism would be seen as aligned

---

1. A version of this thesis appears in Rebecca Esterson, "Allegory and Religious Pluralism: Biblical Interpretation in the Eighteenth Century," *JBRec* 5 (2018): 111–39.

-1-

2   JEWISH ALLEGORY IN EIGHTEENTH-CENTURY CHRISTIAN IMAGINATION

with mystical interpretations and hidden meanings. This significant shift in the discourse is worthy of our attention for its implications regarding the reception history of the Bible. Its effects are visible not only in formal biblical commentary but also in the public discourse and in philosophical, literary, and artistic strata as well.

Christian allegorical interpretation of the Bible had relied on narratives about the nature of Jewish texts and Jewish interpretations since its first instance in Paul's Epistle to the Galatians (4:21–5:26). Paul's interpretation of the Genesis matriarchs Sarah and Hagar, which contrasts slavery, the law, and the flesh on one hand with freedom from the law and the power of the spirit on the other, set the tone for Christian discourses about the Bible and about Jews for the ages. The explicit connection between Hagar the slave and Judaism would come in the third century with the commentaries of Origen, who divided biblical meaning between a Jewish literal sense and a Christian allegorical sense. With the emergence of Jerome's Latin translation and commentaries on the Bible in the late fourth century, Jews were further characterized as slaves to *carnaliter interpretari*. Jerome's heavy reliance on Jewish interlocutors in Palestine for the contextual meaning of scripture came at a time when accusations of Judaizing were rampant, and he sought a hermeneutical partition between his interpretation and that of his Jewish sources. It was an anxiety of influence that would haunt the Christian exegetical tradition going forward. Both Jerome and his enormously influential contemporary, Augustine of Hippo, advanced the notion of split levels of meaning in the Bible: the Jewish literal sense and the Christian spiritual sense. The success of this characterization of Jewish and Christian interpretive abilities can be traced in the work of countless medieval Christian Bible specialists and persisted in the thought of reformers such as Martin Luther in the sixteenth century. Even where Christian scholars exhibited heightened interest in the literal sense, as tended to be the case especially among Hebraists, a distinction between Christian depth of meaning and Jewish carnality was strongly pushed, such as in George of Sienna's claim that "the Jews understand and explain the sayings of the prophets and all of Scripture carnally but we Catholics draw back to the spirit … and therefore in all of the prophecies which may be understood literally about Christ, they see in those same passages only a carnal sense."[2] Constructions concern-

---

2. As quoted in Deeana Copeland Klepper, "Literal versus Carnal: George of Siena's Christian Reading of Jewish Exegesis," in *Jewish Biblical Interpretation and*

INTRODUCTION 3

ing Jewish externality were employed throughout history where a contrast with Christian interpretation was emphasized. The trope became entangled with Christian self-identity and claims of doctrinal authority and occupied a central place in Christian definitions of Judaism as a carnal, worldly, and spiritually deficient tradition. As author Megan Hale Williams writes of this legacy, Jerome's work "contributed greatly to the emergence of a new Christian discourse of the Jew, and to its persistence in the Latin West for at least a millennium."[3] While the trope of Jewish literalism persisted in certain veins of Christian discourse, and persists even today, we can trace its reversal at key moments in early modernity, especially where Christian literalism was on the rise in the guise of reasonableness, common sense, and scientific discovery. This time, rabbinic understanding was marked as nonliteral and allegorical rather than as merely carnal.

The very idea of Jewish allegory, a remarkable reversal of the scheme that had been ubiquitous in premodern Christian thought, had its roots in seventeenth-century Christian discourse about the extrabiblical books of the Jews, especially the Talmud and sources of kabbalah. Scholars at this time debated the value of these sources and their relationship to the New Testament writings, especially regarding the Jewishness of the parables and other rhetorical conventions on display in the words of Jesus and his followers. Out of an interest in Jewish storytelling, then, a debate emerged regarding whether or not the Talmud's stories were allegorical. In the preface to his father's 1639 *Lexicon chaldaicum, talmudicum et rabbinicum*, for instance, Johannes Buxtorf the younger made the case that the Talmud was full of allegories:

> It contains many sound theological observations, although enveloped in the useless shells of allegory; it contains the faithful ruins and vestiges [*rudera et vestigia*] of a collapsed Hebrew antiquity that contribute to confuting the infidelity [*perfidia*] of the Jews in later times, to illustrating the history of the Old Testament, and to elucidating rituals, laws, and customs among the ancient Jews.[4]

Cultural Exchange: Comparative Exegesis in Context, ed. Natalie Dormann and David Stern (Philadelphia: University of Pennsylvania Press, 2008), 206.

3. Megan Hale Williams, "Lessons from Jerome's Jewish Teachers: Exegesis and Cultural Interaction in Late Antique Palestine," in Dormann and Stern, *Jewish Biblical Interpretation*, 77.

4. Johann Buxtorf, *Lexicon chaldaicum, talmudicum et rabbinicum* (Basel: König, 1639), 3. As translated in Josef Eskhult, "Andreas Norrelius' Latin translation of Johan

4   JEWISH ALLEGORY IN EIGHTEENTH-CENTURY CHRISTIAN IMAGINATION

Other seventeenth-century scholars made similar claims, such as Wilhelm Schickard's suggestion that the Jews had forgotten the meaning of the Talmud's allegories, and Johannes Leusden's comparison between the allegories of the Talmud to those of Ovid's *Metamorphoses*.[5] We find evidence of these ideas in secular literature of the time as well. Margaret Cavendish's 1666 work of proto–science fiction, *The Blazing World*, depicts a fanciful alien planet, whose new empress is inspired by the "Jews Cabbala" and the mystical way of interpreting scripture in the Jewish religion on Earth. She takes the advice of her wise Duchess to create her own "Romancical Cabbala, wherein you may use Metaphors, Allegories, Similitudes, &c. and interpret them as you please."[6] These ideas concerning the allegorical books of the Jews expanded in the late seventeenth century and early eighteenth century beyond notions about the Talmud and kabbalah to include ideas about Jewish biblical exegesis more broadly.

This new way of characterizing Jewish interpretation was often derisive, as in Robert Hooke's words distancing his work in microscopy from the perceived obsession with biblical minutiae on the part of rabbis: "*Rabbins* find out *Caballisms*, and *Enigmas* in the figure, and placing of Letters, where no such thing lies hid; whereas in *Natural* forms there are some so small, and so curious, and their design'd business so far removed from the reach of our sight, that the more we do magnify the object, the more excellencies and mysteries do appear."[7] John Toland's accusation against allegorists rang a similar tone in his *Christianity Not Mysterious*: "Everyone knows how the primitive Christians, in a ridiculous imitation of the Jews, they turn'd all the Scripture into Allegory."[8] Toland's assessment of early Christian allegory as an imitation of Jewish interpretation would be repeated by those in the following generations who required a negative foil in defending their reading of scripture. Ironically, early Christian accusations of Jews as literalists had served a similar purpose.

Kemper's Hebrew Commentary on Matthew: Edited with Introduction and Philological Commentary" (PhD diss., Uppsala University, 2007), 20–21.

5. For a discussion of these and other examples of seventeenth-century Christian ideas about the allegories in the Talmud, see Eskhult, "Andreas Norrelius' Latin," 18–28.

6. Margaret Cavendish, *The Blazing World*, ed. Sylvia Bowerbank and Sara Mendelson (Peterborough, Ont.: Broadview, 2000), 210.

7. From Robert Hooke, *Micrographia: Or Some Physiological Descriptions of Minute Bodies Made by Magnifying Glasses* (London: Martyn & Allestry, 1665), 8.

8. John Toland, *Christianity Not Mysterious* (London: Buckley, 1696), 115.

INTRODUCTION   5

Positive associations between Jews and allegory were also made. Christian thinkers sometimes exploited Jewish sources out of a perception that they contained an interpretive depth unmatched in Christian commentaries. Many learned experts believed the mystical books of the Jews, especially the texts of the Zohar, contained ancient wisdom from distant lands, supposing them to be much older than today's historians believe them to be.[9] Some even believed Jewish exegesis to be the foundation upon which the gospels were written, such that the English orientalist and Mishnah enthusiast, Simon Ockley, concluded: "If I had ever had an Opportunity, I wou'd most certainly have gone thro' the New Testament under a Jew ... that they understand it infinitely better than we do."[10] Thus, while Jewish interpretation was derided by some for its association with allegory, it was appropriated by others precisely for its connection to hidden depths of meaning, revealing a tension within the intellectual culture of eighteenth-century Christendom.

Recent scholarship has contributed to our understanding of post-Reformation approaches to the Bible and early modern Jewish-Christian relations in a number of ways. Michael Legaspi, Christopher Ocker, and Jonathan Sheehan, for instance, explore the academic and cultural recentering of biblical studies in European universities and other centers of learning.[11] This turn to reading the Bible as cultural heritage or as part

---

9. Belief in the early dating of the Zohar persisted into the eighteenth and nineteenth centuries, especially in Christian kabbalistic circles, where it was believed to be part of an ancient wisdom predating the New Testament. Guy Stroumsa (*A New Science: The Discovery of Religion in the Age of Reason* [Cambridge: Harvard University Press, 2010], 41) argues that the eighteenth-century fascination with ancient cultures came hand in hand with a fascination with foreign cultures and notes that the texts, practices, and history of the Jews, as "foreigners within," became the locus of decoding for Christian intellectuals. There were also challenges to the early dating of the Zohar, for instance, in the work of Venetian rabbi Leon Modena. See Yaacob Dwek, *The Scandal of Kabbalah* (Princeton: Princeton University Press, 2011).

10. Simon Ockley, "Letter to William Wotton," quoted in the Postscript to the Preface in William Wotton, *Miscellaneous Discourses Relating to the Traditions and the Usages of the Scribes and Pharisees in Our Blessed Savior Jesus Christ's Time* (London: Bowyer, 1718).

11. Michael Legaspi traces the work of eighteenth-century academics, such as Johann David Michaelis, who consign biblical studies to the humanities and read the Bible as classical poetry, thereby making Moses the Homer of classical Israel. See Michael C. Legaspi, *The Death of Scripture and the Rise of Biblical Studies* (Oxford: Oxford University Press, 2010). Jonathan Sheehan argues that the rise of the "cultural

6   JEWISH ALLEGORY IN EIGHTEENTH-CENTURY CHRISTIAN IMAGINATION

of the emerging humanities arose alongside the scientific revolution. Stephen Burnett, for his part, describes the Reformation-era removal of Jews and Judaism from Hebrew learning and translation in Christian circles.[12] Naomi Seidman points to this removal as a source of conflicting notions regarding translation and conversion.[13] And Adam Sutcliffe argues that despite this attempted divorce from things Jewish, a deep-seated and sweeping ambivalence persisted. Sutcliffe writes: "Throughout the Enlightenment the question of the status of Judaism and of Jews was a key site of intellectual contestation, confusion, and debate."[14] This ambivalence manifested both among those that challenged traditional Christian interpretations of the Bible and among those that defended them. Judaism was never absent from the discourse. "Judaic themes were invoked with equal intensity across the entire spectrum of the Enlightenment."[15] Against the backdrop of this scholarship, this book argues that rather than witnessing the final demise of allegory, as some would have it, the eighteenth century saw a discourse emerge about allegorical exegesis that was itself one of these key sites of radical ambivalence concerning Jews and Judaism.

The Myth of Allegory's Demise

Did biblical literalism rise triumphantly alongside modernity and the scientific revolution? Many eighteenth-century figures certainly thought this

---

Bible" in England and Germany was not motivated by secular impulses but rather utilized a sophisticated set of instruments inspired by confessional contexts. See Jonathan Sheehan, *The Enlightenment Bible: Translation, Scholarship, Culture* (Princeton: Princeton University Press, 2005). Christopher Ocker, for his part, demonstrates continuities between late medieval and early modern interest the grammatical and rhetorical elements of biblical texts. The collapse of the literal and spiritual senses that began in the Middle Ages informs the interest in biblical poetics that develops in the centuries following, and demonstrates a corresponding collapse of human and divine authorship. See Christopher Ocker, *Biblical Poetics before Humanism and Reformation* (Cambridge: Cambridge University Press, 2002).

12. Stephen G. Burnett, *Christian Hebraism in the Reformation Era (1500–1660): Authors, Books, and the Transmission of Jewish Learning* (Leiden: Brill, 2012).

13. Naomi Seidman, *Faithful Renderings: Jewish-Christian Difference and the Politics of Translation* (Chicago: University of Chicago Press, 2006), 115–52.

14. Adam Sutcliffe, *Judaism and Enlightenment* (Cambridge: Cambridge University Press, 2003), 5.

15. Sutcliffe, *Judaism and Enlightenment*, 14.

INTRODUCTION

was the case. Cambridge mathematician William Whiston, for instance, argued that the Bible should be read literally rather than according to its "parabolic sense" and used an array of scientific and text-critical tools to make his case. Taking his thesis to its logical extreme, he proposed that even the six days of creation and the Old Testament prophecies should be understood according to their literal sense alone. This was a bold move on both accounts as the natural sciences of the day presented serious challenges to the creation story, and even the most ardent Christian literalists who came before him still held fast to a double meaning to the prophets.[16] Whiston persisted, nevertheless, and argued that a proper understanding of the effects of comets explains the events described in Genesis 1 and that a thorough study of Bible manuscript versions would reveal original prophetic texts that were far more straightforward than had yet been realized. Traditional Christian reliance on more than one sense of scripture, he concluded, should be altogether abandoned along with other patristic perversions.[17] Whiston was an extreme example of the kind of preference for the literal sense that arose at this time, but the rhetoric of literalism pervaded more popular and devotional settings as well, where we find evidence of the belief in God's straightforward revelation through the simple words on the page. This sentiment is reflected in the popular 1773 hymn by William Cowper, "God Moves in a Mysterious Way," which proclaims: "God is His own interpreter, And He will make it plain." The verse reveals the early modern conviction, especially prominent in Protestant circles but also present in Catholicism, that the true meaning of scripture is made apparent to any faithful reader in the plain sense of the text.

This view of the demise of allegorical interpretation in the eighteenth century is backed by some contemporary historians. In his book *The Bible, Protestantism and the Rise of Natural Science*, Peter Harrison points to the Protestant Reformation and its antiauthoritarian turn to *sola scriptura* as the impetus not only for the hermeneutical preference for the plain sense

---

16. For instance, see Deeana Klepper's discussion of Nicholas of Lyra's "double literal sense" and quodlibetal questions concerning the prophets in *The Insight of Unbelievers: Nicholas of Lyra and Christian Reading of Jewish Text in the Later Middle Ages* (Philadelphia: University of Pennsylvania Press, 2007), 32–36, 82–108.

17. Whiston, like his teacher Isaac Newton, rejected the doctrine of the Trinity, viewing it as patristic innovation. This was part of a post-Reformation wave of enthusiasm for the earliest forms of Christian doctrine, forms believed to have not yet been corrupted by creeds and councils.

8   JEWISH ALLEGORY IN EIGHTEENTH-CENTURY CHRISTIAN IMAGINATION

but for the scientific revolution itself.[18] Harrison points to a new kind of natural history, for instance, in the work of John Ray, one that represented an unprecedented, secular approach to the subject. While in the medieval world of Hugh of St. Victor the book of nature and the book of scripture corresponded at every point, Ray presented his classifications of plants without reference to "Hieroglyphics, Emblems, Morals, Fables, Presages."[19] A singular focus on the plants themselves was all that was necessary; whatever relation they bore to other realities remained the work for another author. This separation of the study of nature from the study of the Bible was a critical moment in the demise of allegory. Harrison writes: "The new conception of the order of nature was made possible by the collapse of the allegorical interpretation of texts, for the denial of the legitimacy of allegory is in essence a denial of the capacity of things to act as signs."[20] Thereafter, according to this argument, the Bible, along with nature, lost something of its symbolic potential as it gained a perceived immediacy and certainty of meaning.

Hans Frei makes a similar argument in his seminal work *The Eclipse of Biblical Narrative*. He writes: "Despite the influence of Pietism, the fate of 'spiritual' reading and thus of double meaning in the interpretation of scripture in the later eighteenth century was finally as dim as that of the principle of interpretation through tradition, evaporating the remnants of whatever mystical-allegorical reading on the part of Protestants had survived the seventeenth century."[21] In this period, he argues, we find a double iconoclasm. Not only did the typological and spiritual reading of the Bible evaporate, but the realistic reading did as well. In particular, the creation stories of Genesis and the miracle stories of the gospels came under scrutiny. As scientists called into question these supernatural biblical claims, the text was placed under the critical eye of German positivism and English deism. Scholars turned their attention to a safer form of literal interpretation: philological and historical literalism. Linguists, having inherited the venerable tradition of Christian Hebraism, doubled down

---

18. Peter Harrison, *The Bible, Protestantism, and the Rise of Natural Science* (Cambridge: Cambridge University Press, 1998), 8.

19. From John Ray's preface to *The Ornithology of Francis Willughby*, as quoted in Harrison, *Bible*, 2.

20. Harrison, *Bible*, 4.

21. Hans Frei, *The Eclipse of Biblical Narrative: A Study in Eighteenth and Nineteenth Century Hermeneutics* (New Haven: Yale University Press, 1974), 55.

INTRODUCTION

their efforts to study the text objectively, identifying multiple sources and conflicting manuscripts. These methods allowed readers of the Bible to engage on terms familiar to the sciences: the inspection of artifacts and the testing of theories. Allegorical interpretation came to be seen as naive and simplistic in the face of a new epistemology that sought mathematical certainty and mechanistic order.

Such a view of the plight of allegory in the eighteenth century, however, betrays a certain selectivity on the part of both Harrison and Frei, in terms of whose interpretations speak for the age. Indeed, there is a great deal of evidence to suggest more continuity with premodern interpretive strategies than this narrative allows. The rhetoric of the rise of literalism that we find so prevalent in both the eighteenth century as well as contemporary scholarly descriptions of this period is countered by evidence of significant interpretive threads that understood the Bible to be saying *something else* (*allos agoria*). The present study will demonstrate that allegory did not die with the Enlightenment but took on different forms and responded to different questions. By recategorizing biblical allegory as Jewish, Christian interpreters imagined there to be some distance between allegory and their native way of reading. Allegory came to be viewed as an ancient and foreign mode of exegesis, which could be marginalized or appropriated as needed.

In his conclusion, Harrison points to the Achilles heel of his argument. The stubborn persistence of Neoplatonism in the form of kabbalah, the Great Chain of Being, alchemy, and the like is detectible in the work of many natural philosophers from the early modern period, including Isaac Newton, Robert Fludd, Robert Boyle, and others. Rather than view this trend as "an unconscious reluctance to admit the failure of the old world picture," as Harrison does, I view it as evidence that symbolic or allegorical thinking was not absent after the Reformation.[22] Allegorical biblical exegesis, while certainly no less fraught than it had been in the past, survived the Reformation and the scientific revolution and impacted various cultural, philosophical, and religious milieux where the symbolic potential of language, art, and even the human psyche would be explored and exploited well into modernity. The current study demonstrates the persistence of biblical allegory in eighteenth-century Christian thought and its entanglement with the figured discourse of Jewish and Christian religious identity.

---

22. Quote from Harrison, *Bible*, 271.

10   JEWISH ALLEGORY IN EIGHTEENTH-CENTURY CHRISTIAN IMAGINATION

Allegory Allegations

It may, at first, seem unwise to showcase allegory in a historical study of a century that was decidedly turned off by the term. Many of the figures who will be featured here reveal a semantic preference for "representations," "signs," "emblems," and "symbols" in their interpretive work, and allegory is often enough associated with "enthusiasm," "mysticism," or other heresies of the day. Such ambivalence results from, as Jon Whitman puts it, "the polemic against speaking 'otherwise' that had developed from the late Middle Ages and the Reformation to the Romantic period."[23] Yet it is precisely this troubled framing of allegory that draws our attention to it. For despite their ambivalence toward allegory and their well-formulated distinctions between, for instance, allegory and symbol, many eighteenth-century figures produced interpretations of the Bible—be they theological, philosophical, or poetic—that belied such distinctions.

The ambivalence about allegory itself has deep roots in biblical traditions. Often, the use of the term allegory has been pejorative, either disparaging the methods of some other interpreter, such as Jerome distinguishing his work from "that allegorist" Origen, or pointing to the temptation in one's self to distort the text, as in Martin Luther's warning that allegory is "a beautiful harlot who fondles men in such a way that it is impossible for her not to be loved."[24] In either case, when used pejoratively the accusation usually claims the allegorist left behind the plain sense of scripture and replaced it with something of their own, rendering God's word disposable or, even worse, making God a liar. Thus, allegory is frequently used as a foil to mark the preferred interpretation as distinctly loyal to the original text.

When used pejoratively, allegory tends to be distinguished from some other, preferred form of nonliteral exegesis. Often it has been contrasted with symbolism, as in Samuel Taylor Coleridge's assertion that the Bible, rather than merely allegorical, is "the most perfect specimen of symbolic poetry."[25] William Blake differentiated allegory from vision, the latter

---

23. Jon Whitman, *Interpretation and Allegory: Antiquity to the Modern Period* (Leiden: Brill, 2000), 20.

24. Regarding Origen, see Dennis Brown, *Vir Trilinguis: A Study in the Biblical Exegesis of Saint Jerome* (Kampen: Kok, 1992), 163. Quote of Martin Luther from *Commentary on Genesis* 30:9–11, as quoted in Whitman, *Interpretation and Allegory*, 3.

25. Samuel Taylor Coleridge, *On the Constitution of the Church and State*, ed. John Colmer (London: Routledge, 1976), 139. On the distinction between allegory

INTRODUCTION   11

again representing the superior, biblical mode. In more recent times allegory has been contrasted with typology with the view that typology is rooted in the history in ways that allegory is not. The list of interpreters to make this distinction, a long and venerable one, includes Jean-Guenolé-Marie Daniélou, Eric Auerbach, Hans Frei, and Northrop Frye. This has resulted in something of a consensus view that allegory and typology are rival siblings, one ultimately victorious over the other. Allegory is the foreign intruder sent to replace and deceive, while typology honors and fulfills the promise of the literal sense. We find, however, that these efforts to distinguish between better and worse forms of nonliteral interpretation are often either applied inconsistently or oversimplify their opponent's approach.[26] And, in retrospect, they often expose a political tension rather than an interpretive one. Rather than asking what form of interpretation is being rejected, therefore, it is better to ask the question: *whose* interpretation is being rejected? Who stands in for allegory when allegory's demise is celebrated in favor of some other technique?

Whitman writes that during the early iterations of allegory in Greek and Roman antiquity there was less of a concern for the historicity of the signifying events. In this context allegory "indicates primarily a transfer from one word or concept to another. Something is said (*agoreuein*), and something else (*allos*) is signified."[27] Greek allegorists, he argues, were motivated by the search for an underlying logic (*logos*) in the passages of the story (*mythos*).[28] However, Jewish and Christian appropriations of allegory, beginning around the turn of the first centuries BCE and CE, generally affirmed the veracity of the original meaning of the text. This was done differently by different communities. Whitman's edited volume

---

and symbolism, see Samuel Taylor Coleridge, "The Statesman's Manual," in *Complete Works: With an Introductory Essay upon His Philosophical and Theological Opinions*, ed. W. G. T. Shedd (New York: Harper & Brothers, 1853), 437.

26. For the former, see Peter W. Martens, "Revisiting the Allegory/Typology Distinction: The Case of Origen," *JECS* 16.3 (2008): 283–317. Regarding the later, John David Dawson traces this to Quintilianus and his distinction between trope and figure in *Christian Figural Reading and the Fashioning of Identity* (Berkeley: University of California Press, 2002), 14. Martens argues that Dawson himself succumbs to the pitfalls in distinguishing between allegory and typology in his reframing of the distinction in terms of "figural" and "figurative." See Martens, "Revisiting," 292.

27. Jon Whitman, "From the Textual to the Temporal: Early Christian 'Allegory' and Early Romantic 'Symbol,'" *New Literary History* 22.1 (1991): 162.

28. Whitman, *Interpretation and Allegory*, 35–37.

12   JEWISH ALLEGORY IN EIGHTEENTH-CENTURY CHRISTIAN IMAGINATION

on the subject demonstrates, for instance, how Alexandrian Jews emphasized the performative elements or the behavioral context suggested by the linguistic context of scripture. The midrashic tradition isolated and elaborated on verses or words of scripture not to expose or impose meaning but as a kind of "interposition between the words of scripture."[29] Paul's use of the term *allegory* in Galatians in the first century CE drew connections between earlier events and later events, neither rejecting nor dismissing the historicity of the former.[30] These and other Jewish and Christian ways of characterizing and reading texts relied on a preserved connection to an original canon and an original community. That is not to say that Jews and Christians have uniformly affirmed the truth of biblical accounts: they have not. But it highlights the difficulty in defining allegory according to what is rejected or taken away rather than by what is added. It is precisely this perceived connection to the actual people and events of the Bible that has produced pejorative uses of the term allegory, which display an anxiety about losing this connection. Many forms of biblical interpretation deemed allegorical, however, still maintain the truth of the original account in its most obvious sense.

This project broadly understands allegory to be the "capacity of things to act as signs," as Peter Harrison puts it, without qualification regarding the integrity of the things (sacred texts in this instance) themselves.[31] Put another way, an allegorical interpretation views a text as having more than one meaning. Rather than determining the precise contours of a definition of allegory, however, this book will analyze how the term is used discursively to define the religious identity of self and other. A study of allegory in the long eighteenth century requires us to investigate figures who distance their own methods from allegory, begging the question of how and why they did so. As Whitman notes, allegory shouldn't be thought of as a single "kind" of interpretation, but a "series of critical negotiations" between a text and its readers.[32] And it is allegory's troubled past that is precisely what allows us a pathway into anxieties about text, history, and religious identity.

In the last half-century, literary critics and philosophers have reversed the Romantic distinction between allegory and symbol and have effectively

---

29. Whitman, *Interpretation and Allegory*, 41.
30. Whitman, "From the Textual," 162–64.
31. Harrison, *Bible*, 4.
32. Whitman, *Interpretation and Allegory*, 5.

INTRODUCTION   13

"rehabilitated allegory" as a category for understanding hermeneutics, pointing to the subjectivity of signs and the figured nature of language more broadly.[33] Scholars have also challenged the notion that allegory springs from an essentially Greek or Western heritage. For instance, in his study of allegoresis in Chinese poetry Zhang Longxi rejects misconceptions of Chinese literature as radically monistic, literal, natural, and impersonal.[34] The present study will build on this scholarly attention to the persistence of allegory not in an attempt to demonstrate that *all* interpretation is allegory but to argue that the political, social and religious utility of allegory explains its presence in even those environments supposedly hostile to it.[35] Allegory ensures a certain flexibility in a textual tradition by allowing connections to contexts foreign to that of the text's origins. By seeking out and uncovering a hidden meaning, the reader is able to either hold on to something they are in danger of losing or introduce innovation into a community that would be otherwise suspicious. As Moshe Idel writes of kabbalah, allegory brings to life "a whole literary universe, mostly a biblical one, compounded of dead persons, destroyed cities [and] shattered temples."[36] Early modern readers of the Bible were no less concerned with the question of the relevance of biblical places and characters than their ancestors were, and they employed a familiar range of hermeneutical methods in their interpretations, even if their discourse about these methods bears the markings of their political itineraries. The

---

33. See, for instance, Whitman, *Interpretation and Allegory*, 15–20, and part 2, "The Late Middle Ages to the Modern Period" with notable contributions from Azade Seyhan, Rainer Nägele, and Tobin Siebers. See also Susanne Knaller, "A Theory of Allegory Beyond Walter Benjamin and Paul de Man," *The Germanic Review* 77 (2002): 83–101. Knaller uses the phrase "rehabilitation of allegory" in reference to the work of Walter Benjamin. Gadamer also uses the phrase in discussing the direction of aesthetics and hermeneutics; Hans-Georg Gadamer, *Truth and Method*, trans. Joel Weinsheimer and Donald G. Marshall (New York: Continuum, 2004), 79–81.

34. Zhang argues for a likeness between traditional Chinese interpretations of the Confucian *Shi jing* and Jewish and Christian interpretations of *The Song of Songs*. See Zhang Longxi, *Allegoresis: Reading Canonical Literature East and West* (Ithaca, NY: Cornell University Press, 2005).

35. See Whitman's summary of this position, most famously articulated by Northrop Frye, in *Interpretation and Allegory*, 16–17.

36. Moshe Idel, "Kabbalistic Exegesis," in *Hebrew Bible/Old Testament: A History of Its Interpretation*, ed. Magne Saebø (Göttingen: Vandenhoeck & Ruprecht, 2000), 1.2:461.

14 JEWISH ALLEGORY IN EIGHTEENTH-CENTURY CHRISTIAN IMAGINATION

following chapters will examine five cases from diverse, though not disconnected, contexts that reveal various facets of this phenomenon.

Structure of the Book

The opening chapter presents a case study from England in which a heated and public intra-Christian debate about the allegories of the Jews would reveal sharply contrasting viewpoints. Some pointed to Jewish allegories as the source of confusion regarding the truth of scriptures, while others saw Jewish allegory as the key to rescuing revealed religion in an age of skepticism. The chapter begins with a noteworthy instance of Christian scientific literalism in the work of William Whiston. Successor to Isaac Newton as Lucasian Professor of Mathematics at Cambridge, Whiston believed that the application of scientific and historical discoveries to the study of the Bible would reveal a text that cohered perfectly "without any recourse to Typical, Foreign and Mystical Expositions."[37] He blamed any contradiction or confusion of meaning on Jewish manuscript corruption and the interference of Jewish allegorical methods of interpretation. Once these corruptions were exposed and resolved, Whiston believed God's plain and straightforward message to humanity would be revealed and the perfect harmony between science and Christian thought would resound. The self-described freethinker Anthony Collins would publish a lengthy rebuttal to Whiston and offer a reverse position on the usefulness of Jewish allegories. It was Collins's positive framing of rabbinic and kabbalistic exegesis in tones of whimsical irreverence toward his adversary that would trigger an explosive reaction and a decades-long public debate on the part of his readers. In surveying the published responses to Collins we find perplexing combinations of ideas regarding Jewish allegory, ideas whose contradictions stand out against the overarching appeal to enlightened rationality. Jewish allegory is successful as a trope, despite the open inconsistencies on display where it appears, because it appeals as a method for addressing deep concerns about the reasonableness of the Christian Bible in the age of Enlightenment.

---

37. William Whiston, *The Accomplishment of Scripture Prophecies: Being Eight Sermons Preach'd at the Cathedral Church of St. Paul in the Year MDCCVII* (Cambridge: Cambridge University Press, 1708), 13.

INTRODUCTION

15

Chapter 2 explores the assumed relationship between Jewish conversion and biblical allegory that characterized Christian eschatological and exegetical activity in the early eighteenth century. In particular, this era saw the rise of the study of kabbalah at centers of Protestant learning, where some believed it to be a key to the kind of *unfolding* or *revealing* of history and salvation that both conversion and proper biblical interpretation described. This chapter examines the work of the convert and Christian kabbalist Johan Kemper, who understood his own conversion to mirror the process of decoding the Bible's secrets. He believed his Jewish identity prefigured his Christian identity like the Old Testament prefigured the New. Kemper's Hebrew-language commentaries on the Zohar and the New Testament, produced while he was a lecturer at Uppsala University, demonstrate key ambivalences regarding Judaism as both foundational and adversarial to Christianity, ambivalences that also manifest in his autobiography. His efforts to simultaneously exploit and erase his own Jewishness will invoke an examination of the phenomenon known today as "philosemitism" that permeated spaces of higher learning in the eighteenth century, though the term itself will provide an opportunity to investigate the historicity at hand.

Kemper's case demonstrates that the narrative of literalism's rise in early modernity has misrepresented the significance of Christian kabbalah in this era. European universities of the time sought rabbinic and kabbalistic texts for their libraries and recruited converted Jews who could apply these sources to Christian teaching. Natural philosophers of the day were familiar with kabbalistic themes and incorporated them into their theories and models. Christian interest in rabbinic and kabbalistic sources increasingly related to ideas about the discovery of ancient wisdom, which could reveal the secrets of the universe and the secrets of the Bible simultaneously. Kemper's allegorical conversion embodied these expectations. It would be the mere fact of his conversion and the *idea* that his Christianized kabbalah held the key to interpreting the Bible, more than the actual content of his commentarial work, that would constitute his legacy at the Swedish university. The commentaries themselves were laden with hints and allusions to talmudic sources that went underappreciated or unnoticed by his Christian students and translators, and the manuscripts were never published.

Chapter 3 examines the work of the German Jewish philosopher Moses Mendelssohn, who, when pressed to give his reasons for not converting to Christianity, responded by disparaging Christian creedal

16 JEWISH ALLEGORY IN EIGHTEENTH-CENTURY CHRISTIAN IMAGINATION

formulas that limited language and text to a single, determined meaning. In surveying Mendelssohn's Hebrew-language Bible commentaries and his German-language philosophy, we find not only a defense of rabbinic hermeneutic modes that produce multivocal readings but also a subtle but steady critique of Christian literalism. Mendelssohn inhabited a complex set of social contexts and attempted to respond to the various intellectual and political realities of his diverse readership, both Jewish and Christian, orthodox and secular. His work countered certain stereotypes regarding Jews and Judaism with a theory of the Hebrew language and Jewish religious life that exhibited morality, rationality, flexibility, and spiritual vitality. He also repeated negative stereotypes regarding the opacity and moral impurity of the Yiddish language, demonstrating his own participation in the contradictions and paradoxes of the *Aufklärung*.

This third chapter also explores Mendelssohn's response to the Christian convention of interpreting the Bible and human religious history along parallel paths, or of believing the relationship between the two Testaments to be both typological and teleological in nature. This tradition tended to view Judaism as an early stage in the developmental progress of humanity and the Old Testament as a remnant of a primitive, authoritarian culture. Mendelssohn presented an alternative view of history as cyclical rather than linear and thereby characterized Judaism as a modern religion in its own right rather than an infantile stage in the development of humanity. The Old Testament was not, as his friend Gotthold Lessing described it, a primer for school children. His midrashic interpretations of Bible stories had much in common with Christian typology, but, he would insist, the moral development encoded in the Bible applies to the individual only and not humanity as a whole. Furthermore, a person's moral capacity is not determined by their location on the timeline of human progressive history. Such an arrangement would be the work of a cruel God. Thus, even Christian allegorizing in the form of typology is cast in Mendelssohn's light as rigidly determined rather than flexible and accommodating.

Mendelssohn's approach attempted to preserve the Bible's multiple layers of meaning and also insisted on the particularity of some of these layers for Jews. Jews understood very well their symbols, he argued, but the symbols themselves neither are universal nor can they be understood universally. His general theory that all language necessarily carries multiple meanings and requires interpretation allowed him to mine rabbinic commentaries for treasures of meaning that could connect Jewish readers to their tradition. His insistence on the particularity of biblical

INTRODUCTION   17

revelation also informed a vision for religious pluralism. If the text of the Bible could mean different things for different readers simultaneously, religiously diverse communities could live harmoniously in a single state. Mendelssohn thereby responded to ideas about Jewish allegorizing with a philosophy of language that recast rabbinic multivocality as theologically and politically nimble and recast Christian literalism as the brittle and dead letter.

Immanuel Kant was an early admirer of Mendelssohn's but ultimately distanced himself from Mendelssohn and openly rejected many of his ideas, including those about Judaism, language, and history that are relevant here. Chapter 4 considers these themes through Kant's ambivalent relationship with another contemporary of his, the scientist-turned-mystic Emanuel Swedenborg, that reveals his most urgent anxieties concerning the allegorical nature of language and scripture. Swedenborg's insistence that a spiritual world corresponded to the natural world the same way that a spiritual sense corresponded the literal sense of the Bible was attractive to Kant, who was drawn to notions of an otherworldly "community of spirits," and whose "moral sense" interpretation of the Bible sought to leave behind the external husk of scripture like a soul leaves behind its body at death. Kant's ultimate rejection of this kind of speculative metaphysics aligns with his ultimate rejection of Swedenborg, whose allegorical interpretations of the Old Testament, Kant would write, made "the mistake of including Judaism."[38]

This fourth chapter also demonstrates that both the character of Kant's anti-Judaism and his principles for interpreting scripture relate to the development of his moral philosophy.[39] His attempts to redraw

---

38. Immanuel Kant, *The Conflict of the Faculties*, trans. Mary J. Gregor (Lincoln: University of Nebraska Press, 1992), 65.

39. The scholarly discourse on the distinction between anti-Judaism and anti-Semitism reveals many tension points in the telling of this history. Many of the instances discussed in this book do indeed demonstrate characteristics typically identified as anti-Semitic, such as irrationality, fantasy, and protoracism. I will be using the broader term anti-Judaism, in part because of my interest in showing consistency across generations, particularly when it comes to hermeneutics and the religious other. My position is aligned with David Nirenberg in viewing the focus on Jews and Judaism as woven into long-standing patters of thought and self-identity in the west. See David Nirenberg, *Anti-Judaism: The Western Tradition* (New York: Norton, 2013). For more on the distinction, see Robert S. Wistrich, *A Lethal Obsession: Anti-Semitism from Antiquity to the Global Jihad* (New York: Random House, 2010); Gavin

18 JEWISH ALLEGORY IN EIGHTEENTH-CENTURY CHRISTIAN IMAGINATION

the borders of reason paralleled efforts to exclude parts of the Bible seen as morally problematic and to euthanize Jewishness from pure religion. Various anxieties of influence emerge in Kant's thought, however, showing his borderlines to be more porous than they first appear. This becomes apparent through analysis of Kant's equivocation regarding Swedenborg, allegory, the Old Testament, and Jews. Kant famously argued that Judaism was no religion at all but a political entity concerned with externalities, legalism, rewards and punishments. He also believed the New Testament to be morally advanced over the Old Testament, which merely documented Jewish ideas about a punishing God. However, we find notable contradictions in his views on these matters, as in his reliance on the Ten Commandments as foundational to moral religion. Furthermore, we find that despite Kant's rejection of Swedenborg's allegorical correspondences, his own approach to scripture produced interpretations nearly identical to Swedenborg's. That his sharpest attack on Swedenborg comes in a chapter titled "Antikabbalah" will further allow us to wade through the eighteenth-century scholarly rhetoric concerning Jewish mysticism and interpretation.

Chapter 5 explores William Blake's poetic reformulation of biblical figures and his provocative distinction between *vision* and *allegory*. While vision is associated with inspiration and immediacy, allegory is associated with memory and with what is backward looking, formulated, and artificial. The Bible, Blake writes, is no allegory but "Eternal Vision or Imagination of All that Exists."[40] In making this distinction, Blake echoes the sentiments of philosophers and poets of his age who wished to reject the dogmatic and arbitrary methods of past generations in favor of more experiential modes. We find that rather than describing a technique of representation whereby one thing is signified by the image of another thing, a technique that pervades Blake's poetry and illustrations, allegory instead functions for Blake as a particular mode of being. Those things he calls "allegoric" are the aspects of religion that are repressive and authoritarian.

I. Langmuir, *Toward a Definition of Antisemitism* (Berkeley: University of California Press, 1990); and Jeanne Favret-Saada, "A Fuzzy Distinction: Anti-Judaism and Anti-Semitism (An Excerpt from *Le Judaisme et ses Juifs*)," *Journal of Ethnographic Theory* 4.3 (2014): 335–40.

40. William Blake, "A Vision of the Last Judgement," in *The Complete Poetry and Prose of William Blake*, ed. David Erdman (Berkeley: University of California Press, 2008), 554.

INTRODUCTION   19

As with Kant anti-Judaism emerges in Blake's work as a mechanism for discarding what is unwanted from biblical religion, and his allegoric mode is most often represented with allusions to Jewish things. Blake makes Jews the unfortunate symbol for those things he is troubled by in corrupted forms of Christianity: false piety, legalism, and clerical duplicity. Motivated in part by the rhetoric of deists around him, Blake adopts the position that the God of the Old Testament is a vengeful tyrant, which he then incarnates as the miserable Urizen. In Urizen Blake provides Christianity's ancient heresy, Marcionsim, a most vivid expression and anticipates the troubling success of the trope of the *angry God of the Old Testament* into modernity. Blake's Jewish God is the God of allegories, the God of pretense and deception. This all comes despite Blake's more positive appropriation of Jewish sources elsewhere, including imagery and concepts from the Hebrew Bible and from kabbalah. Like Kant then, Blake's ambivalence toward Jews and Judaism parallels an ambivalence toward biblical allegory: anxieties about the foreignness of biblical language are displaced onto the religious other.

The cases in this study counter the narrative of the demise of allegory in the Enlightenment. They also demonstrate the ways religious identity and Jewish-Christian relations continued to shape biblical hermeneutics into modernity. The conclusion discusses the biblical criticism that was born of these dynamics and developed in the generations to follow. For example, Elizabeth Cady Stanton's *The Woman's Bible* utilized source criticism to isolate threads in the text that were favorable to women's rights and regarded the rejected material as having been corrupted by Jews who were bent on deception. The anti-Jewish threads evident in nineteenth-century biblical criticism, in the name of literalism and historical certainty, have their roots in an age characterized by a double ambivalence toward Jews and allegory, despite the persistent and substantive influence of both on Christian thought.

This is a study of the use of allegory in a particular period in history, a period in which assumptions about ontological connections between nature, scripture, reason, and spirit were challenged and changed. Exegetical and literary articulations of semiotic relationships in language and text were impacted by these changes. Despite the claims of some eighteenth-century critics as well as some critics today, allegory did not breathe its last breath in this century. It did, however, show up in new contexts where it was allied to different communities than it had been previously and where it was rejected or embraced using new criteria for interpreting and knowing the truth. Each of the exegetes considered here found their own way through the hermeneutical challenges of their time by conceptually marrying multivocality and Jewish identity, sometimes positively and sometimes negatively. This was a surprising turn, given the history of the Christian discourse of Jewish literalism, one that adds to our understanding of the entanglement of religious identity and biblical exegesis.

1
ENLIGHTENED CONTRADICTIONS: AN ENGLISH CONTEXT

A curious argument arose in England in the first half of the eighteenth century regarding the allegories of the Jews. Some believed Jewish allegory to be nefarious, the source of all confusion regarding the meaning of the Bible, and a threat to Christian institutions. Others believed the allegories of the Jews were divinely inspired and a resource to Christians who needed help interpreting the scriptures. The association between Jews and allegory is itself a surprising one, given the rhetoric about Jewish literalism that dominated in previous generations. It was also an imagined one developed and maintained by Christians whose discourse about these things was with other Christians. It both relied on and reversed familiar tropes concerning Jews and Judaism recycled by Enlightenment-era theologians and their critics in debates involving the Bible and its true meaning. Old stereotypes were applied in emerging disciplines and when they did not suitably respond to the needs of the moment, troublesome ambiguities and contradictions resulted. As Diego Lucci writes:

> Enlightenment interpretations of Judaism were indeed diverse and often conflicting, ranging between two extremes: from the original source of wisdom and the foundation of an admirable political model that had been gradually perverted by false prophets and malicious priests, to an ill-grounded series of superstitions that subsequently became the primary cause of the deterioration of social and political life in Western civilization.[1]

---

1. Diego Lucci, "Judaism and the Jews in the British Deists Attacks on Revealed Religion," *Hebraic Political Studies* 3.2 (2008): 178–79.

22   JEWISH ALLEGORY IN EIGHTEENTH-CENTURY CHRISTIAN IMAGINATION

The growing tendency to associate Jewish exegesis with allegory was one source of such contradictions.

It is helpful to understand this development against the backdrop of two related trends in biblical studies: the interpretive energy put into a literal reading of Old Testament prophecies, and the political energy put into defending Christianity amid a perceived attack on its foundation in the Bible. Jewish interpretation was utilized in both arenas, often in dizzying combinations of the kinds of extremes described by Lucci, in order to illuminate the Bible's relationship to true religion.

Driven by historical and humanist investigations of the Bible, seventeenth-century scholarship and debate had centered on the coherence of the Bible as a whole and particularly the relationship between the Old and New Testaments. The question of *integritas Scripturae* emerged as a primary theological concern in the wake of the work of Hugo Grotius, for example, who investigated the immediate, contextual meaning of the Hebrew prophetic texts rather than their fulfillment in the gospels. Related questions arose around the ways that the apostles or Jesus himself cited Old Testament prophecies, and whether or not mistakes or mistranslations were on display in New Testament scripture quotations. These questions continued to dominate in the early eighteenth century, when concerns about the integrity of scripture comingled with debates on the nature of true religion, that is, whether it was revealed to humankind through God's word in text, or whether it could be discerned through the study of nature and reason alone. Those who saw themselves left on the battlefield to defend revealed religion had to do so with the epistemological tools of the day and could not rely on an appeal to either the supernatural through biblical miracles or premodern typological and allegorical explanations. Challenges to revealed religion and Christian orthodoxy in the name of reason took on different forms in eighteenth-century Netherlands, Germany, England, and France. The legacies of Descartes, Spinoza, Leibniz, Newton, and Locke, to name just a few, produced a wide array of philosophical debates, and impacted religious and exegetical discourses in a number of interconnected ways. This chapter will explore the English context, where the emergence of what came to be known as deism triggered a series of debates that would be fertile ground for the kind of discourse about Jewish allegory that concerns us presently. Here we find that ideas about Jewish allegory were employed by both challengers and defenders of biblical religion in ways that exposed core inconsistencies of thought despite appeals to reason and sober rationality. The trope of Jewish allegory was successful, if also contradictory, because it addressed urgent anxieties about the Bible that characterized this context.

Two notes on the context and the phenomenon of deism are important at the start. First, the term *deist* was itself discursive and used against those whose work aimed, allegedly, to destabilize or destroy revealed religion. Those known today as the English deists rarely self-identified as such. A second point relates to the first, namely, that it is important avoid a "teleological history of secularization," to borrow a phrase from Wayne Hudson.[2] Hudson's revisionist history of English deism attempts to decouple dissent from secularism and highlights the religious commitments of many of England's most critical thinkers as well as the intra-Christian context of many of the era's fiercest debates. The deists radicalized their ontologies with "no difficulty in combining a sincere Christian supernaturalism with philosophical ideas which could be turned against it."[3] A similar emphasis is made by Jonathan Sheehan in his treatment of *The Enlightenment Bible*. Sheehan posits that the "cultural bible" produced by the Enlightenment did not come about by attack, but by the development of a set of instruments aimed at internal, religious reform. Sheehan and Hudson position themselves as corrections to narratives of "the rise of modern paganism," as framed by Peter Gay, and the progression of secularism described by historians such as Jonathan Israel.[4] One key lesson from these histories, therefore, is that perceived attacks against Christianity were mostly internal ones, and the extent to which the deists intended to undermine Christianity has been exaggerated. To some extent, at least, it was the responses to these critics, rather than the critics themselves, that were so destabilizing to the orthodox position, as they revealed notable weaknesses and contradictions of terms. We will trace the serpentine path of one particular debate from this period that raged between those who saw Jewish allegory as the root of all biblical confusion and incoherence

---

2. Wayne Hudson, *The English Deists: Studies in Early Enlightenment* (Brookfield, VT: Pickering & Chatto, 2009), 1.

3. Hudson, *English Deists*, 9.

4. Peter Gay, *The Enlightenment: An Interpretation. The Rise of Modern Paganism* (New York: Knopf, 1976); and Jonathan Israel, *Radical Enlightenment: Philosophy and the Making of Modernity, 1650–1750* (Oxford: Oxford University Press, 2001). See Hudson's treatment of Israel in Hudson, *English Deists*, 18–19. See also Diego Lucci, *Scripture and Deism: The Biblical Criticism of the Eighteenth Century British Deists* (Bern: Lang, 2008).

24   JEWISH ALLEGORY IN EIGHTEENTH-CENTURY CHRISTIAN IMAGINATION

and those who believed Jewish allegory to be the key to resolving the very same confusion and incoherence. This will involve a study of one particular deist attack from the self-described freethinker Anthony Collins and the defenders of biblical religion who came before and after him. We will begin with Collins's adversary, William Whiston, whose singlehanded war on allegory used scientific discovery and the study of Hebrew and Judaism as arsenal.

Whiston's War on Allegory

Whiston, like so many of his contemporaries, embodies the historian's familiar refrain that science and religion were not yet separate disciplines in the early eighteenth century. Whiston's work in biblical chronology, Josephus translation, early church history, and biblical manuscript study interfaced with his work in mathematics and astronomy in ways unique to his age. Among his many books demonstrating this interface was his *Astronomical Principles of Religion, Natural and Reveal'd*, in which he applied his exegetical skills and scientific reasoning to the task of determining, among other things, the location of hell. Using a "curious mixture of physico-theological reasoning and prophetic admonition," as one scholar has put it, Whiston determined that the place of darkness and fire described in scripture could be none other than a comet.[5] He compared the comet to the description from Rev 14 of the smoke of torment rising and witnessed by the angels. A comet, he reasoned, can likewise be seen "ascending from the Hot Regions near the Sun, and going into the Cold Regions beyond Saturn, with its long smoking Tail arising up from it, through its several Ages and Periods of revolving."[6] Whiston's comet-hell was in part a response to the recently published theories of Tobias Swinden, who speculated that the location of hell, given the everlasting fire described in the Bible, must be on the surface of the sun. Swinden had been inspired by illustrations of solar flares drawn through access to new telescope technologies and speculated that the flares were the burning damned. Denouncing those who would believe in a metaphorical hell only, Swinden asserted, "It is evident therefore, that the general and final

---

5. Roomet Jakapi, "William Whiston, the Universal Deluge, and a Terrible Spectacle," *Folklore: Electronic Journal of Folklore* 31 (2005): 7–14.

6. William Whiston, *Astronomical Principles of Religion, Natural and Reveal'd: in Nine Parts* (London: Senex and Taylor, 1717), 156.

1. ENLIGHTENED CONTRADICTIONS

Sentence, by which the Wicked shall be adjudged to everlasting Fire, must have it in no Figures or Allegories, but plain and proper Speech only; because the Guilty must perceive thereby what is their Doom."[7] The question of whether hell could be seen on the sun or on comets with the use of scientific instruments excited those who imagined the Bible's literal truth would be confirmed with each new invention and each new optical lens.

Whiston's incorporation of astronomy into his exegesis was made possible by his mentorship with Isaac Newton. A student of Newton and his successor as Lucasian Professor of Mathematics at Cambridge, Whiston inherited several of Newton's positions and interests regarding natural philosophy and theology. However, the question of how these two men aligned (or not) over their approaches to the Bible is yet to be settled, and a word should be said about this before proceeding.

James Force, whose research centers on Newton and his influence, argues that Whiston's approach to the Bible is essentially Newtonian in nature and that Newton was a behind-the-scenes promoter of Whiston's Boyle Lectures on biblical literalism, which were published as *The Literal Accomplishment of Scripture Prophecies.*[8] Force's evidence for what he calls Whiston's "literal Newtonian interpretation" has been challenged in more than one review, and the positive relationship between Newton and Whiston has been disputed by Jed Buchwald and Mordechai Feingold.[9] Furthermore, Whiston's biblical literalism bumps up against Newton's interest in alchemy and symbolism. Newton's symbolic interpretations of tabernacle and temple, for instance, suggest an approach somewhat dif-

---

7. Tobias Swinden, *An Enquiry into the Nature and Place of Hell* (London: Bowyer, 1714), 41.

8. James Force, *William Whiston, Honest Newtonian* (Cambridge: Cambridge University Press, 1985), 77–88. The Boyle Lectures can be found in William Whiston, *The Literal Accomplishment of Scripture Prophecy. Being a Full Answer to a Late Discourse, of the Grounds and Reasons of the Christian Religion* (London: Senex & Taylor, 1724).

9. See, for instance, the reviews by Simon Schaffer in *British Journal for the History of Science* 19 (1986): 226–28; Anita Guerrini in *JR* 67 (1987): 100–1; and Mordechai Feingold in *Eighteenth-Century Studies* 21 (1987): 141–42. See also Jed Z. Buchwald and Mordechai Feingold, *Newton and the Origin of Civilization* (Princeton: Princeton University Press, 2013), 333–38. On the similarity between Newton and Whiston's view of the Godhead, see Stephen Snobelen, "'God of Gods, and Lord of Lords:' The Theology of Isaac Newton's General Scholium to the Principia," *Osiris* 16 (2001): 187–88.

26 JEWISH ALLEGORY IN EIGHTEENTH-CENTURY CHRISTIAN IMAGINATION

ferent from Whiston's in its reliance on coded meaning. Describing the relationship between the Old Testament prophecies and the New Testament Apocalypse through types, Newton writes that they are "like twin prophecies of the same things, and cannot be properly understood apart from each other. For that book, sealed by the hand of Him who sits upon the throne, is the very book of the law, as will be shown later, and its seals are opened in the Apocalypse. We must now therefore study the world of Israel, and expound the significance of its parts and ceremonies." [10] This symbolically layered interpretation of the prophets was precisely the kind of extravagance Whiston worked so hard to avoid.

Whatever differences we can parse between their interpretations of the biblical prophecies, an important commonality between Newton and Whiston can be discerned in their shared fixation on deciphering and preserving an uncorrupted version of the biblical text. Both men employed comparison between the Greek, Latin, and Hebrew versions of the Old Testament, and they shared a suspicion of the Hebrew Masoretic Text, viewing it as a corrupted version. More will be said on this below. Fundamentally, the exegetical writing of both men exhibited the conviction that the antiquity of a text or tradition demonstrated its truth. Born out of a Protestant distrust of tradition, Newton, Whiston, and others among their contemporaries viewed religious developments in both Christianity and Judaism from the second century forward as corruptions. The Talmud and the Council of Nicaea alike came under scrutiny, and the scholar's aim was discovering the purest, most ancient, most holy Bible. Of their many shared conclusions, Arianism or the rejection of the Trinitarian formula of Athanasius and the church fathers was by far the most controversial and ended with Whiston's banishment from Cambridge University in 1710. Much more popular, and with farther reaching consequences, was Whiston's assault on allegorical interpretation, which he promoted with renewed vigor thereafter in London.

In particular, Whiston was responding to debates regarding two parts of the Bible: Genesis, specifically the creation story and the flood, and the Old Testament prophets and their connection to New Testament events. On the one hand, developments in natural history and astronomy called into question the validity of the Genesis narratives. On the other, manuscript

---

10. Isaac Newton, *Prolegomena ad lexici prophetici partem secundam in quibus agitur De forma sanctuarij Iudaici*. Ms. 434, trans. Michael Silverthorne, published online at The Newton Project, December 2013, https://tinyurl.com/SBL6706a.

discoveries and textual criticism called into question the assumed relationship between the Hebrew prophets and the Christian Messiah. Both cases centered on whether biblical truth claims could be defended by means of "general providence" alone (i.e., by means of the ordinary processes and forces of nature) or whether traditional notions of God's active intervention by means of "special providence" was required. With the rise of scientific principles and text criticism, the two pillars of biblical revelation—namely, miracles and prophecy—were challenged as never before. Enter William Whiston with his toolbox of Newtonian physics, textual dexterity, scholarly rigor, and zealousness for the truth of the printed word of God.

Whiston's views on allegory were in part a response to the deist attacks on Thomas Burnet and his controversial *Telluris Theoria Sacra*, published in the 1680s. The reception of Spinoza in seventeenth-century England triggered discussions about the reasonableness of belief in biblical miracles, which became a major topic of discussion in the eighteenth century.[11] Burnet's work attempted to straddle two positions seemingly at odds in Spinoza's wake: the inerrancy of scripture and God's operation via the laws of nature. Burnet attempted an explanation of creation that matched the biblical account using natural causes and with as little recourse to special providence as possible. This made the hexamaeron, or six-day creation, a particularly difficult stumbling block. He believed that the world was created in the order and manner described in Genesis, but that the length of time itself could only be understood allegorically. That it did not literally take six days was no innovation. As far back as Augustine, Christian exegetes had been relativizing the measurement of time *in the beginning*. But Burnet's turn to allegory in an otherwise scientific study stood out. His qualification was viewed as a weakness by his challengers, the growing body of skeptics who would come to be known as deists.[12] That one could be so convinced regarding the science behind the Bible, but make use of allegory where science had no explanation, became a point of ridi-

---

11. Henry More and Ralph Cudworth, for instance, wrote in defense of miracles in response to Spinoza. See Rosalie L. Colie, "Spinoza in England, 1665–1730," *Proceedings of the American Philosophical Society* 107.3 (1963): 183–219.

12. Burnet had many critics, including Charles Blount, Christianus Wagner, Herbert Crofts, and Erasmus Warren. On the deist response to Burnet, see Force, *William Whiston*, 35–38. See also William Poole, *The World Makers: Scientists of the Restoration and the Search for the Origins of the Earth* (Oxfordshire: International Academic Publishers, 2010), 56–68.

28 JEWISH ALLEGORY IN EIGHTEENTH-CENTURY CHRISTIAN IMAGINATION

cule. Whiston thought he could do better and was determined to defend the biblical account of creation without the crutch of Burnet's "parabolick sense."[13] Whiston's support of the Genesis events relied, once again, on the physics of comets. He argued that the impact of colliding spheres on their natural course rapidly changed the landscape of the earth and that the six days of creation describe exactly what it would have looked like to an observing set of eyes. No reliance on allegory or rhetorical flourish was needed; the text meant precisely what it says. In Whiston's configuration, therefore, a reliance on allegory suffered the same weakness as a reliance on miracles: they both required divine intervention into the natural order of things. He set out to demonstrate that both allegory and miracles could be set aside as proofs for Christianity with the aid of the new sciences.

That the biblical text could have only one meaning, and that its meaning was to be understood literally, became fundamental to Whiston's overall hermeneutical approach. He outlined this approach in a best-selling publication responding to Burnet's, which he illustrated with elaborate astronomical charts and pointedly titled *A New Theory of the Earth, from Its Original, to the Consummation of All Things, Where the Creation of the World in Six Days, the Universal Deluge, and the General Conflagration, as Laid Down in the Holy Scriptures, Are Shewn to Be Perfectly Agreeable to Reason and Philosophy*. Among his postulates for interpretation, Whiston writes, "The Obvious or Literal Sense of Scripture is the True and Real one, where no evident Reason can be given to the contrary."[14] If the reader finds the style of the Genesis creation story difficult to understand, he argues, this is because it was never intended to be a philosophical account but a historical one describing the dramatic events of a natural cosmic disruption.

Whiston's Boyle Lectures as well as his 1722 follow-up book, *An Essay towards Restoring the True Text of the Old Testament*, applied his methods to the Old Testament prophecies.[15] Like Genesis, interpretations of prophetic literature had become a point of controversy for their reliance

---

13. William Whiston, *A New Theory of the Earth, from Its Original, to the Consummation of All Things, Where the Creation of the World in Six Days, the Universal Deluge, And the General Conflagration, As Laid Down in the Holy Scriptures, Are Shewn to Be Perfectly Agreeable to Reason and Philosophy* (London: Roberts, 1696), 64.

14. Whiston, *New Theory*, 95.

15. William Whiston, *An Essay towards Restoring the True Text of the Old Testament, and for Vindicating the Citations Made Thence in the New Testament* (London: Senex, 1722).

on double meanings. Without recourse to double meanings, however, the connection between the Testaments was less obvious, and the foundations of the Christian faith vulnerable to scrutiny. To meet this challenge, Whiston set out to prove that the messianic prophecies referred to events surrounding the birth, life, and death of Jesus alone and not to the immediate circumstances of the Judahite and Israelite kings and kingdoms to which they were pronounced. Traditional Christian reliance on more than one sense of scripture was to be abandoned here along with other patristic perversions: "I observe that the Stile and Language of the Prophets, as it is often peculiar and enigmatical, so it is always single and determinate, and not capable of those double Intentions, and typical Interpretations, which most of our late Christian Expositors are so full of upon all Occasions."[16] The books of the prophets do contain historical information, he concedes, but the prophetic statements therein are of a different nature and refer to future events only.

To demonstrate the literal meaning of the prophecies "without any recourse to Typical, Foreign and Mystical Expositions" as well as their perfectly accurate citation by Jesus and the apostles, Whiston postulated the corruption of the text by second-century Jews, whose intent, he insisted, was to confound Christianity.[17] Just as the Athanasian Creed brought confusion and falsity to Christian notions of the Father and the Son, the Jews had manipulated the text of the Bible to mislead its followers during the early Christianity period. Whiston set out to prove that the Masoretic Text was the corruptive tool to blame for the resulting confusion for the Christians who relied on it. This accusation of Jewish textual corruption had always existed in Christendom and gained strength and complexity in the late twelfth and thirteenth centuries.[18] Such accusations also flourished in Islam. Whiston was therefore weaving an old story into his text-critical work: a familiar anti-Judaism into new manuscript discoveries and analysis, all in the name of revealing a version of the Bible that could be read literally and scientifically.

In his *Essay towards Restoring the True Text of the Old Testament*, Whiston cites the Talmudic principle of *tiqqun sopherim* as a starting

---

16. Whiston, *Accomplishment of Scripture*, 13.

17. Whiston, *Accomplishment of Scripture*, 13.

18. See Irven Resnick, "The Falsification of Scripture and Medieval Christian and Jewish Polemics," *Medieval Encounters* 2.3 (1995): 344–80.

30 JEWISH ALLEGORY IN EIGHTEENTH-CENTURY CHRISTIAN IMAGINATION

point for his accusation against the Hebrew Masoretic Text.[19] He faults the "later Jews" for making alterations to the text, particularly regarding matters of chronology and the messianic prophecies, in order to "stop the power of the Gospel."[20] Acknowledging their own religious convictions, Whiston imagines that these rabbis were "lying for God," but blames them nevertheless for all modern difficulties in interpretation.[21] In his subsequent work, *The Literal Accomplishment of Scripture Prophecies*, Whiston presents a detailed study of the prophecies in question, placing them side by side with their New Testament fulfillments in two columns. Marginal notes explain every discrepancy with a description of the corruption to the text made by Jews. Using the Septuagint, the Samaritan Pentateuch, and the Roman Psalter for comparison, Whiston notes where the Hebrew text misleads. For instance, concerning the famous fulfillment of the prophecy of the virgin birth in Matt 1:22–23 and its controversial relationship to Isa 7:14, he writes: "This appears to have been the Old Reading of the Septuagint, before the Jews corrupted their copies."[22] Where no existing manuscript provides a prophecy to correlate with a New Testament citation, the Jews are blamed for its absence.[23] With the latest tools of biblical scholarship at hand, therefore, Whiston proposed to reconstruct the original text, which would, he believed, present a straightforward description of the Messiah born in Bethlehem. The Hebrew language is the unnamed vehicle of deception in Whiston's theory, easily manipulated by those who mastered it and put to use steering unsuspecting Christians away from the truth. Early translations, in safer languages, could be relied on in most cases for their accuracy, he reasoned, having safeguarded the true text just in time before the Masoretes engaged in their craft.

Most significant for our present purposes is Whiston's association of allegory with the contaminating nature of Jewish interpretation, which he makes in a supplement to *An Essay towards Restoring the True Text of the Old Testament*. The supplement takes up the case of the Canticles (i.e., Song of Songs) and argues against its inclusion in the canon. Whiston does not challenge the traditional attribution of authorship to King Solomon, but says that it was written late in Solomon's life when he was

---

19. Whiston, *Essay*, 221.
20. Whiston, *Essay*, 223.
21. Whiston, *Essay*, 232; quote on 224.
22. Whiston, *Literal Accomplishment*, 2.
23. Whiston, *Literal Accomplishment*, 4.

influenced by Egyptian ways and entrenched in idolatry. Any moral content that could be derived from the Canticles would depend on a reading that was "entirely mystical and allegorical."[24] The literal sense alone is depraved and as such has no place in holy scripture. Whiston uses the Canticles as an opportunity to declare allegory "that later Jewish Method of Interpretation," pointing to Philo as the father of allegory and to Philo's Egyptian (that is, idolatrous) heritage.[25] He argues that allegory takes a hold on biblical tradition only after the fall of Jerusalem and is used by the earliest Christians only when they are engaged in debate with Jews.[26] The inclusion of the Canticles in the canon came in the second century when allegory was in fashion and, importantly, at the same time the Jews were engaged in their textual corruptions, so goes Whiston's argument.

However, while Whiston's understanding of the role of Jews in the history of religion centers on their corruption of scripture, more positive elements of his interaction with Judaism manifest the knotty relationship between early modern Christian thinkers and their hermeneutical exploitation of Jews and Judaism. Adam Shear points to the fact that Whiston's lifetime coincides with the period of Jewish settlement in England as evidence for what he calls Whiston's "Judeo-centric Christianity."[27] His Arianism made Jewish acceptance of Jesus as divine unnecessary for their salvation. And Jewish national restoration was seen by Whiston as an important precursor to, rather than result of, the second coming of Christ. Even more striking was Whiston's incorporation of *mitzvot*, *kashrut*, and the Saturday Sabbath into his notions of what true Christian practice should look like. The purest form of Christianity, again, would have been the earliest and consequently would reflect the early Jewish context of Jesus's Judea. Whiston is very much a product of his time in his fascination with Jewish customs and inherited the project from such Hebraists as Johannes Buxtorf and his 1603 *Synagoga Judaica*.

---

24. William Whiston, *A Supplement to Mr. Whiston's Late Essay, towards Restoring the True Text of the Old Testament: Proving, That the Canticles Is Not a Sacred Book of the Old Testament; Nor Was Originally Esteemed as Such, Either by the Jewish or the Christian Church* (London: Senex, 1723), 12.

25. Whiston, *Supplement*, 41.

26. Whiston, *Supplement*, 21.

27. Adam Shear, "William Whiston's Judeo-Christianity: Millenarianism and Christian Zionism in Early Enlightenment England," in *Philosemitism in History*, ed. Jonathan Karp and Adam Sutcliffe (Cambridge: Cambridge University Press, 2011), 93–110.

32   JEWISH ALLEGORY IN EIGHTEENTH-CENTURY CHRISTIAN IMAGINATION

His "chimerical philosemitism," to borrow Shear's phrasing, was also not unique.[28] Christians across Europe had long viewed the conversion of the Jews as integral to bringing on the messianic age. More will be said about eighteenth-century ideas about conversion and allegory in the next chapter. What is important for now is Whiston's distinctive and elaborate documentation of Jewish textual corruption and the accompanying link between Jews and allegory.

Collins's Counterattack

Whiston had many critics, but one response in particular ignited an extensive public debate and inspired dozens of published responses and counterresponses from learned defenders of the faith in the following years. This provocative response came from Anthony Collins, a well-read and well-connected public intellectual known at the time for his 1713 *A Discourse in Freethinking*. His response to Whiston, titled *A Discourse of the Grounds and Reasons of the Christian Religion*, was itself a celebration of freethought and public debate centered precisely on the question of allegory's origins in Judaism and its contribution to Christian exegesis.

Collins's book is a scathing attack on Whiston, his logic, and his conclusions, yet it opens with a sixty-page preface defending and even praising his adversary, titled "An Apology for Mr. Whiston's Liberty of Writing." In it he generously attempts to stave off the fury of his readers against Whiston. "It is very possible, that in opposing the opinions of that ingenious and learned gentleman, I may be undesignedly instrumental in raising up against him the passions of some readers; who may think, that the opinions he maintains, are such, as should not be allow'd to be advanc'd or defended; and that he ought to suffer in his person or fortune for maintaining them."[29] In defending Whiston as an "honest man and lover of truth" Collins extols the importance of free debate for the advancement of truth and the strength of society and the church. His preface celebrates disagreement as the design of providence and argues that God created humans to be diverse in opinion.[30] He then expresses gratitude for Whiston's contribution, which provides such a rich occasion for

---

28. Shear, "Millenarianism and Christian Zionism," 110.
29. Anthony Collins, *A Discourse of the Grounds and Reasons of the Christian Religion* (London, 1724), iv.
30. Collins, *Grounds and Reasons*, xxxviii.

1. ENLIGHTENED CONTRADICTIONS   33

posing a contrary response. It is precisely because Whiston's views are so controversial that they are so compelling as an opportunity for free debate. With a note of teasing, then, Collins writes that Whiston's views are "so much better than all other such learned divines as himself, as he exceeds them in the liberty he takes of proposing his conjectures and sentiments."[31] It is posed as a compliment, on the part of the free thinker, but one that would hardly be received as such by its intended recipient, and of this Collins was surely aware. The entanglement of irony and genuine enthusiasm on Collins's part sets the tone for the remainder of the book. One thing is clear concerning the preface, however: Collins need not have worried about the vilification of Whiston in response to his *Grounds and Reasons*. With few exceptions, readers were united in vilifying Collins and the dangerous heresies perceived to be contained therein, particularly his reliance on Jewish allegory to rescue the Christian Bible from persecution. Before turning to its explosive reception, a summary of its contents is in order.

Grounds and Reasons argues that, rather than salvaging the Old Testament, Whiston was showing it to be defective and thereby had undermined all biblical religion. Collins then presents an alternative solution to the problem of the gospel citations of the Old Testament. Jewish interpretation, rather than Jewish corruption, is the key. The book begins with the statement that "Christianity is founded on Judaism, or the New Testament on the Old." A series of arguments is then built upon this point of departure, beginning with the claim that Jesus and the apostles established Christianity by citing Old Testament prophecies. The Old Testament alone is the canon of Christianity and cannot be abandoned or altered. If these proofs of prophecy are found to be invalid, the whole of Christianity is proven false. Finally, the proofs of Christianity from the Old Testament cannot rely on their literal fulfillment. As Whiston demonstrated so effectively, because the citations of the Old Testament in the New are either inaccurate or confusing, and because the Hebrew scriptures do not plainly predict the coming of Christ as told in the gospels, the prophets must be interpreted allegorically. Using an assortment of terms for the phenomenon, Collins argues that the "allegorical," "secondary," "typical," "mystical," or "enigmatic" sense is the only path remaining for Christians if they are to proceed with their Bible intact.

---

31. Collins, *Grounds and Reasons*, xlii.

34 JEWISH ALLEGORY IN EIGHTEENTH-CENTURY CHRISTIAN IMAGINATION

With a critical investigation of each of the alternative manuscript sources suggested by Whiston, Collins questions the very notion that more reliable sources for the Old Testament could be identified as well as whether Whiston was qualified for such a task. He asserts that "a Bible restor'd, according to Mr. Whiston's Theory, will be a mere Whistonian Bible, a Bible confounding and not containing the true Text of the Old Testament."[32] Collins points to the need for an interpretive approach grounded in the prophecies of the Old Testament that could explain the enigmatic nature of New Testament citations. For this Collins relies on the theories of Dutch scholar Willem Surenhuis, whose legendary encounter with a wise rabbi led him to believe in the revelatory nature of the Mishnah and the genius of Jewish methods for interpreting scripture.[33] Recounting Surenhuis's discovery, Collins describes the anonymous rabbi as an astute interpreter of the New Testament as well as the Old, "well skill'd in the Talmud, the Cabbala, and the allegorical books of the Jews."[34] When presented with the problem of how the New Testament authors inaccurately cite Hebrew scriptures, the rabbi revealed the solution: the New Testament is a mystical interpretation of the Old, properly interpreted only by the methods of kabbalah. This was all to the delight and relief of Surenhuis, whose faith had waivered on precisely these points, and Collins likewise celebrates the breakthrough.

According to Collins, Surenhuis's auspicious encounter with this "learned allegorical Rabbin" led him to the ten rules by which Jews cite and interpret scripture. These rules were clearly in play at the time of Jesus's life, according to Surenhuis, and resolve any confusion over New Testament prophecy citations. Collins quotes them in full from his source on Surenhuis, the periodicals of Michel de la Roche, who writes that the rules were "how the Ancient Allegorical Writers, and others, interpreted the Scripture in such a Manner, as to change the mean Literal Sense of the Words into a Noble and Spiritual Sense."[35] Collins translates the ten rules from Latin into English, something de la Roche himself avoided because of their difficulty. As laid out in his translation, the rules present an astonishing degree of liberty on the part of the interpreters, who are permitted to alter the text of the Bible by rearranging the words or letters, or "adding

---

32. Collins, *Grounds and Reasons*, 255.
33. Collins and others use the Latinized version of his name, Surenhusius.
34. Collins, *Grounds and Reasons*, 55.
35. Michel de la Roche, *Memoirs of Literature* (London: Knaplock, 1722), 6:115.

other words to those that are there, in order to make the sense more clear, and to accommodate it to the subject they are upon; as, is manifest, is done by the apostles throughout the New Testament."[36] Evoking the kabbalistic practice known as *tzeruf otiyot*, or combination of letters, Collins's list presents a radical method of interpretation that would appear no less destructive to his readers than Whiston's. And yet, he presents it as clearly superior to Whiston's, a fact that would set his readers on edge.

It is worth noting that Collins does not provide a loyal translation of Surenhuis and he curiously removes the explicit mention of an "allegorical sense" from the list, which appears in the fifth rule. He instead emphasizes the removal, addition, or rearrangement of words, letters, and punctuation on the part of Jewish interpreters.[37] Whether this was an act of carelessness or intentional erasure on Collins's part, his readers were nevertheless left with a summary of rabbinic interpretive methods that had gone through too many of its own transmutations to be recognizable from its originating source. The mischief behind Collins's efforts is made evident when he concludes this summary list with a comparison between Surenhuis's encounter with kabbalah to Luther's meeting with the devil: "The Rabbin establishes christianity; and the devil protestantism!"[38] This line will be cited by many of Collins's readers, both early modern and contemporary, as evidence of either his sarcasm or his contempt, which they then apply to his book as a whole. An alternative reading is possible, however, when one considers that Luther's nightly encounters with the devil provided precisely the kind of theological debate and intellectual labor that Collins so frequently defended as the vehicle for religious integrity. Whatever his intention, this section of *Grounds and Reasons* evokes a chaotic display. Whiston, the kabbalist, the Dutch scholar, the apostles, the prophets, and the devil all meet in Collins's arena in a brutal exchange of ideas, mistranslations, provocations, and fumbled citations. The result is nevertheless more constructive than the casual reader perceives.

Collins's ironic summary of the Jewish rules of interpretation is followed by a more serious consideration of the benefits of allegorical reading. Collins counters Whiston's notion that the literal sense of

---

36. Collins, *Grounds and Reasons*, 60.

37. The fifth rule treats the "sensus allegoricius elicitor," which Collins translates as: "the transposing of words and letters." See Collins, *Grounds and Reasons*, 60; de la Roche, *Memoirs of Literature*, 116.

38. Collins, *Grounds and Reasons*, 61.

36   JEWISH ALLEGORY IN EIGHTEENTH-CENTURY CHRISTIAN IMAGINATION

prophecy, properly reconstructed, would show an open attack on Jewish unbelief by citing Surenhuis's gentler way of understanding prophecy: "That the design of the evangelist was not to oppose the Jews, and prove them, that Jesus was the true Messias; but to shew to those, who did believe Jesus to be the true Messias, how the whole divine œconomy of former times, having always the Christ as it were, in view, had form'd all things to resemble him."[39] Viewed retrospectively, the movement of providence in scripture reveals repeating patterns, the recurrence of themes and personalities. Biblical history is reflected in the life of Christ but is not predictive in any manner that should coerce or condemn. The greater prophecy simply imitates the smaller prophecy. Using what appears to be the principle of *kal va-homer*, the argument from a minor premise to a major premise, Collins links events of the Old Testament to the coming of Christ the Messiah: Sarah's conception in old age is compared to Mary's conception of Jesus, Abraham's offering up of Isaac is compared to Christ being offered on the cross, and Isaiah's prophecy to Ahaz of the birth of the young child is compared to the birth of Christ.[40] Readers would recognize these comparisons from the types and anti-types established by the early church fathers, but here they are reframed as essentially Jewish in nature.

Collins surmises from his consideration of the scholarship of Suren-huis that Paul as well as the gospel writers must have been educated in the ways of kabbalah, gaining the ability to interpret the mysteries of scripture.[41] Christians since ancient times have employed allegory when relating the Old and New Testaments, he acknowledges, but Collins suggests a more rigorous path than simply following patristic interpreters. One must first become like a Jew and then be "converted by type and allegory."[42] Only then will one know the truly sublime nature of allegorical reasoning. He writes that a Christian must understand that Jesus used Jewish language

---

39. Collins, *Grounds and Reasons*, 63.
40. Collins, *Grounds and Reasons*, 63–64.
41. An interesting corollary to this idea developed several decades later with Krishna Mohan Banerjea (1813–1885), a Bengali convert to Christianity. In his 1875 book *The Arian Witness*, he argues that the Vedas are closer to the spirit of Christianity than the Hebrew Scriptures and contain the hidden mysteries of Christianity, includ-ing the anticipated coming of Christ. See R. S. Sugirtharajah, *Asian Biblical Hermeneu-tics and Postcolonialism: Contesting the Interpretations* (New York: Orbis, 1998), 4–5.
42. Collins, *Grounds and Reasons*, 95.

when he called his followers to be allegorically "born again" with "ears to hear."[43] The book of Revelation as well, he writes, might disappoint the reader when taken literally, but should be read "in the cabalistic style" as a "master-piece of mystical-prophecy." He concludes, in a line that would make him infamous, that "Christianity is the allegorical sense of the Old Testament, and is not improperly called mystical Judaism."[44]

Collins was aware of the difficulties he created for his readers in showing Jewish exegesis to be both as arbitrary as Whiston's *and* a reasonable and satisfying solution to the problem of interpreting the prophecies cited (or miscited) in Christian scriptures. The difference between them, he argues, is that Whiston's exegesis, unlike Jewish exegesis, suffers from being *both* arbitrary and unreasonable. He writes: "And I add, that if the allegorists scheme be weak and enthusiastical, his scheme is yet more so, by receiveing the weak and enthusiastical part of their scheme, and rejecting the rational part."[45] Jewish allegory is raised up by Collins as the unexpected champion of rational exegesis, though rational in an unconventional sense. In exploiting the theories of Whiston, Collins showed that science and literalism could not make an enlightened philosophy out of the Bible. He presented an alternative: only by understanding its internal logic, the closest thing to it being rabbinic exegesis, will readers be satisfied regarding its integrity. Such a conclusion would prove to be simply too outrageous for many of his readers to fathom, a fact which Collins seems to have anticipated given the provocations punctuating the chapters of his *Grounds and Reasons.*

Jewish Allegory as Imagined by Collins's Challengers

In 1754 John Leland reflected on the thirty years of quarreling that Collins's *Grounds and Reasons* had inspired: "Few books have made a greater noise than this did at its first publication."[46] Indeed, the book caused an immediate outcry from its readers and those who heard rumors regarding its content. Some who authored book-length responses did so with a nod to the authorities, as did Edward Chandler, bishop of Coventry, whose

---

43. Collins, *Grounds and Reasons*, 254.

44. Collins, *Grounds and Reasons*, 92.

45. Collins, *Grounds and Reasons*, 244.

46. John Leland, *A View of the Principal Deistical Writers That Have Appeared in England in the Last and Present Century* (London: Dod, 1754), 110.

38   JEWISH ALLEGORY IN EIGHTEENTH-CENTURY CHRISTIAN IMAGINATION

book was addressed to the king and dedicated to royal efforts to defend Christian piety against the destroyers of religion. Others framed their work as a response to the distress of their congregants, who had heard of the controversy and desired a learned response. A survey of these published answers to Collins reveals a few trends. Nearly all of his readers interpreted *Grounds and Reasons* to be an open attack on the foundations of Christianity that mocked both the biblical prophecies and their fulfillment in the gospels. Many readers occupied themselves, in response, with the question of what the Jews of Jesus's time were expecting to happen in light of their prophetic scriptures. If it could be demonstrated that Jews were expecting a messiah, this would be evidence of the clear and direct nature of the messianic prophecies. As a result, readers targeted their scholarly efforts at demonstrating that at least some of the prophecies can and should be interpreted literally. Few relied on Whiston for this endeavor, recognizing the failure of his particular approach. Many sought a kind of middle ground, showing that some prophecies were demonstrably literal (Chandler counted twelve of these) and that some relied on the logic of allegory.

This middle way was not without its own troublesome contradictions in logic, however, a point Collins would make in his own published rebuttal, *The Scheme of Literal Prophecy Considered*. A reliance on a double sense for only the more challenging prophecies was a logical inconsistency. More important, Collins was unconvinced by the arguments for the selection of prophecies deemed clear and straightforward. Collins granted that some Jews were expecting a messiah, but argued that this was due to allegorical interpretation and not literal interpretation. Only those Jews who embraced nonliteral interpretations, such as the Essenes, had the expectation and not those "letter men" like the Sadducees, he writes.[47] To accuse him of undermining the foundation of Christianity is itself a self-destructive move, he argues, since Christianity has relied on the allegorical sense of the Old Testament since its inception.

While his many adversaries (Collins counted thirty-five by the time of his response in 1727) accused him time and again of attacking the foundations of the Christian faith, they nevertheless tended to affirm the connection between Judaism and allegory that both he and Whiston emphasized. It is an association that only seems to have grown

---

47. Anthony Collins, *The Scheme of Literal Prophecy Considered; in a View of the Controversy, Occasion'd by a Late Book, Intitled, a Discourse of the Grounds and Reasons of the Christian Religion* (London: T. J., 1726), 19–22.

1. ENLIGHTENED CONTRADICTIONS

stronger as this chain of biblical debates gathered new links. In fact, the published responses consistently affirm Collins's characterization of Christian scriptures as clear and literal and Jewish scriptures as secretive and allegorical even while judging his positive characterization of Jewish allegory to be disdainful. Edward Chandler, for instance, reasoned that Paul in his early missionizing efforts attempted to use plain speech to bring people to Christ but was viewed with suspicion by the Jews due to the "lack of ornamentation" in his words "and that mystical skill wherein their Judaizing teachers seemed to have the advantage of him." Paul and other early Christians were thereby forced to use allegory when speaking with Jews, who were "afflicted" with its logic.[48] Another instance is found in the writings of Thomas Curteis, who described the "very full and plain directions" given to Christians in their Bible, while the case was different for Jews:

> God has not left us, as He has many other Large and Populous Nations, to the imperfect Light, and uncertain Guidance of our Natural and Depraved Reason, neither has he given us the Intimations of His Holy Will, under a Veil of dark Types and Shadows, as He did to the Jews; but He has graciously afforded us the most Clear and Perfect Revelation of what we are to Believe and Obey, that ever was vouchsaf'd to the World.[49]

Various theories were expressed by Collins's challengers regarding the reason behind the "Veil of dark Types and Shadows" that they believed characterized Jewish existence in ancient times. Edward Chandler remarked that some things had to be hidden from Jews so that they would abandon neither the Mosaic laws nor their important role in bringing about the death of Christ. If they knew the truth of their purpose, he wrote, they would be unable or unwilling to carry it out.[50] In another instance, Samuel Chandler parsed the kinds of allegories found in the Bible, concluding that there were two reasons God used allegorical methods with the Jews: to

---

48. Edward Chandler, *A Defence of Christianity from Prophecies of the Old Testament; Wherein Are Considered All the Objections against this Kind of Proof, Advanced in a Late Discourse of the Grounds and Reasons of the Christian Religion* (London: Knapton, 1725), 261.

49. Thomas Curteis, *A Dissertation on the Unreasonableness, Folly, and Danger of Infidelity; Occasion'd by a Late Virulent Book, Intitul'd A Discourse on the Grounds and Reasons of the Christian Religion* (London: Willkin, 1725), 207.

50. Chandler, *Defence*, 216–18.

40 JEWISH ALLEGORY IN EIGHTEENTH-CENTURY CHRISTIAN IMAGINATION

lure them to God's protection in troubled times and to cultivate a hope for the Messiah.[51] They could only be led and encouraged, it seemed, with the help of divine storytelling rather than plain speech.

William Warburton wrote along similar lines in his three-volume magnum opus *The Divine Legation of Moses*, which responded to Collins amid a larger study of the Old Testament. His principal argument was that the Jews, unlike other ancient cultures, had no belief in the afterlife or the "doctrine of a Future State" and were restrained instead by the threat of punishment related to their present circumstances. This was, he argued, because of their attraction to Egyptian superstitions and polytheism and the need to keep them from returning to the carnal pleasures of life in the "fleshpots" found, paradoxically, in the land of their captivity.[52] Warburton's particularly brutal interpretation of Jewish history came with an equally callous appeal to contemporary Jews, which appears in *The Divine Legation of Moses* as a "Dedication to the Jews." Here he attempts to recruit Jews for the cause of countering a common enemy in the deists and freethinkers, who, he writes, blur the boundaries between Jew and Christian. In the same breath, however, his Jewish audience is condemned to be forever strangers belonging nowhere. Their only hope, according to Warburton, would be to accept the completion of their "partial, imperfect and preparatory" religion by converting to Christianity and thereby meriting naturalization as citizens of England on an individual basis. This he declares to be the "will of heaven."[53]

Warburton accuses Collins of attempting to prove Jesus an imposter, but agrees that there is a double sense to be found in the Hebrew scriptures. He understands the double sense to be a necessity for the Jewish religion, which required a reliance on "the hyperbolical genius of Eastern Speech" because of its preparatory nature.[54] It was important, wrote Warburton, that the scriptures of the Jews be "conveyed under the covert language

---

51. Samuel Chandler, *A Vindication of the Christian Religion* (London: Chandler, 1725), 258.

52. William Warburton, *The Divine Legation of Moses Demonstrated: On the Principles of a Religious Deist, from the Omission of the Doctrine of a Future State of Reward and Punishment in the Jewish Dispensation*, 3 vols. (London: Gyles, 1738–1741), 2:298–302.

53. Warburton, *Divine Legation*, 2:93–104.

54. Warburton, *Divine Legation*, 3:202.

of their present œconomy,"[55] so that they would not know the temporary nature of their law and could be kept in compliance with it. Warburton uses examples of Jewish traditions to illustrate their allegorical logic, such as the connection between Passover and the exodus from Egypt and the association made between the destruction of Jerusalem and the end of the world.[56] His disagreement centers on Collins's logic that a return to Jewish allegory is the key to interpreting the New Testament. The second sense of scripture is made obscure in the Old, he argues, and made plain in the New. To return to Jewish methods of interpretation would be regressive.[57]

Despite their chorus of condemnation, Collins's challengers doubled down on notions that Jewish allegorizing somehow constituted or paved the way for Christian transparency. This common cause came with its own contradictions, however. Some supposed that the Jews were unaware of the allegorical logic of their scriptures and their ceremonies. This version of the formula, whereby Jews were limited to a literal sense of their own allegories, had much in common with premodern notions of Jewish literalism. Others, however, portrayed Jews as masters of allegory, skilled in rhetoric and symbolism for the sake of some mystical purpose. This was the viewpoint exploited by Collins, and reaffirmed by many of his readers, even those who condemned him as heretical and dangerous. His offense was due to his aligning Christ and Christianity with Jewish allegory and not his depiction of Jewish allegory as such. Still others presented a mixed view, depicting Jews as simultaneously unaware of their allegories but also repelled by plain speech.

The contradictions between and within the various theories about Jewish allegory did nothing to inhibit the success of the trope. In the following decades, it would continue to find purchase even in the most esteemed settings. The celebrated biblical scholar Robert Lowth, for instance, would present his expert opinion on biblical allegory in his 1753 *Lectures on the Sacred Poetry of the Hebrews*. His lectures identify three types of allegory in the Bible: continued metaphor (such as the imagery of agriculture and threshing to describe God's justice), parable or storytelling, and a third type which he calls "mystical allegory." Lowth identifies mystical allegory as those places in scripture where the same words meaningfully describe two things, or two real events, simultaneously. This type of allegory, he

---

55. Warburton, *Divine Legation*, 3:203.
56. Warburton, *Divine Legation*, 3:206–9.
57. Warburton, *Divine Legation*, 3:210.

42   JEWISH ALLEGORY IN EIGHTEENTH-CENTURY CHRISTIAN IMAGINATION

writes, has its foundation in the things of the Jewish religion. While the first two types of allegory came from the imagination of the authors, who were free to choose whatever imagery they liked, mystical allegory was the natural language of the "Divine Spirit" and always employed images that came from the history or the sacred rites of the Jews.[58] Jewish things, it would seem, have an inherent ability to double-signify, and God made use of this quality when inspiring the biblical prophets. Lowth's sober analysis of Hebrew figurative language lived in a different disciplinary space than the deist controversies surrounding Collins's *Grounds and Reasons*. It nevertheless relied on a similar logic concerning Jewish interpretation nearly thirty years later, demonstrating the staying power of these ideas despite the perception by many that they constituted a fundamental attack on Christian faith.

Interpreting Anthony Collins

Before concluding this brief exploration of an early eighteenth-century English context, a survey of contemporary interpretations of Anthony Collins will shed further light on the significance of his ideas. Conflicting theories exist among historians and biographers on precisely how satirical *Grounds and Reasons* was intended to be and whether or not Collins's admiration for Surenhuis and the allegories of his rabbi were genuine. Scholars such as James O'Higgins, David Berman, Silvia Berti, Wayne Hudson, and Hans Frei each present a different version of Anthony Collins. Some view him as an atheist, others as a deist, still others as a practicing Christian, as evidenced by his continued membership in the Church of England. Each of the scholars cited so far, however, agrees with the standard view that Collins was attacking the foundations of Christianity with his *Grounds and Reasons*, and making the Christian scriptures "absurd" (a word found frequently in the secondary literature) for their reliance on Jewish allegory. The evidence for this view reveals an assortment of reconstructive activity. Indeed, Collins himself never admitted to being anti-Christian. Frei points to the fact that Collins was a disciple of John Locke as evidence of his skepticism regarding allegorical methods. In Frei's view, Collins would have believed, as a follower of Locke, that

---

58. Robert Lowth, *Lectures on the Sacred Poetry of the Hebrews*, trans. G. Gregory (London: Tegg, 1839), 114–20.

1. ENLIGHTENED CONTRADICTIONS

43

the "lost rules governing nonliteral interpretation are completely arbitrary nonsense and the interpretation itself therefore nonsensical."[59] Alternatively, O'Higgins points to *Grounds and Reasons* as evidence of Collins's ultimate break with Locke and with Christianity. Collins, "by denying the validity of the Messianic prophecies, struck at the roots of Christianity precisely as Locke had conceived it."[60] As for his reasons, Berti suggests that Collins was motivated by Jewish polemical arguments against Christianity. She cites the listing of three rare Hebrew manuscripts in his library with decidedly anti-Christian content.[61] Her research highlights the indebtedness of both Toland and Collins to Jewish sources, concluding that "the most conscious and fruitful radical English Enlightenment owes the incisiveness and force of its criticism of Christianity not so much, as is often said, to a total, atheistic condemnation of the Judeo-Christian tradition, as to a rationalistic and scathing utilization of the polemic spirit of Judaism."[62] Her argument puts Collins's work somewhere on the spectrum between ironic and paradoxical, suggesting he attacked the foundations of Christianity with Judaism, since it is precisely Christianity's foundation in Judaism on which he insisted. The most inventive reconstruction of Collins's true intentions, however, comes from Berman, who speculates regarding his closeted atheism. Berman cites an argument against the existence of God rumored to have been authored by Collins and circulated in secret. He proposes to reconstruct the alleged document himself and does so in a four-point argument for atheism drawing on ideas from Collins's published writings.[63] In attempting to say what Collins himself could not, evidently, say, he speculates somewhat freely regarding Collins's true beliefs, and this effort extends to an outline of *Grounds and Reasons* in nine summary points. The first seven points Berman loyally paraphrases

---

59. Frei, *Eclipse*, 70.

60. James O'Higgins, *Anthony Collins: The Man and His Works* (The Hague: Nijhoff, 2012), 8, 171.

61. Collins does cite these sources in a footnote, which appears in a section of the text explaining why modern Jews, unlike their ancestors, do not utilize allegory and instead mock allegory as a Christian innovation. The section attempts to explain modern Jewish anti-Christian and anti-allegorical sentiments. See Collins, *Grounds and Reasons* 82, note b.

62. Silvia Berti, "At the Roots of Unbelief," *Journal of the History of Ideas* 56.4 (1995): 573.

63. David Berman, "Anthony Collins and the Question of Atheism in the Early Part of the Eighteenth Century," *Proceedings of the Royal Irish Academy* 75.C (1975): 102.

44   JEWISH ALLEGORY IN EIGHTEENTH-CENTURY CHRISTIAN IMAGINATION

from the text. The last two points, however, amount to speculative reconstruction, stating that the typological fulfillment of biblical prophecies is absurd and "Christianity has no basis."[64] Such a reading, which appears to have a great deal of scholarly support, nevertheless requires an interpretation of Collins that is itself allegorical. On the surface, *Grounds and Reasons* makes no such claim, and at least one scholar suggests there is something to be gained from taking Collins at his word.

Jewish historian David Ruderman, for his part, argues for the seriousness of Collins's underlying purpose, even if it was cloaked in irony, and considers the possibility that Collins was offering a sincere response to Whiston's theories. Acknowledging the sizeable amount of literature supporting the standard view, he presents an alternative stating: "I simply would like to read Collins in a different way."[65] The results of such a reading prove to be instructive for highlighting the underappreciated trend in Christian Hebraism among New Testament scholars in the eighteenth century. Ruderman points to both Collins's source (de la Roche) and Mishnah scholars in England such as William Wotton, who took the issue very seriously, as did Surenhusius's followers on the continent. Such men, steeped in Hebrew studies and Judaica already, were drawn to comparisons between New Testament and early rabbinic texts and their methods for citing scripture. De la Roche wrote that the New Testament authors "have done nothing in the present Case but what was practiced by the ancient Hebrew Theologers."[66] Whatever playfulness or irreverence one may detect in Collins's purported interest in Jewish allegory, the contemporary sources he cited were sincere and represented a growing inclination to interpret the Christian scriptures with the aid of the rabbinic methods. Collins quoted Cambridge professor Simon Ockley, for instance, who wrote: "If I had ever had an Opportunity, I wou'd most certainly have gone thro' the New Testament under a Jew. Whatsoever some of our gentlemen may think, this I am well assur'd of, that they understand it infinitely better than we do."[67] Even if Collins

---

64. Berman, "Anthony Collins," 99.

65. David B. Ruderman, *Connecting the Covenants: Judaism and the Search for Christian Identity in Eighteenth-Century England* (Philadelphia: University of Pennsylvania Press, 2007), 66.

66. From Roche's *Memoirs of Literature*, as quoted in Ruderman, *Connecting the Covenants*, 72.

67. Ockley, "Letter to William Wotton," as quoted by Collins, *Grounds and Reasons*, 78.

1. ENLIGHTENED CONTRADICTIONS   45

was wholly sarcastic, therefore, many of his sources and their contemporaries were not. As we have seen, Jewish allegory was absurd or offensive to some, but others would profess it to be divinely inspired. Collins's work drew attention to these more positive formulations in order to challenge the arguments of his opponent. Rather than undermining Christianity on the whole, therefore we would do better to interpret Collins as undermining a particular trend in Christian interpretation of the Bible, one modeled in Whiston's scientific and iconoclastic literalism.

Christianity faced unprecedented challenges in the eighteenth century, and the latest in historical and scientific methods of exegesis had not always served it well. In the minds of some, it had left behind a text that no longer cohered. New methods of interpretation were needed; the reliance on allegorical reading, which had been foundational for so much of patristic and medieval exegesis, was viewed by many as naive and out of touch with advancements of modernity. Whiston's attempt to recover a lost Bible that described history more plainly was the result of a crisis in Christian hermeneutics, and Collins's response exploited the difficulty inherent in such a project. However layered or confounding his intentions may have been, the author of *Grounds and Reasons* exposed a fundamental flaw in the work of his contemporaries: the appeal to reason to prove the fundamentals of religion was producing unreasonable combinations of proofs. The ambivalence directed at both allegory and Jews by the defenders of the faith revealed major inconsistencies of thought in an era that favored logic and reason. Whether Collins aimed his efforts at rescuing allegory and Judaism (and with them Christianity) or at condemning allegory and Judaism (thereby condemning Christianity), or some other, more clever combination of these ideas, is still up for debate. What is clear is that the concept of Jewish allegory itself would become cemented in the minds of his readers. The imagined relationship between Jews and allegory would be reaffirmed in the wake of his dispute with Whiston, appearing in both positive and negative formulations in the decades to come. The contradictions embedded in these ideas about Jewish allegory would also reemerge in other contexts, as we will see in the following chapters.

2
ALLEGORY AND CONVERSION:
JOHAN KEMPER'S CHRISTIAN KABBALAH

In the opening to his Hebrew language commentary on the Zohar, written between 1710 and 1713, Johan Kemper, a converted Jew from Kraków then lecturing at Uppsala University in Sweden, assures his readers that his explanations meet the strictest kosher standards.[1] He compares his interpretations to a knife used for ritual slaughter, employing graphic metaphors related to the slaughter of birds and animals drawn from tractate Hullin of the Talmud. His knife has been inspected with both fingernail and flesh; it slices without interruption and without being concealed by the skin it pierces. He has reached into the glands and examined the lungs, squeezed and poked any cysts for signs of infection, and declares that his work passes inspection with no evidence of tear, blemish, or adhesion. And what does such a meticulous interpretation of the Zohar, the legendary esoteric Torah commentary of mysterious origins, reveal? Kemper summarizes his findings: that the true Messiah is Jesus the Nazarene and that he is the embodied form of Metatron and one person of the triune God. None of this is explicitly stated in the text of the Zohar itself, of course, but Kemper believed the combination of his rabbinic training and his Christian faith could expose the meaning hidden in its pages. The Jews, who Kemper asserts have not understood this as the true message of the Zohar, are the ones who are "torn" with a defective knife. They are *treyf*, unkosher, confused. Kemper offers his commentary as a means to heal their wounds and to counter the lies they have inherited. Employing a second halakic metaphor for the proper disposal of leavened foods before Passover, he

---

1. Johan Kemper, *Maṭeh Mosheh o Maḳel Ya'aḳov*, MS Uppsala University Library, Heb. 24, fol. 2a. Hul. 17b, 27a, 47a.

48   JEWISH ALLEGORY IN EIGHTEENTH-CENTURY CHRISTIAN IMAGINATION

offers his *Liqqute ha-Zohar* as a candle to search between the cracks and a torch to burn the *hametz* of their interpretations (*perushim*).

How did such a commentary come to be produced at Uppsala University in a country that had, by royal decree, banished Jews from its lands? Who was Kemper's intended audience, given the paucity of Jewish readers in his orbit who would recognize the talmudic references and the ostensible irrelevance of these same references to his Christian students and colleagues? To whom was he declaring his own work kosher? Kemper's Hebrew manuscripts, which provide commentary not just on the Zohar but also on the Gospel of Matthew, are aimed at decoding biblical and rabbinic sources to reveal what he understood to be their underlying christological sense. None of his works in Hebrew were published, save for a few heavily annotated excerpts, despite the efforts of his most devoted disciples to produce Latin translations for a wider audience.[2] Kemper's presence at the Swedish university and his enigmatic manuscripts may seem of limited significance given their lack of immediate impact.[3] However, both the story of his conversion and his methods of interpretation have caught the attention of twentieth and twenty-first century historians who study kabbalah and Jewish-Christian relations for several reasons. His blend of Christian and Jewish exegetical material, in the associative style of midrash and all in Hebrew, illustrates the kinds of border crossings that excited the halls of European universities for complex and conflicting reasons in early modernity. His commentaries stand, therefore, at the intersection of ideas and movements characteristic of the early eighteenth century. We will survey some of this scholarship in the present chapter.

What has yet to be explored in the scholarship on Kemper, however, is the relationship between biblical allegory and conversion that he exemplifies. Whoever Kemper may have imagined reading his commentaries in the years to come, his most important audience was, in a sense, himself. His work of decoding sacred texts was a means of understanding his own life's story. He believed his Jewish identity to be an allegory for his Christian identity, the same way that the Old Testament was an allegory for

---

2. Aside from the Latin translations of Kemper's work on Matthew by his student Anders Norrelius, Eric Benzelius, chief librarian of Uppsala University, petitioned the Academic Senate to support the Latin translation of his Zohar commentary. See Eskhult, "Andreas Norrelius' Latin," 63.

3. For a summary of the careers of Kemper's closest students, see Eskhult, "Andreas Norrelius' Latin," 70–72.

2. ALLEGORY AND CONVERSION: JOHAN KEMPER   49

the New. This is most plainly expressed in the two different titles he gave his first treatise of Zohar commentary. He titled the work both *Matteh Mosheh*, "Staff of Moses," employing his Hebrew name Moses Aaron, and *Maqqel Ya'aqov*, "Rod of Jacob," employing his baptized name Johannes Christianus Jacobi. His work discloses a type and antitype relationship not just in the text of the Zohar or the text of the Bible but also between his two interconnected selves. In this, Kemper embodies the imagined eschatological function of conversion that we find so prevalent in his generation. Christian expectations of Jewish conversion saturated the theories and theologies of thought leaders in this time. Kemper saw himself as the incarnation of these expectations and therefore uniquely suited to interpret scripture finally for Jews and Christians alike, to reenact both the receiving of the law and the witness of its fulfillment in Christ. Christian narratives about history and salvation manifest, therefore, in Kemper's allegorical conversion. A study of Kemper's life and work will illuminate the kind of discourse about Christian kabbalah that characterized the eighteenth century, and the imagined relationship between biblical allegory and Jewish conversion this discourse revealed.

Moses Aaron's Allegorical Conversion

Kemper's autobiographical *Unterthäniger Bericht* (*Humble Report*) tells the story of his conversion from Judaism to Christianity and his migration from Kraków to Schweinfurt to Uppsala. Born Moses Aaron, he became fatherless at the age of two and as a consequence of the family's instability and his facility with learning, he found himself in the homes of rabbis and of Christians educated in various religious contexts in rabbinic texts and in the Bible. According to his *Unterthäniger Bericht*, it would be the interpretation of the biblical prophecies that captured his imagination and triggered persistent questions about their fulfillment. He began to wonder who had interpreted them correctly between his rabbis and his Christian teachers. His early struggles, weighing Christian and Jewish interpretations of the prophecies, are framed in dialogue with his worried mother. He would bring her prooftexts from the Talmud and the Hebrew scriptures, pointing to a threefold division of ages that indicated a messianic age already in progress. Other hints and references to groupings of threes in the Bible were placed before his mother, raising the possibility that the Trinitarian view of God and history might be right. She responded with trepidation and tried to put an end to these inquiries.

50   JEWISH ALLEGORY IN EIGHTEENTH-CENTURY CHRISTIAN IMAGINATION

He writes: "But it caused her only sorrow and distress. She wept bitterly over this and said: I have only one child and of all things he has to make me experience disgrace! She had many sleepless nights because of that and caused me great suffering as well. This was the first obstacle which I encountered with my conversion."[4]

Kemper reports that he returned to the study of the Talmud to assuage his mother's fears and took a wife at a young age with whom he had a son. Here he identifies his wife Siphra as the "second obstacle" to his conversion. Despite the strong persuasion of these two Jewish women, however, the cataclysmic events of the Jewish world would finally pull him away from them. Rumors of the imminent arrival of the Messiah gripped the communities around him leading up to the year 1695. The apostasy and death of Shabbetai Tzvi decades earlier had shaken the faith of those who believed him to be the Messiah, but rumors persisted, calculations were redrawn, and an influential Lithuanian Rabbi by the name of Zadok convinced the Jews of Poland, Silesia, Moravia, and Bohemia that the day would finally be September 5 of that year. Kemper himself prepared for the day with fasting and ritual immersions and comforted himself with the thought that his mother's guidance would be affirmed. When the day arrived with sunshine instead of the predicted darkness and "venomous haze," a profound disillusionment settled over the expectant communities, and Kemper withdrew finally from his faith and his mother, despite her weeping and begging.[5] With little expressed concern for the fate of the family he left behind, Kemper describes being welcomed into the home of German theologian Johann Friedrich Heunisch, where he finally converted. His rejection of Judaism is expressed in exegetical terms recalling the hazy-day expectations of those who were fooled by Rabbi Zadok: "The Jews regard Scripture as something opaque and imperfect that no one can

---

4. Johan Kemper, *Unterthäniger Bericht an einen Hoch-Edlen und Hoch-Weisen Rath zu Schweinfurth von der wunderlichen Güte Gottes, welche Er, der Allerhöchste, erwiesen mir armen Menschen, Mosi Aaron, einem durch Gottes Gnad bekehrten Rabbi, auß Crackau gebürtig, Nechst Angehengter demüthigen Bitt Ihm die heilige Tauff wiederfahren zu lassen* (Schweinfurt: Drechsler, 1696). English translation by Niels Eggerz in "Johan Kemper's (Moses Aaron's) Humble Account: A Rabbi between Sabbateanism and Christianity," in *Continuity and Change in the Jewish Communities of the Early Eighteenth Century*, vol. 12 of *Early Modern Workshop: Jewish History Resources* (Ohio State University, August 17–19, 2015), 28.

5. Kemper, *Unterthäniger Bericht*, 30.

2. ALLEGORY AND CONVERSION: JOHAN KEMPER

understand without the Talmud."[6] If the Jews were in the dark concerning the Messiah's arrival, their understanding of scripture was also clouded. This is followed by a critique of Jewish texts, ways, and understanding, condemning them all as confused, shallow, and flawed.

Kemper was not the sole author of his biographical account. Reverend Heunisch himself played a major role in shaping the conversion narrative, something that was common practice when it came to producing the *Lebensläufe* of converted Jews. As Elisheva Carlebach writes, the convert and his sponsors would typically craft the document together. "Collectively, then, the narratives constitute a unique layering of material shaped by both the imagination of the convert and the vision of those who played an instrumental role in converting him or her, mirroring two distinct sets of expectations."[7] Due to its coauthorship, Kemper's *Unterthäniger Bericht* demonstrates features common to convert autobiographies produced in German lands in early modernity. Carlebach suggests that this genre was intended to relate stylistically to the practice of confession. Such documents cast the early life of the convert as a secret that has now been revealed.[8] Another common feature was an emphasis on the Jewish childhood and education of the convert. Unlike medieval narratives of conversion, there was less of a focus on the miraculous events that inspired conversion and more of an emphasis on the early Jewish foundation of the individual in question. They may have experienced flashes of insight or been drawn to Christian interpretations, their "paths strewn with signposts of their future fulfillment in Christianity,"[9] but the cause of their conversion related to their solid foundation in Jewish learning and to questions and desires that arose from this study, as if an upbringing immersed in Jewish texts naturally pointed to an eventual conversion to Christianity.

The reason for the emphasis on Jewish education in conversion stories related to Christian expectations of the endtime. As Carlebach's work demonstrates, conversion narratives in the sixteenth through the eighteenth centuries played a central role in Christian ideas about the unfolding of history.[10] Both missionaries and converts incorporated the

---

6. Kemper, *Unterthäniger Bericht*, 31.

7. Elisheva Carlebach, *Divided Souls: Converts from Judaism in Germany, 1500–1750* (New Haven: Yale University Press, 2008), 94.

8. Carlebach, *Divided Souls*, 89.

9. Carlebach, *Divided Souls*, 99.

10. Carlebach, *Divided Souls*, 67–87.

52   JEWISH ALLEGORY IN EIGHTEENTH-CENTURY CHRISTIAN IMAGINATION

drama of the eschaton into their narratives, interpreting the turning of the Jews to Christ as a strong indicator of the apocalypse. This expectation was excited even further after the rise and fall of Shabbetai Tzvi, inspiring a spike in missionary activity and conversions. Thereafter, Christians and converted Jews alike became especially fixated on the false messiahs of the Jews, Jewish deceit, and Jewish gullibility. Lists of Jewish messiahs became popular in pamphlets and other writings, indicating a generalized enthusiasm concerning the failed expectations of the Jews. For converts like Kemper, an expertise in rabbinic learning prior to their conversion served to bolster notions that Christianity was the fulfillment of Judaism and that the Old Testament, read honestly by a Jew, pointed plainly to Christ, the first-century Messiah, and to his imminent return. They were held up as the embodiment of Jewish allegory decoded, the unfolding of messianic prophecy in real time.

One of Kemper's first activities as a Christian demonstrates the allegorical quality of his conversion as he understood it. Between the time of his baptism and his move to Sweden, Kemper relocated to Altdorf, where he was commissioned by the German Hebraist Christof Wagenseil to copy, among other things, a Yiddish Purim play containing a subversive and irreverent retelling of the biblical Esther story. It may seem a strange undertaking for the earnest theologian and the newly baptized Jew, but as Rachel Wamsley has shown, such plays were sought after at the time by Christians curious about Jewish customs. This was, in part, because they were often hidden away or even destroyed by Jews, who feared they might come into the wrong hands. The Purim spiel is an intentionally transgressive event. It celebrates the ritual performance of inverted norms, tricks, and disguises. Purim is a night of topsy-turvy roleplaying, the imaginary acting out of moral transgression, before things are set right again the following day. For this reason, a given community might want to avoid the gaze of interlopers likely to misquote or misinterpret the play. For the Christian ethnographer, not only was the Purim play hard to come by, but its decipherment required a willing translator-informant, and Kemper would play just such a role in Wagenseil's employment. Reading his work closely, particularly the layout and contents of the title page, Wamsley argues that Kemper was no passive conduit, but filled the page with ironies and inside jokes that framed his own conversion more than anything else. For example, a familiar layout greets the reader in a hand-drawn columnar archway, a common feature of title pages in Jewish books. But here the gate appears as a hinged triptych, evoking medieval Christian devotional objects and displaying a Trinitarian scheme.[11] His annotation to the gate image opens with a talmudic citation and ends with a remark about his own name change: "All gates are locked but for the gates of tears. May that be a witness and remembrance for all time that I signed my name, busy with the work of heaven, Johan Christian Jacob, formerly Moses Cohen of Krakow, for changing one's name changes one's fortune, and there is no fortune for Israel."[12] Kemper used familiar Jewish formulas but also inserted notes about his own journey and religious identity. He also employed Christian conventions such as the spelling out of the Tetragrammaton, which would have been avoided by a Jewish scribe. Wamsley finds it suiting that the backdrop for Kemper's personal conversion would be a Purim spiel, as he "continuously plays against type, seizing on the transgressive reversals native to the Purim play to destabilize the social and textual forms he is called to reproduce."[13] She likens Kemper to the "Purim Rav," a mock rabbi who puts on a performance of expounding the Torah, but in such a way that reverses or overturns accepted interpretations with counterexegesis. Whether or not Kemper understood his work in such a playful light, he clearly saw his new identity as the religious counterpoint to his former identity. He had passed through the archway and turned to look back. He was reborn a Christian in the image and likeness of a Jew. He had become a biblical allegory unfolded.

Kabbalah at a Swedish University

While living in Altdorf, Kemper built a reputation for himself as a tutor for students with an interest in Hebrew and rabbinic learning. It was two students from Sweden who ultimately convinced him to return with them to their homeland, having heard that the king was actively searching for an able *Judaeus conversus* to teach Hebrew and rabbinic studies at Uppsala University. Kemper would indeed meet with the approval of the royal administrators and spent the next fifteen years as Lecturer of Talmudic and Rabbinic Hebrew. At Uppsala he was admired by his students as a model of the marriage of ancient Jewish sagacity and true Christian faith,

---

11. Rachel Wamsley, "Characters against Type: Conversion, Mise-en-Page, and Counter-Exegesis in a Seventeenth Century Purim Play," *Lias* 44.1 (2017): 71–73.

12. Johan Kemper, *Eyn sheyn purim shpil*, as translated by Wamsley, "Characters against Type," 84.

13. Wamsley, "Characters against Type," 62.

54   JEWISH ALLEGORY IN EIGHTEENTH-CENTURY CHRISTIAN IMAGINATION

or in the words of his disciple and Latin translator, Anders Norrelius, a "Rabbi moistened with the waters of the salvation-bringing Baptism and of the sound spring of wisdom."[14] But it was his facility with kabbalah that was Kemper's most celebrated quality. He writes that he was pressured by the faculty at Uppsala to interrupt his Hebrew translation of the New Testament to produce his *Liqqute ha-Zohar*, which they believed would have a greater impact on the successful conversion Jewish readers. Kemper's role at Uppsala, as a converted Jew and as a kabbalist, will be further clarified with a brief summary of the trends in early modern Christian Hebraism, trends that emphasized both conversion and kabbalistic interpretation.

In 1510 the emperor of the Holy Roman Empire, Maximilian I, appointed a commission of theological experts to council him on an important matter brought by the Jewish convert to Christianity, Johannes Pfefferkorn. The matter at hand was whether or not to approve the destruction of Jewish books in an effort to force conversion to Christianity. Johann Reuchlin, an accomplished humanist and Christian Hebraist, offered the only dissenting opinion. Though outnumbered, his argument swayed the emperor, and the books in question were spared. A legal and public debate between Pfefferkorn and Reuchlin ensued, fueled by their supporters. On the one side were the theologians at the University of Cologne, who were convinced by Pfefferkorn's professed insider knowledge of the Talmud's dangerous qualities. On the other side was a collection of humanists convinced by Reuchlin's view that Jewish texts were essential to Christian scholarship. Reuchlin himself continued to research and publish in his related areas of interest, Hebrew philology and Christian kabbalism, providing fresh ammunition for both sides of the debate. While the more hostile perspective of Pfefferkorn and his supporters would persist, the study of Jewish books would be an expanding field over the coming centuries, and with it various perspectives on the usefulness of postbiblical Jewish sources to Christianity circulated. The study of rabbinic sources was not new to Christian scholarship at this time. What Reuchlin and his contemporaries, such as Giovanni Pico della Mirandola and Guillaume Postel, contributed was an emphasis on Jewish esotericism and, in particular, on the Zohar as a precious source of ancient Jewish wisdom.

---

14. Anders Norrelius, *Prolegomena*, translated in Eskhult, "Andreas Norrelius' Latin," 315.

2. ALLEGORY AND CONVERSION: JOHAN KEMPER   55

What came to eventually be published under the title of the Zohar (meaning "radiance") in the sixteenth century was a collection of esoteric commentaries on the weekly Torah readings and other teachings that had been in circulation among the Jews of Castile in the thirteenth century. The teachings were believed to have been recorded by second-century Jews under the leadership of Rabbi Shimon bar Yochai but were thought to contain the wisdom of still earlier generations. These texts exhibited themes from other esoteric writings, such as the Bahir and Sefer Yetzirah, but also elaborated a vast and complex mythology of the ten aspects of God personified, that is, the *sefirot*. The texts are notoriously enigmatic, drawing on a vast set of cosmic symbols and relationships that required facility with rabbinic methods to skillfully decipher. The intertextual layering of earlier Jewish sources did not discourage Christian interest in the Zohar, however. Its peculiar manipulation of numbers, letters, genders, and biblical themes excited the curiosity of Christian humanists and philosophers, who imagined that a universal language of spirit and nature could be eventually discerned through the proper interpretation of the world's signs and cyphers.

To the dismay of the Jewish communities who circulated it and who believed at least some of the material in question should not be printed or translated from the original Aramaic lest it be misunderstood, Christian readers from the time of Reuchlin and Postel advocated for a wide circulation of the Zohar. Published Jewish translations of the Zohar came with careful abridgements or disclaimers that the translated material contained only the *peshat* of the text, protecting the most esoteric meaning (or *sod*) hidden away.[15] The aim of its Christian distributors was exactly the opposite. Postel, for his part, translated the Zohar into Latin in a spirit of unveiling the most ancient, most holy "revelation of revelation." The fourfold sense of scripture, which early Christians had preserved imperfectly, would be made clear in the Latin Zohar.[16] Postel believed the Zohar to be a confirmation of Christian teaching authored by Christ himself, in an ultimate sense, the true Oral Torah to compliment the Hebrew scriptures.

---

15. Boaz Huss, "Translations of the Zohar: Historical Contexts and Ideological Frameworks," *Correspondences* 4 (2017): 89.

16. Bernard McGinn, "Cabalists and Christians: Reflections on Cabala in Medieval and Renaissance Thought," in *Jewish Christians and Christian Jews: From the Renaissance to the Enlightenment*, ed. Richard H. Popkin and Gordon M. Weiner (Dordrecht: Springer, 1994), 25.

56   JEWISH ALLEGORY IN EIGHTEENTH-CENTURY CHRISTIAN IMAGINATION

He posited that the one who finally put it to writing was the high priest Simon the Just from the Gospel of Luke, who received the baby Jesus at the temple in Jerusalem and praised God that he could finally see revelation unveiled: "for my eyes have seen your salvation, which you have prepared in the presence of all peoples, a light for revelation to the Gentiles and for glory to your people Israel" (Luke 2:30–32, NRSV).[17] Postel presented a view of history that divided time between the Jewish era, or the era of the Written Torah identified with the authoritative, masculine, and aloof God the Father, and the era of the Oral Torah, the Zohar, which was identified with femininity and the messianic age.[18] In Postel's view, the Zohar was the scripture for the coming age, intended for kabbalistic Christians, who were the real Jews "much more truly than those literal Jews of long ago."[19] We see in this arrangement a typological view of the relationship between Judaism and Christianity. It unfolds over time, revealing what was only hinted at previously. It is, in some ways, the antithesis of Pfefferkorn's approach, which sought to obliterate the Judaism of his ancestors. Both approaches are, in a sense, conversionary, replacing an "old" with a "new" and embracing the customary supersessionism, but the one retains a reverence for the older form, however romanticized, while the other seeks to destroy it. In this, perhaps, we can discern a parallel to ambivalence directed at allegory, or to anxieties concerning the integrity of a sacred text whose interpretations stray too far from the letter. Thereafter Christian kabbalah came to be either embraced or vilified, mirroring Reformation-era attitudes toward biblical allegory more broadly.

Postel's sixteenth-century Latin translation of the Zohar would eventually be replaced by Christian Knorr von Rosenroth's seventeenth-century Latin translation, the enormously influential *Kabbalah Denudata*, which provided extensive commentary claiming to prove that Jewish esotericism confirmed the truth of Christianity. On the frontispiece of early editions

---

17. Some Christian kabbalists identified Simon of the New Testament with Shimon bar Yochai. Postel had a different configuration, and believed Shimon bar Yochai was the Zohar's later translator, believing it to have been originally written by Simon the Just in Hebrew. See Judith Weiss, "Guillaume Postel's 'Idea of the Zohar,'" *Aries: Journal for the Study of Western Esotericism* 19.2 (2019): 256.

18. See Weiss, "Idea of the Zohar," 253–54.

19. "Sumus vero nos Christiani Judaei longe quam olim literales fuissent veriores," as quoted in Marion Leathers Kuntz, *Guillaume Postel, Prophet of the Restitution of All Things: His Life and Thought* (London: Nijhoff, 1981), 130, n422.

2. ALLEGORY AND CONVERSION: JOHAN KEMPER

of the *Kabbalah Denudate* we find an illustration of a figure whose gaze is fixed on the sun. The sun is depicted as a circle around ten smaller circles, three above separated from seven below, signifying a divine Trinity governing the *sefirot*. The figure has a set of keys around her arm and holds an unrolled scroll, with Gen 1:1 in Hebrew on one side and John 1:1 in Greek on the other, as though the Old Testament and New Testament creation stories were two sides of the same scroll able to be unlocked by one whose interpretive gaze is fixed on the divine.

Due in large part to translations, anthologies, and commentaries such as *Kabbalah Denudata*, Christian interest in kabbalah was widespread in early modernity, impacting the discourse among thought leaders such as Leibniz and Newton.[20] It was also a discourse with a heavy presence from Jewish converts to Christianity. This was the case in the centuries before Reuchlin and Postel and continued to be the case in the centuries that followed.[21] Various reasons have been articulated for the role of converts in the circulation of Christian kabbalah. Bernard McGinn and others have pointed to affinities between Jewish and Christian thought that kabbalah lays bare and to mutual influences between Christians and Jews that can be traced in kabbalistic texts and ideas that converts were able to exploit.[22] I would add that conversion and kabbalah had a functional similarity, from a Christian perspective, in that they both reinforced a particular hermeneutic narrative, a story of fulfillment or unveiling through embodied interpretation.

Converts were also instrumental in circulating the idea that the Zohar, and kabbalah more generally conceived, represented an ancient, universal form of religion dating back as far as Adam in Eden. Examples include Paulus de Heredia and Flavius Mithradates, who were sources of Pico's views on the oral transmission of kabbalah from ancient times.[23] From

---

20. See Allison P. Coudert, "Leibniz, Locke, Newton and the Kabbalah," in *The Christian Kabbalah: Jewish Mystical Books and Their Christian Interpreters*, ed. Joseph Dan (Cambridge: Harvard University Press, 1997), 149–80.

21. See McGinn, "Cabalists and Christians," 14–16. McGinn distinguishes between Jewish "Kabbalah" and the Christianized "Cabala."

22. See, for instance, McGinn, "Cabalists and Christians," 15, 29 n. 36; Shalom Sadik, "When Maimonideans and Kabbalists Convert to Christianity," *JSQ* 24.2 (2017): 145–67. On Christian influence on the Zohar, see Yehuda Liebes, "Christian Influences on the Zohar," in *Studies in the Zohar*, trans. Arnold Schwartz, Stephanie Nakache, and Penina Peli (Albany: State University of New York Press, 1993), 139–61.

23. On Pico's relationship to Heredia see Gershom Scholem, "Zur Geschichte der Anfänge der christlichen Kabbala," in *Essays Presented to Leo Baeck* (London: East &

58   JEWISH ALLEGORY IN EIGHTEENTH-CENTURY CHRISTIAN IMAGINATION

the Renaissance on, this view had enormous appeal to those who believed they could discern a *prisca theologia* that had been preserved or encoded somehow in the symbolically rich texts of ancient cultures. In theological circles, the universal wisdom of antiquity was interpreted to be a foreshadowing of the Christian message or of a Christian age to come. The religions of the past were seen as mere vehicles for preserving the sacred, secret truth, which would be unsealed only at the inauguration of the final age. The Jewish convert to Christianity was therefore the embodiment of such a notion, having brought from their childhood the wisdom of the ancients, but also having not realized the essence of their inherited knowledge until it was discovered and disclosed at the baptismal fount.

In comparing notions related to the myth of Jewish antiquity from new Christians in the Iberian context, Jerome Friedman suggests that those who converted to Catholicism and those who converted to Protestantism made distinct contributions. Particularly in the era of the Renaissance and Reformations, Jewish Catholics tended to embrace kabbalah, believing the truth of the ancients could be discerned with proper study of esoteric traditions and by reading the Bible through kabbalistic techniques such as *gematria* or *notarikon*. According to these methods, individual Hebrew letters signify either numbers or whole words, which can be recombined in ways that draw out inner, alternative meanings. "By moving from the verbal to the mathematical text and back again, a scholar could force the Bible to yield its most esoteric secrets."[24] Protestant converts, on the other hand, tended to renounce such extravagances, along with traditional notions of a fourfold sense of scripture, and participated in the Christian Hebraism of their contemporaries for the sake of understanding the plain sense of scripture. Protestant notions of Jewish antiquity were driven by efforts to return to a more primitive form of apostolic, or Ebionite, Christianity rather than a decoding of the text. Jewish Christians in the Protestant context contributed practically to the production of Hebrew texts, but

---

West, 1954), translated into English by Debra Prager as "The Beginnings of the Christian Kabbalah," in Dan, *Christian Kabbalah*, 30–35. On Kemper's familiarity with the work of Heredia, see Hans Joachim Schoeps, *Philosemitismus im Barock: Religions und Geistesgeschichtliche Untersuchungen*, (Tübingen: Mohr, 1952), 117.

24. Jerome Friedman, "The Myth of Jewish Antiquity: New Christians and Christian-Hebraica in Early Modern Europe," in Popkin and Weiner, *Jewish Christians and Christian Jews*, 37.

2. ALLEGORY AND CONVERSION: JOHAN KEMPER 59

also conceptually to what the reformers believed to be a more authentic, original Jesus movement.[25]

If it is true that Protestant converts to Christianity were less implicated in the rise of Christian kabbalah than their Catholic counterparts in the sixteenth century, this was not the case in the seventeenth century when Protestant scholars such as Surenhuis, Henry More, Franciscus Mercurius van Helmont, and Knorr von Rosenroth discovered kabbalah and put its instruments to work in solving the philosophical puzzles of the Enlightenment. As a case study, Uppsala University's department of Oriental Languages proves that there was less of a distinction between kabbalah and more sober forms of Hebraism in Protestant centers of learning in the late seventeenth and early eighteenth centuries. Kabbalah and Hebraism constituted a single field of study aimed at explicating "the sacred antiquities of the Jews."[26] Kemper's employment in the department epitomizes this phenomenon.

Uppsala was rising in recognition as a center of European intellectual advancement. In the wake of Descartes's visit to Sweden in 1650, the nation's natural philosophers were moved by a spirit of freedom of thought and King Charles XI proclaimed that scientific studies at Uppsala would be released from ecclesial oversight: "The doctrines of the Christian faith may not be subjected to philosophical criticism, but for the rest, philosophy shall be free, in practice and discussion."[27] Adding to this climate of liberal education was a fascination with Old Testament monarchical narratives on the part of the Carolean autocracy, which drew parallels between Swedish history and ancient Israel. Eskhult writes: "Thus, the March across the ice-covered Belts in Denmark were in panegyrical poetry compared to Israel's crossing of the Red Sea in the midst of the waves upon the dry ground. Likewise, Charles XII's introduction of extra taxes on rich people was justified by reference to a similar event in biblical Israel (2 Kings 15, 20)."[28] It

---

25. Friedman, "Myth of Jewish Antiquity," 38–42. Gershom Scholem goes so far as to define Christian kabbalah as a Catholic phenomenon. See Scholem, "Beginnings," 17.

26. Enoch S. Price, "The Curricula in Swedenborg's Student Years," published serially in *The New Philosophy* 34–38 (1931–1935). See also Eskhult, "Andreas Norrelius' Latin," 56–63.

27. Quoted from the decree of Charles XI, see Cyriel Sigrid Ljungberg Odhner Sigstedt, *The Swedenborg Epic: The Life and Works of Emanuel Swedenborg* (New York: Bookman Associates, 1952), 8–9.

28. Eskhult, "Andreas Norrelius' Latin," 54.

60   JEWISH ALLEGORY IN EIGHTEENTH-CENTURY CHRISTIAN IMAGINATION

was a point of national pride, therefore, that Uppsala would become an internationally recognized center for the advanced study of the Old Testament.

Like other European nations, Sweden experienced a wave of interest in kabbalah and rabbinic sources due to the perception that such studies would aid Christian understanding of scripture and would assist in efforts to convert Jews. The cross-currents of Pietism and Neoplatonism fostered the growing focus on the Hebrew Bible for devotional purposes and for the sake of metaphysical speculation. The Swedish monarchy encouraged scholarly investigation of Jewish texts, despite the royally mandated absence of Jews from the kingdom, and the surge of dissertations on rabbinic topics in Sweden left "all other European countries far behind" as one historian has put it.[29] Jewish commentaries, such as those by Maimonides, Abravanel, Ibn Ezra, and Rashi, were made available in university libraries, and it became a national priority to find a converted Jewish scholar, a university "Rabbi," to guide the study of such sources.

A scan of the scholarship on Kemper and his role at Uppsala reveals the recurrence of the term "philosemitism" by way of contextualization. Hans Joachim Schoeps, whose studies on the subject were formative in the mid-twentieth century, acknowledges the meager contribution of philosemitism relative to anti-Semitism, noting it to be "a mere sluggish trickle compared with a wide river."[30] Schoeps nevertheless frames Kemper's arrival in Sweden as a leading example of the philosemitic trends that characterized the study of Judaism during the Baroque period. The term philosemitism has been problematized by today's historians of early modern Europe, especially given the missionizing intentions of the many efforts in this direction.[31] King Charles XI exemplified the murkiness of Swedish philosemitism in his remarks to Laurentius Norrmannus, who was sent to Germany in search of a Jewish convert to teach at Uppsala prior to Kemper's arrival. Implying a kind of religious espionage, the king instructed Norrmannus to "find Jewish entrenchments and how to

---

29. Hans Joachim Schoeps, *Barocke Juden, Christen, Judenchristen* (Bern: Francke, 1965), 64, as translated by George Dole in *Studia Swedenborgiana* 7 (1990): 15.

30. Hans Joachim Schoeps, "Philosemitism in the Baroque Period," *JQR* 47 (1956): 139.

31. See, for instance, Sutcliffe, *Judaism and Enlightenment*, 6–11; and Eliane Glaser, *Judaism without Jews: Philosemitism and Christian Polemic in Early Modern England* (Basingstoke: Palgrave Macmillan, 2007).

2. ALLEGORY AND CONVERSION: JOHAN KEMPER 61

undermine them."[32] However, less nefarious examples of enthusiasm for Jewish sources can be detected in the words of Uppsala's faculty. Theology professor Daniel Djurberg penned a treatise on the Zohar, which was accompanied by the following dedicatory poem by Norrmannus extolling the value of kabbalah for the Christian interpreter:

> Who does here appear as a new teacher of the old synagogue
> And from where shines such a good light forth in the dense darkness?
> Whoever you are, I recognize the metals drawn out from a better mine
> And the property left by the old Fathers.
> The cloud is scattered and the world turns bright.
> Ben Jochai gives light to the Christians.[33]

Overloaded with metaphors, Norrmannus's ode to the Zohar is an appropriate point from which to consider the place of allegory in Protestant kabbalism. It suggests that kabbalah provided an outlet for an interest in double meanings that Protestant literalism had inhibited, a rehabilitation of allegory in contexts where it had waned.[34] The prevalence of kabbalah in Protestant centers of learning, such as Uppsala University, belies any notion that biblical allegory was out of fashion by the eighteenth century. On the contrary, we find a renewed interest in biblical symbolism by the faculty whose study of ancient and foreign cultures drew out exoticized notions of Hebrew and other "oriental languages." Kemper's interpretive efforts, directed at the Zohar and the New Testament, were well suited to this climate. Kemper the convert was more than a professional biblical allegorist at Uppsala, however. He was a walking allegory himself, a Jew and a Christian, the sign and the signified all at once. His life's journey was an interpretive act, or as he put it in the opening of *Matteh Mosheh*: "I have crossed the Jordan river of the Zohar to gather from amongst its

---

32. Mats Eskhult, "Rabbi Kemper's Case for Christianity in his Matthew Commentary, with Reference to Exegesis," in *Religious Polemics in Context: Papers Presented to the Second International Conference of the Leiden Institute for the Study of Religions*, ed. Arie van der Kooij and T. L. Hettema (Assen: Van Gorcum, 2004), 152.

33. Laurentius Norrmanus, opening poem in Daniel Djurberg, *Specimen doctrinae mysticae de via salutis juxta testimonium Scripturae Sacrae et consensus Antiquitatis* (Uppsala, 1696), as translated in Eskhult, "Andreas Norrelius' Latin," 63.

34. See Klaus Reichert, "Christian Kabbalah in the Seventeenth Century," in Dan, *Christian Kabbalah*, 136.

62 JEWISH ALLEGORY IN EIGHTEENTH-CENTURY CHRISTIAN IMAGINATION

words here and there and they will be joined together."[35] With messianic purpose, therefore, Kemper saw himself as uniquely qualified to enter the inner worlds of scripture, to recombine the words there in order to draw out and report on their true sense.

Kemper's Matthew Commentary

Like Postel before him, Kemper believed the New Testament contained the teachings of the Oral Torah or the secret meaning of the Written Torah, the Old Testament. In his view, the word made flesh was the spoken word, the true interpretation of the Hebrew scriptures.

> This Torah was spoken orally by the Messiah to all the patriarchs and to the true prophets, and it was as clear as the sun, but they were commanded to write it in a hidden way that would have to be explained orally to the masses, and especially the teaching of the Gospel that the holy mouth spoke to you. This secret may be revealed, but to others it must be by way of parable that needs a commentary, and this is the true, just and correct Oral Torah.[36]

Kemper's commentary on the Gospel of Matthew, *Me'irat Einayim* (1704), attempts to elucidate this quality of the New Testament by drawing out connections between New Testament verses and Old Testament and rabbinic sources. The commentary accompanies his Hebrew translation of the gospel and includes a prologue explaining his intention and methodology. The entire work, translation and commentary, was subsequently translated by Norrelius into Latin, and the pages of the Latin and Hebrew were then collated together in their present form, where they reside at Uppsala University Library, never having been published. However, while Norrelius's Latin communicates the earnestness of Kemper's efforts, it fails to preserve Kemper's many hints and allusions to rabbinic discursive language, some of it directed at anti-Christian material in the Talmud. Reading Kemper's Hebrew, one encounters an intricate dialogue with talmudic sources that

---

35. Kemper, *Maṭeh Mosheh*, introductory page.

36. Johan Kemper, *Avodat ha-Qodesh*, MS Uppsala University Library, Heb. 26, fol. 134a, as translated in Elliot Wolfson, "Messianism in the Christian Kabbalah of Johann Kemper," in *Millenarianism and Messianism in the Early Modern European Culture: Jewish Messianism in the Early Modern World*, ed. M. D. Goldish and R. H. Popkin (New York: Springer, 2001), 151.

would have been lost on a Christian audience, as it was lost in translation. This is the case with the title of the gospel translation, which appears in Kemper's Hebrew in three words: *Even Gilyon Matityahu*. The two-word Latin translation *Evangelium Matthiæ* misses the joke encoded in Kemper's title. Tractate Shabbat 116a of the Babylonian Talmud contains discussions related to the value of the *gilyonim*, the scrolls or gospels of the heretics, and plays on the Greek word *euangelion* with the Hebrew terms '*aven gilyon*, meaning "false gospel," or '*avon gilyon*, meaning "sinful gospel." Kemper borrowed this pejorative transliteration from the Talmud but used a variant with a slight change in spelling, thereby modifying the meaning. By changing the letter *vav* to a *bet*, the phrase now read '*even gilyon*, meaning "stone gospel," a possible reference to the "stone that the builders rejected," which he expands on later in the commentary.[37] Kemper's title is a play on a play on words, using the mock *euangelium* against itself and disclosing a new meaning for the Greek-turned-Hebrew terminology in the process.

In his prologue to the commentary, Kemper quotes the Aramaic formula, "a hint is enough for the wise man."[38] He encourages his readers to look for hints in his own commentary, as he has chosen to use as few words as possible to convey depths of meaning. Like the title of his translation, these hints come in the form of subtle allusions to texts and formulas that would have been well known to a reader with his background. Another example of this can be found a few lines earlier in the prologue, where he invokes the language of the Song of Songs and suggests his commentary is like a tower built with turrets, from which the reader can stand and look out over the vast corpus of biblical and rabbinic teaching (Song 4:4). The Old Testament and the Talmud alike will be accessible in his commentary for "from within and without the forest comes the ax to it."[39] This line, a direct quotation of from the Talmud, at first seems to be a simple metaphor for the Old Testament, as the part of the ax that comes from within, and the Talmud, as the part that comes from without, when applied to the Christian scriptures. The talmudic context of the metaphor, however, tells another story. The section in question, from b. Sanh. 39b, considers a string of biblical characters, from Obadiah to Ruth and David, who are

---

37. See Johan Kemper, *Even Gilyon Matityahu*, MS Uppsala University Library, Heb. 32, fol. 170r.

38. Kemper, *Even Gilyon Matityahu*, fol. 98r.

39. Kemper, *Even Gilyon Matityahu*, fol. 96v.

64 JEWISH ALLEGORY IN EIGHTEENTH-CENTURY CHRISTIAN IMAGINATION

either converts themselves or who come from within or without a given community but enact some kind of reversal of fortune. The Talmud states that Obadiah came from the place of two wicked people, referencing Ahab and Jezebel, but also prophesies concerning the Edomites, who came from two righteous people, Isaac and Rebecca. "Obadiah was an Edomite convert. Consequently, he prophesied with regard to Edom. And this is as people say: From and within the forest comes the ax to it, as the handle for the ax that chops the tree is from the forest itself." The proverb is repeated, this time in the name of Rabbi Shimon bar Yochai, whom Kemper would have associated with the Zohar's authorship. The second talmudic reference to the ax from within and without is made concerning David, a descendant of Ruth the Moabite, who went on to defeat the Moabites in battle. Ruth herself was, of course, the model convert, and Kemper may have had this in mind when he went on to quote her directly, stating that he hopes to finish a translation of the entire New Testament and that the endeavor may be "complete from the Lord" (Ruth 2:12). Neither Obadiah nor Ruth were converts to Christianity, of course, but it is their respective conversions rather than their confessional identities that seem to be the subject of Kemper's hints. They are implicated in the fateful reversals that would unfold for their respective communities. Kemper hoped that he would be implicated in the conversion of the Jews, that he would be the ax from within and without that could finally fell the forest. He even implicates himself when he inserts a first-person pronoun into another gemaric expression: "So please lift up for yourselves the potshard so that you may find underneath me a jewel."[40] The jewel lies underneath Kemper himself. He stands in for the biblical text as the subject of interpretation.

Two examples from his commentary on Matthew will demonstrate key aspects of Kemper's method and message. In commenting on Matt 8:26, wherein Jesus commands the seas to calm, Kemper makes the curious connection between the biblical image of the serpent and Christ the Messiah. Weaving together Old Testament and New Testament imagery, he writes:

> Observe that Moses lifted his staff over the sea and divided it, and this staff is a *remez* of the Staff of mightiness, which is Jesus, as it is written: 'The Lord will extend your mighty scepter' (Ps 110:2); and consequently that staff turned into a snake, because 'snake' by means of gematria is

---

40. Kemper, *Even Gilyon Matityahu*, fol. 98r.

2. ALLEGORY AND CONVERSION: JOHAN KEMPER 65

equal to the Messiah, and therefore that staff swallowed up the snakes that the magicians made.[41]

This association would not have been entirely lost on Christian readers, who would have inherited typological comparisons between Jesus and Moses's staff-turned-serpent in Exod 4 and 7 as well as in Num 21. This instance in particular, however, betrays a Sabbatian influence. While kabbalistic references to the "holy serpent" have their origins in thirteenth-century Spanish kabbalah it became a central figure in the late seventeenth-century messianism of Shabbetai Tzvi and his prophet, Nathan of Gaza.[42] Kemper's reading is backed by the numerological equivalence between the Hebrew words for messiah and serpent: *mashiah* and *nahash* both add up to 358 according to the *gematria* system. Kemper's use of the term "dragon" in the same paragraph to refer to the serpent bears the mark of Nathan's zoharic *Treatise on the Dragons*, and Shabbetai Tzvi himself used the figure of the snake in his personal signature.[43] We detect in Kemper's commentaries, therefore, another kind of conversion: devotional language related to the former Messiah, a seventeenth-century imposter, is redirected to the first-century Jesus. Other Sabbatian terms and concepts found in Kemper's commentary include his repeated use of the term "Holy King," his reference to the three *partsufim* or faces of the divine,[44] and, most importantly, his treatment of Jewish law with its simultaneous fulfillment and retraction, a theme to which I will return below.[45]

A second example comes from Kemper's commentary on Matt 21:42, which is itself an interpretation of "the stone that the builders rejected" from Ps 118:22. Kemper weaves in further textual layers by drawing on rabbinic sources. In particular, he incorporates Rashi's interpretation of Gen 28 concerning the stone that Jacob placed under his head before his mystical dream of the stairway. Employing the kabbalistic methods of *sod*, *remez*, and *peshat*, Kemper demonstrates the layering of tradition and text

---

41. Kemper, *Even Gilyon Matityahu*, fol. 124v, as translated in Eskhult, "Rabbi Kemper's Case," 157.

42. Gershom Scholem, *Sabbatai Sevi: The Mystical Messiah*, trans. R. J. Zwi Werblowsky (Princeton: Princeton University Press, 1976), 235–36, 309, 813.

43. Scholem, *Sabbatai Sevi*, 235.

44. Schoeps, *Barocke Juden*, 66–67, as translated by George Dole for *Studia Swedenborgiana* 7 (1990): 16–17.

45. Regarding the *partsufim*, see Schoeps, *Barocke Juden*, 66–67, as translated by George Dole in *Studia Swedenborgiana* 7 (1990): 16–17; Wolfson, "Messianism," 153.

66   JEWISH ALLEGORY IN EIGHTEENTH-CENTURY CHRISTIAN IMAGINATION

that need uncovering for the truth of Christianity to be revealed. On the stone that the builders rejected, he writes:

> This is a matter of *sod*, namely he took the stone, (Gen 28:11) which (in turn) is a *remez* of the Messiah, because Jacob placed his head on the stone of justice, since he believed in the Messiah.... Observe, it is not the literal sense that Rashi refers to, when he, drawing from the Talmud, says that Jacob took more than one stone, when he made a kind of gutter, etc., and the Holy, blessed be he, made these into one. The secret is that Jacob took three stones, a hint of the Trinity, and they became one, that is Unity.[46]

According to Kemper's reading, Rashi provided a hint of the triune God when he expanded on the biblical text, adding to it the idea that many stones were needed to create an indentation for Jacob's head and that God then made the stones one. The very fact that the stones appear in the plural form in the Torah, and that Rashi used this plural form to expand on the meaning, is an indication that there were exactly three stones, according to Kemper, and that these three stones represent the Trinity. That a plural form in Hebrew is an indication of the number three, which refers to the Father, Son, and Holy Spirit, is a method used elsewhere by Kemper. His phrase in Hebrew, *shillush ha-yihud*, conveys the theological "three in one."[47] There is precedent for this move in earlier Christian exegetical practices, as the presence of plural forms in Gen 1:26, "Let us make humankind in our image," is taken as evidence of the presence of the Trinity at creation as early as Justin Martyr in the second century.[48] The stone that the builders rejected, however, appears in the singular form in the Psalms and in Kemper's own translation of Matt 21:42. It is only through its midrashic association with other sacred texts and with the Jewish commentarial tradition, in Kemper's hands, that its plurality is revealed and its christological sense is professedly disclosed.

According to Kemper, the Trinitarian truth of the Torah was known to all of its Jewish authors and commentators, including Rashi and the

---

46. Kemper, *Even Gilyon Matityahu*, fol. 170r, as translated in Eskhult, "Rabbi Kemper's Case," 157.

47. See, for instance, Kemper, *Even Gilyon Matityahu*, fol. 105v.

48. Justin Martyr, *Dial.* 62.2. On Justin's interpretation in dialogue with Jewish interpretation of the same verse, see Daniel Boyarin, *Border Lines: The Partition of Judaeo-Christianity* (Philadelphia: University of Pennsylvania Press, 2004), 40.

2. ALLEGORY AND CONVERSION: JOHAN KEMPER 67

talmudic sages, but is lost on the typical Jewish reader. The general population of Jews were in the dark when they read and studied their texts, but nevertheless preserved the truth when they passed along their interpretive traditions. As Elliot Wolfson puts it, "the open secret of Christianity is the esoteric truth of Judaism."[49] In his commentary on the Zohar, Kemper blames Satan for the Jews' forgetfulness and their inability to recall the true meaning of scripture: "He who has a brain in his head will conclude that the patriarchs point to the Trinity, and Satan assisted them in this matter, until the point that the wisdom of the kabbalah was also lost. But know that even today they have very ancient and just customs that instruct about the Trinity, but they cover their faces with a mask."[50] The Jews are rebuked for hiding their faces with a mask, even as the three faces of God are concealed in holy texts. A holy mystery contends with a wicked disguise in Kemper's construction.

Kemper represents the ambivalence of Christian kabbalists of his time in his depiction of Judaism as both the foundation of Christianity and its greatest adversary. In considering how Kemper is unique among the Christian kabbalists of early modernity, Wolfson points to his need "to preserve the nomian framework of the kabbalah even as he sought to undermine that framework by proving the truths of Christianity on the basis of the traditional texts."[51] This "hypernomianism," is fed by Kemper's rabbinic background and his effort to extend the law beyond the boundaries of Judaism. Accordingly, the law becomes even more relevant in a Christian context. And while a spiritualized explanation of the laws of circumcision, for instance, does have other Christian corollaries, his insistence that the close reading of kabbalistic texts is key to a true Christian understanding of the law is distinctive. For instance, Kemper's Trinitarian interpretation of the customary kabbalistic prayer "for the sake of the unification of the blessed holy One and his presence" is backed by an understanding of the nature and relationship between the divine attributes, that is, the *partsufim*. His formula suggests that Jews everywhere, as Wolfson puts it, "unwittingly affirm the trinity" whenever they recite it.[52]

This does not, Kemper would insist, negate the wisdom of the talmudic sages. The sages knew the truth of the gospels and encoded it in their

---

49. Wolfson, "Messianism," 141.
50. Kemper, *Maṭeh Mosheh*, fol. 49b, as translated in Wolfson, "Messianism," 161.
51. Wolfson, "Messianism," 141.
52. Wolfson, "Messianism," 159.

68   JEWISH ALLEGORY IN EIGHTEENTH-CENTURY CHRISTIAN IMAGINATION

own commentaries. Kemper echoes Christian Hebraists of the seventeenth century in characterizing the Talmud as full of allegories. His critique in a novel one, however, in suggesting that the Jews who read the Talmud according to its literal sense alone (*peshat*), have missed its secret message (*sod*).[53] The Talmud, like the Torah, has layers or senses, and when properly interpreted bears testimony of Christ, he argues. The talmudic rabbis are described as masters of the truth and masters of deceit all at once: "[The] masters of the Talmud were cunning, and all of the words that they uttered were parables and riddles, and words that draw the heart."[54] They have also, paradoxically, preserved the truth so that skilled guides, such as Kemper, can use the Talmud as a mechanism for finally revealing the truth of the Christian Bible. As someone who inhabited both worlds, Kemper divides the Jews into two camps: the sages who knew the truth of their encoding (in some combination of heroism and wickedness) and the reading public who miss the point. An ignorant literalism is associated with Jews while an enlightened literalism is attached to Christians and to the New Testament as Oral Torah. It may seem too great a contradiction to stand that the Talmud would simultaneously be a source of trickery and divine revelation. In a sense, though, Kemper's commentaries are performative of the Christian ambivalences toward Jewish books that emerged alongside the Christian kabbalah beginning in the sixteenth century. Kemper's commentaries also reflect the ambivalences of the eighteenth century when they make both positive and negative associations between Judaism and allegory.

Kemper read Jesus into every story of the Hebrew Bible and into every Jewish custom using the Hebrew term for type: *mashal*. Jesus is the *shekinah*. Jesus is the *'afikoman*, the *mezuzah*, the fiftieth day after Pesach. Jesus is Torah, Shabbat, Metatron. Jesus is Abraham, Isaac, Jacob, Moses, and Job. He is the ark, the stone, and the temple: "the goal, archetype, end and fulfilment of all prophecies, holy prototypes and prefigurations" as Norrelius puts it.[55] Again, there is precedence for such a hermeneutic in Christianity, regarding the Bible at least, and Kemper's conversion explains much of his interpretation even if the format is in an associa-

---

53. Wolfson, "Messianism," 158r–v.

54. Johan Kemper, *Beriah ha-Tikon*, MS Uppsala University Library, Heb. 25, fol. 160a, as translated in Wolfson, "Messianism," 167.

55. Anders Norrelius, *Prolegomena*, translated in Eskhult, "Andreas Norrelius' Latin," 319.

2. ALLEGORY AND CONVERSION: JOHAN KEMPER

tive, midrashic style. However, we can also trace such an interpretive fixation through Sabbatianism. Nathan of Gaza borrowed the methods of the marrano Solomon Molko, who introduced Christian allegories into his commentaries. Nathan used Molko's interpretations and substituted his own Messiah when interpreting Job, for instance, as an allegory for Shabbetai Tzvi.[56] About which sources influenced Kemper's own biblical interpretation we can only speculate. But it certainly bares the markings of a tortuous genealogy, one with forays into Jewish contexts, Christian contexts, and contexts whose Jewish and Christian strands are indistinguishable. His personal history as and his life's work tell the story of religious nomadism, and allegory is the vehicle for the passage of ideas back and forth across religious borders.

It is perhaps not surprising that none of Kemper's commentaries were printed or circulated in his lifetime, given their inaccessibility. Christians in his orbit would have been largely oblivious to his subtle talmudic allusions, even if they were generally impressed by his dexterity with rabbinic literature. Jews, who had a better chance of noticing his references, had been banished from the land. It was the conversion narrative, his *Unterthäniger Bericht*, that would attract the most attention from his contemporaries. The specific meanings of verses in Matthew and the Zohar, which he revealed in his commentaries, had less of an immediate impact than the narrative of an allegorical conversion that his presence manifested.

Boaz Huss and Judith Weiss are two scholars who frame certain kabbalistic endeavors as an interest in the "idea of the Zohar" rather than an interest in the content of actual Zoharic texts.[57] A similar phenomenon is detectable in Kemper's recruitment to and employment at Uppsala University. It was the *idea of his conversion*, rather than his interpretive contributions, that stimulated notions of biblical allegory and the unfolding of the Christian messianic age. That his own conversion narrative was likely heavily influenced by the views and desires of his Christian sponsor amplifies the allegorical quality of his life's story. In a sense, his story remains secreted—we have access only to the conventional symbols and metaphors that have been imposed upon it. If his commentaries are any indication of the true inner journey of conversion, his heritage in rabbinic learning continued to be a fountain of inspiration and the scaffold

---

56. Scholem, *Sabbatai Sevi*, 309.

57. Boaz Huss, *The Zohar: Reception and Impact*, trans. Yudith Nave (London: Liverpool University Press, 2016), 36–66; Weiss, "Idea of the Zohar," 248–49.

through which he understood his religious life. That biblical allegory was the available framework for his conversion tells us, perhaps, more about the Christian discourse concerning Jews and Judaism in this context than his authentic biography. The remainder of his story will be forever hidden from view, subject to the interpretations and speculations of those who read him.

3
Unmasking Plurality:
Moses Mendelssohn on Language and Religion

The German Jewish philosopher Moses Mendelssohn was the subject of a great deal of speculation on the part of his Christian readers regarding his true intentions. Some who encountered his work were so impressed with his appeal to reason and liberty of conscience they were sure he must secretly be a Christian or that his philosophical commitments would soon lead to his conversion. He was publicly confronted several times in this regard and pushed to defend his Jewish identity in contrasting tones of harsh accusation, sanctimoniousness, cordiality, and the cool appeal to reason. In one anonymously published essay, "The Search for Light and Right, in a Letter to Moses Mendelssohn," his challenger suggested that Mendelssohn was hiding behind a veil, much the same way that Moses did when his shining face was too much for his people to bear. He writes:

> Moses, the lawgiver of the Jews and of the Christian church that emerged from the oldest faith, spoke in former times to his people with his face veiled because, according to tradition, the children of Israel could not bear the radiance of his face. In the period of the so-called New Testament, the Christians boasted of seeing Moses with his face uncovered. This figurative expression probably signifies nothing more than that there was a time when the eyes of as-yet-unenlightened nations were still unable to bear the truth pure and whole, and that there came another time when people dared to take a longer glimpse at the bright sun and considered themselves strong enough to throw away the veil, and, speaking frankly, to teach in an unconcealed manner what had otherwise only been cloaked in hieroglyphics and more than halfway veiled in figurative expressions.[1]

---

1. August Friedrich Cranz, "The Search for Light and Right in a Letter to Mr. Moses Mendelssohn, on the Occasion of this Remarkable Preface to Menasseh ben

72 JEWISH ALLEGORY IN EIGHTEENTH-CENTURY CHRISTIAN IMAGINATION

Mendelssohn is then admonished to unveil himself in the manner of Christian transparency and give up the ways of Jewish expression, which is "cloaked in hieroglyphics" and "veiled in figurative expressions." The hiding of his identity and the keeping of imagined secrets were viewed as markers for his Jewishness. His conversion is therefore described not in terms of creedal adoption but in terms of lucidity or plainspokenness. He should come out and say what he really means.

Mendelssohn's response to this letter came in the form of his 1783 opus *Jerusalem oder über religiöse Macht und Judentum (Jerusalem, or on Religious Power and Judaism)*. *Jerusalem* responds to many of the accusations by the letter's author, August Friedrich Cranz, whose identity itself was unveiled only after Mendelssohn had begun writing *Jerusalem*. In his response, Mendelssohn presents his views on religious tolerance and the perils of coercion, church and state separation, and the value of Jewish particularism to the German national project. He also reinterprets hieroglyphics and figurative speech itself, as we will see, and ends the book with a return accusation regarding masked intentions. Those who would have all people unified under one religion, Mendelssohn writes, are the ones who wear "the mask of meekness in order to deceive you." They hide behind notions of brotherly love and tolerance but "secretly forge fetters which it means to place on reason."[2] Mendelssohn points instead to the faces behind the mask, which reveal plurality and difference. Why feign uniformity when God has stamped every human with different facial features? To be unmasked is to recognize true diversity in body and in speech. He posits that words, like faces, cannot be made uniform. They carry various meanings for various users, and to deny these facets is to deprive them of any meaning at all. If made to agree in formulas or creeds, people would simply interpret the words differently, infusing them with "inner differences." Mendelssohn's appeal to religious pluralism is thereby intrinsically linked to his appeal for interpretive pluralism. In both cases the true, natural variety of God's creation is celebrated: "let us not feign agreement where diversity is evidently the plan and purpose

---

Israel" (1782), as translated in *Moses Mendelssohn: Writings on Judaism, Christianity and the Bible*, ed. Michah Gottlieb (Lebanon, NH: Brandeis University Press, 2011), 55–56.

2. Moses Mendelssohn, *Jerusalem: Or on Religious Power and Judaism*, trans. Allan Arkush (Lebanon, NH: Brandeis University Press, 1983), 136.

3. UNMASKING PLURALITY: MOSES MENDELSSOHN   73

of Providence."[3] Countering accusations of Jewish trickery, Mendelssohn argues in *Jerusalem* that Judaism uniquely contributes an appreciation for interpretive multiplicity and thereby benefits a pluralistic state. Mendelssohn's response to accusations of Jewish allegorizing is therefore a defense of both Judaism and interpretive plurality.

The preceding chapters considered various responses to the challenges posed to biblical religion in the Enlightenment and the figured discourse of Jewish interpretation utilized by Christian interpreters of the Bible. Jewish interpreters were forced to respond to challenges that were, in many ways, similar to those facing Christendom but also came with difficulties unique to Jewish contexts. Such challenges included, but were not limited to, iconoclastic forms of biblical criticism initiated by Spinoza in the seventeenth century, and contestations of the veracity of the Masoretic Text, such as those illustrated already in the work of William Whiston. Jewish biblical scholars, like their Christian counterparts, struggled to demonstrate the reasonableness of traditional modes of interpretation in an Enlightenment context, but Jews had the added challenge of contending with Christian discursive uses of rabbinic exegesis, such as those sampled above. This chapter will consider one enormously influential Jewish response to this context in the case of Moses Mendelssohn, admired in his day as the "German Socrates" and revered in our day as the founder of modern Jewish philosophy and instigator of the Jewish Enlightenment, or *Haskalah*. Mendelssohn responded to anti-Jewish trends in his intellectual environment, addressing questions regarding Jewish identity and interpretation coming from his contemporaries in both his German-language philosophical works and his Hebrew-language commentaries. The intricate, and at times conflicting, lines of reasoning in his published works, bear witness to the difficulty in responding to his diverse audiences, Jewish and Christian, traditional and modern. Or perhaps the ambivalences expressed at times in his writing tell the story of his own hybridity. Either way, his contributions to the present study are considerable. His celebration of the complexities of human language and of revealed texts is especially noteworthy, given the connection we find being made between Jews and allegory by his contemporaries. Mendelssohn's embrace of multivocality was more than an academic defense of traditional modes of exegesis, however. It had practical implications regarding

---

3. Mendelssohn, *Jerusalem*, 138.

74 JEWISH ALLEGORY IN EIGHTEENTH-CENTURY CHRISTIAN IMAGINATION

the possible coexistence of diverse religious communities. By recognizing the many senses of biblical language, aided by rabbinic sources, he understood himself to be unmasking plurality. His advancement of religious coexistence did not prevent him from offering his own reverse critique, however, in response to Christian ideas concerning the limits of Jewish biblical interpretation. As this chapter will demonstrate, Mendelssohn characterized Christian creedal traditions as disingenuous for suggesting the same confessional language would be understood uniformly, rejected Christian views of religious history as linear and progressive, and depicted Christian understanding of the language the Bible as limited to the dead letter. These critiques were made carefully, and at times only implicitly, due to his social location in a state where Jews had no civil rights. Mendelssohn nevertheless responded to ideas about Jewish allegory not only by affirming rabbinic exegetical methods that celebrate multiple meanings but also by offering an innovative critique of Christian literalism.

Opposing Histories

Before turning to Mendelssohn's biblical commentaries, a word on historiography related to the intellectual and scientific culture of the European Enlightenment is required. One finds among the histories a range of descriptions, from those that depict a time of relative isolation and even stagnation to those that speak of unprecedented integration and advancement among the Jews of Europe. Hillel Levine, for instance, writes that the Jewish community was "curiously unshaken" by the changing winds of European epistemology.[4] Among the many reasons for this disengagement, he points to the Jewish concern for history over nature, the effects of persecution in turning the Jewish community inward, and the messianic hopes of a people in exile, which made divine intervention a difficult reality to compromise. The work of Gershom Scholem traces the emergence of the *Haskalah* to the aftereffects of the Sabbatian controversy, when a radical nihilism swept over European Jewry. He describes a skepticism and desire for assimilation resulting from a movement that ultimately self-destructed, "where the world of rabbinic Judaism had already been

---

4. Hillel Levine, "Paradise Not Surrendered: Jewish Reactions to Copernicus and the Growth of Modern Science," in *Epistemology, Methodology and the Social Sciences*, ed. R. S. Cohen and M. W. Wartofsky (Dordrecht: Reidel, 1983), 204.

3. UNMASKING PLURALITY: MOSES MENDELSSOHN 75

completely destroyed from within."[5] However, another side has been illuminated in the revisionist histories of Jonathan Israel, David Ruderman, Noah Efron, and others.[6] Ruderman, for his part, argues that there was an increase in Jewish integration in medical schools and universities in this time period and consequently a growing positive awareness of the secular sciences, and that the intellectual achievements of Anglo-Jewry should be added to the standard view that the German *Haskalah* was the source and inspiration of the Jewish Enlightenment.[7] Opportunities for Jewish integration were ultimately made possible, argues Ruderman, by the separation of metaphysics and the natural sciences in European universities, weakening official truth claims that required the exclusion of non-Christian perspectives.[8]

Mendelssohn, at the forefront of the *Haskalah*, manifests the contrasting emphases that we find in these histories. Mendelssohn believed Judaism could provide key insights into the potential for an enlightened and pluralistic Germany, and that Jewish participation modeled the coexistence of diverse communities in a unified state. He also wrote disparagingly of the state of Jewish intellectual life, suggesting his Bible translation and commentary would be "the first step toward culture from which my nation, alas, is so estranged that one is almost ready to despair of the possibility of improvement."[9] Alternating views of Judaism, as both already sophisticated and in need of rehabilitation, are present in Mendelssohn's work, and in this he reflects the various contexts laid out by our histories as well as something of the complexities of Jewish self-identity in early modern Europe.

---

5. Gershom Scholem, "Redemption through Sin," in *The Messianic Idea in Judaism: And Other Essays on Jewish Spirituality* (New York: Schocken, 1995), 141.

6. See Noah J. Efron, *Judaism and Science: A Historical Introduction* (London: Greenwood, 2007); and Israel, *Radical Enlightenment*.

7. See David B. Ruderman, *Jewish Thought and Scientific Discovery in Early Modern Europe* (New Haven: Yale University Press, 1995); Ruderman, *Jewish Enlightenment in an English Key: Anglo-Jewry's Construction of Modern Jewish Thought* (Princeton: Princeton University Press, 2001).

8. Ruderman, *Jewish Thought*, 11. The history of this separation and the emergence of secular theology in the seventeenth century is explored in Amos Funkenstein, *Theology and the Scientific Imagination from the Middle Ages to the Seventeenth Century* (Princeton: Princeton University Press, 1986).

9. From "Letter to August Hennings, June, 1779," as translated in Gottlieb, *Moses Mendelssohn*, 188.

In terms of trends in biblical studies, a few things can be said about the particular state of Jewish scholarship in this time period. First, the polyphonic nature of Jewish hermeneutics made the embrace of traditional interpretations of scripture in the face of advancements among Jews engaged in the natural sciences less problematic. A discrepancy between nature and scripture was not necessarily cause for alarm in a rabbinic tradition at home with diverse interpretations.[10] On the other hand, the scholarly pursuits of Christian universities into language and manuscript study did not receive the same attention in Jewish centers of learning. As Edward Breuer argues, the study of talmudic law and Jewish mystical traditions prevailed over biblical grammar and exegesis as the focus of interpretive activity, limiting overall engagement with the rapidly developing field of biblical criticism. Breuer writes: "Despite the many important accomplishments of early modern Jewish scholarship, the general area of Bible and language study was pervaded by a palpable sense of decline."[11] Whether or not detachment from the expanding field of biblical criticism constituted a blessing or a disadvantage is a matter of perspective, of course, but it is also important not to exaggerate this gap. The ground had been laid for Mendelssohn and his partners in the earlier work of Judah ben Bezalel Loew of Prague (1525–1609), whose influential critique of Ashkenazi education included an appeal for more formal study of Hebrew grammar, the Bible, and science.[12] Further, Maimonides's philosophical approaches to the Bible continued to be a source for Jews and Christians alike in this period, and Spinoza's contribution to biblical criticism cannot be overstated. Eighteenth-century biblical studies was by no means a frontier breached by Christians alone, even though Jews were largely excluded from centers of advanced study and from the public discourse about the Bible and its interpretation.

The challenge for Mendelssohn and his followers, the *Maskilim*, was to engage the field of modern biblical scholarship as it was developing

---

10. For examples of how this played out in the work of Jewish scientists, see Efron, *Judaism and Science*; and Noah Efron and Menaḥem Fisch, "Astronomical Exegesis: An Early Modern Jewish Interpretation of the Heavens," *Osiris* 16.1 (2001): 72–87.

11. Edward Breuer, *The Limits of Enlightenment: Jews, Germans, and the Eighteenth-Century Study of Scripture* (Cambridge: Harvard University Press, 1996), 71.

12. See David Sorkin, *The Religious Enlightenment: Protestants, Jews, and Catholics from London to Vienna* (Princeton: Princeton University Press, 2001), 169; and Breuer, *Limits of Enlightenment*, 72–74.

3. UNMASKING PLURALITY: MOSES MENDELSSOHN

in Germany while not compromising the authority of medieval Jewish sources, which they understood to be the key to biblical interpretation. Breuer writes: "they were all committed to maintaining rabbinic hegemony in the normative interpretation of Scripture. In upholding exemplary features of medieval Jewish culture, eighteenth-century Maskilim embraced a literature that was self-consciously and thoroughly imbued with a sense of its own particularism."[13] This rabbinic particularism was perceived by some to be at odds with the universalist spirit of the Enlightenment, and the resulting dissonance threatened to put a barrier between Jewish and Christian biblical scholarship during this period.

Mendelssohn's Bible Translation and Commentary

Mendelssohn saw himself as uniquely suited to bridge the two worlds of Jewish tradition and enlightenment scholarship. At once committed to rabbinic authority, Hebrew language study, and philosophical theories of language, Mendelssohn's approach involved a dedicated engagement with multiple ways of knowing and multiple audiences. This is evident in his German-language publications, such as *Jerusalem*, as well as his Hebrew-language Bible commentaries, which will be the focus of this section. We will begin with his commentary on Ecclesiastes, which built on established traditions of explicating the *peshuto shel miqra* "the plain sense of scripture," while integrating rabbinic and philosophical notions of language's capacity to communicate multiple meanings simultaneously.

Mendelssohn opens his commentary on Ecclesiastes, *Sefer Megillat Qohelet*, with a bold presentation of the medieval model of four methods of interpretation and an appeal to logic: "There are four ways to interpret our holy Torah. They are, as is well known, *peshat, derush, remez*, and *sod*. All of them are words of the living God, at once correct (Jer. 23:36, Ps. 19:10), which is neither contrary to the ways of reason and logical thinking, nor strange and astonishing to the human intellect, as I shall explain with God's help."[14] This statement is a defense of an old hermeneutical system for a new age and, although aimed at a Jewish audience and written

---

13. Breuer, *Limits of Enlightenment*, 21.

14. Moses Mendelssohn, "Biur Megilat Kohelet," as translated by Edward Breuer in *Moses Mendelssohn's Hebrew Writings* (New Haven: Yale University Press, 2018), 123. Breuer keeps with Mendelssohn's spelling of *derush* rather than the more common *derash*.

78 JEWISH ALLEGORY IN EIGHTEENTH-CENTURY CHRISTIAN IMAGINATION

in Hebrew, responds to anxieties in Christian biblical scholarship regarding allegorical interpretation. All language, Mendelssohn argues, written or spoken, can be interpreted in multiple ways, and this should be neither controversial nor difficult to comprehend. After all, he will go on to argue, do we not have plenty of evidence from the world around us that this is in the natural order of God's universe? All aspects of the created world demonstrate layers and levels of intentionality on the part of the Creator via their multifaceted purposes. Limbs and other body parts perform various functions, as do the elements of nature.

> For example, He created the nose to smell, to breath, to excrete excess mucus, and for facial beauty; He created air for creatures to breathe, to produce sound, for the wind to blow and the rain and dew to fall, for a flame to rise, and the like. These are [cases of] multiple purposes attained through one intermediary, and there are many other examples. As such is it not implausible that [Divine] Wisdom intended for one utterance to have many divergent meanings, all of them being true. This is what our Sages meant when they said "One Scriptural verse can be interpreted in a number of senses."[15]

All things have the potential for multiple and complex purposes, the nature of which scientists still labor to understand. If, with common sense, we can understand the levels of meaning in everyday speech and other natural phenomenon, Mendelssohn argues, how much more so with a sacred text? Language, especially sacred language, participates in this divine design.

Mendelssohn's commentary goes on to develop a theory of the primary and secondary meanings of language. Language uses both conventional and spontaneous signs; it carries a generally intended meaning as well as subtle nuances that convey levels of intentionality on the part of the speaker. In Mendelssohn's conception the *peshat*, the primary sense, can be gleaned from a loose reading of the text by paying attention to the general meaning with little concern for the particularities of word choice and rhetoric. On the other hand, the secondary meaning can be detected only through a careful study of the subtleties and particularities of the text. Just as one might analyze the specific words, their ordering, and the tone of another person's speech in order to understand the implicit connotations of what they are saying, so too rabbinic interpretation discovers

---

15. Mendelssohn, "Biur Megilat Kohelet," 128. The quote is from b. Sanh. 38a.

levels of meaning in every nuance, Mendelssohn explains. The *derash*, or the secondary intention of the text, requires the isolation of specific terms to be studied as well as the detection of words missing from the text or what is left unsaid.

As an example, Mendelssohn cites Gen 44:18, where Judah appears to defer respectfully to his brother Joseph, now a powerful Egyptian official, when he remarks, "you and Pharaoh are alike." The primary meaning of the verse is that Judah wished to praise and honor Joseph, whose true identity he had not yet realized. The secondary meaning, uncovered in midrashic sources, however, presents the opposite. Here, Judah's message is paraphrased: "You will end up being stricken with leprosy, just as Pharaoh was stricken on account of my great-grandmother Sarah."[16] The midrashic interpretation takes notice of the fact that nothing explicitly positive is said about either Joseph or Pharaoh in the text. Judah simply states that they are alike, leaving open the possibility that his true intention was to curse the man who lorded his power over his family. The repressed history of conflict between his ancestors and the Egyptian ruling class, and perhaps something of the repressed strife between Judah and Joseph from their youth despite Joseph's still masked identity, is encoded here in this brief interaction. In short, Judah's remarks, according to the secondary meaning, contain a veiled threat. It is a curious choice on Mendelssohn's part as an explanation of the multivocality of scripture. It is one thing to discern repressed levels of animosity in an exchange between estranged brothers or between an oppressor and his subject. It is another thing to suggest sacred scripture would participate in such a fundamentally human form of aggression. Mendelssohn's larger point seems to be that the layering of intentionality in language is something we can understand intuitively and with the use of reason. Two opposing meanings can logically be conveyed with a single statement. His choice of text might also relate to the larger subject of the work, the book of Ecclesiastes, which embraces contradiction out of despair for the vexed conditions of mere mortals. Mendelssohn's concern is the apparent contradictions regarding divine justice and the immortality of the soul. His commentary proceeds to outline different voices in the text and subtle secondary intentions for

---

16. Mendelssohn, "Biur Megilat Kohelet," 125. The midrashic source is Gen. Rab. 93:6.

80 JEWISH ALLEGORY IN EIGHTEENTH-CENTURY CHRISTIAN IMAGINATION

the sake of an overarching logical consistency from the wide-angle perspective of providence.

Mendelssohn's greatest and most ambitious work of biblical scholarship is his five-volume German translation of the Pentateuch in Hebrew characters and with Hebrew commentary, *Sefer Netivot ha-Shalom* (*The Paths of Peace*). Commonly referred to as the *Bi'ur* "Commentary," Mendelssohn spearheaded this collaborative effort after beginning a German-language translation for his son's education. Written for a Jewish audience, it nevertheless responded to the ways that Christian Bible translation and scholarship had veered off course in Mendelssohn's view.[17] The title, *Paths of Peace*, countered notions that the Torah of the Jews emphasized legal obligations or ancient mythology, presenting instead a spiritual guidebook with relevance to its readers in the present. His translation of the Tetragrammaton as "the Eternal" rather than the more common "Lord" (*der Herr*) countered notions of an Old Testament God of vengeance and tyranny with a God for the Enlightenment age.[18] Finally, his extensive scholarly defense of the Masoretic Text in the introduction responded to trending notions of Jewish manuscript corruption. In all of this, Mendelssohn sent the message that Judaism was not only capable of interpreting the biblical text for modernity, but that it was uniquely suited to doing so.

In the introduction to *Sefer Netivot ha-Shalom,* Mendelssohn meditates on the problem of literalism and translation. It is a problem of utmost concern, as there are instances when a literal, word-for-word translation can mislead and confuse the intended meaning of the text. One who translates this way is a deceiver.[19] A good translation will understand the layers of meaning and adjust accordingly. He proposes a methodology to guide his own translations: where the *peshat* and the *derash* agree, or where the two senses diverge but are nonetheless still both true, he translates according to the *peshat.* Where they contradict one another such that they cannot both be true, he translates according to the *derash.* Using the commentaries of Rashi, Rashbam, Ibn Ezra, Nahmanides, and other

---

17. For a discussion of Mendelssohn's views on Christian translation practices, see Breuer, "Editor's Introduction," in *Moses Mendelssohn's Hebrew Writings,* 223–24.

18. For a discussion of Mendelssohn's translation of the Tetragrammaton compared with Luther's, see Seidman, *Faithful Renderings,* 169. See also Breuer, *Moses Mendelssohn's Hebrew Writings,* 225, n19.

19. See Mendelssohn's introduction to *Sefer Netivot ha-Shalom,* entitled "Or Li-Netivah," in Breuer, *Moses Mendelssohn's Hebrew Writings,* 274.

3. UNMASKING PLURALITY: MOSES MENDELSSOHN   81

medieval rabbinic sources as guides, Mendelssohn considers the primary and secondary meanings to the passages he translates and makes word choices accordingly, to best guide his readers. In every instance where the *peshat* can carry multiple meanings, it must be preserved, as it is "the way of someone who has mastered a language to sometimes aim at different meanings in one utterance."[20]

In a technical sense, therefore, Mendelssohn understood his translation to be guided by traditional rabbinic interpretations not only to discern multiple meanings in a given verse but also to decide which ones to preserve: what must be made plain and what can remain hidden. He claims a kind of precision of methodology that satisfies philological as well as philosophical questions about textual interpretation in terms not unfamiliar to the Christian scholastic tradition. Where the introduction to his translation most strongly challenges Christian exegesis is in his explanation of the origins of and necessity for proper cantillation when reading scripture out loud.

Mendelssohn maintains that God spoke the words of the Torah precisely as they are recorded in scripture (this comes with a lengthy defense of Mosaic authorship). Furthermore, he insists that God spoke with intonation, that is, with certain changes in pitch, pauses, and the enunciation of vowel and consonant sounds that fluctuated according to the intended meaning of the words. These inflections were passed on to Moses, who passed them on orally to his people, and the generations preserved them as carefully as they did the letters of the words in written form. The task of preserving the cantillation became especially urgent when the people were in exile and a system of notation had to be developed, lest it be forgotten. Finally, and most importantly, the inflections transmitted orally and recorded by the Masoretes are necessary for the understanding of *both* the primary and secondary intentions of the text. Without attention to the rhythm and modulation of the sounds, the words of Torah are like "dry bones which have no life" (Ezek 37:4–5).[21] Reading without cantillation is, of course, how Christians read the text, and here Mendelssohn is responding, implicitly, to the old trope of Jewish interpretation of the dead letter. To the Christian claim that the "the letter kills, but the Spirit gives life" (2 Cor 3:4), Mendelssohn presents an alternative, Jewish perspective

---

20. Mendelssohn, "Or Li-Netivah," 293.
21. Mendelssohn, "Or Li-Netivah," 252.

on the spirit of the text. Without proper cantillation, without the intonation breathed into it by the Divine, the text is lifeless and its inner truth cannot be known. Rabbinic tradition is here cast as the key to accessing the life force and full spectrum of meaning of the Bible not only because of its exegetical and intellectual talents but also because of its melodies. Christianity is cast as the unfortunate keeper of the shell of the text only.

As has so often been the case with Mendelssohn's reception, we find opposing stances when it comes to contemporary evaluations of his translation and Bible commentary project. For instance, while Breuer celebrates *Sefer Netivot ha-Shalom* as "one of the best-published and well-received Hebrew works of the nineteenth century," Naomi Seidman writes that the translation had "no lasting appeal" and that its format was obsolete within a couple of decades.[22] While Breuer presents ample evidence to support a more effective reception, Seidman's critique is useful from a hermeneutical perspective, as it challenges the very notion of translation as a vehicle for dialogue and the kind of cultural conversion often associated with Mendelssohn.

As Seidman writes, Mendelssohn became "an emblem of the very possibility of authentic Jewish-German intercourse."[23] He was famously figured as a character in Gotthold Ephraim Lessing's play *Nathan the Wise* and in Moritz Oppenheim's painting of the two philosopher friends, which presents the Christian Lessing and the Jew Mendelssohn engaged in conversation over an open book and a chess board. But Seidman views Mendelssohn's willing participation in his emblematic status as revealing, not simply a desire for cultural exchange but also an internally conflicted self-identity. "When one takes into account the duality within the German Jew as within the German language itself, German-Jewish Bible translation emerges not as a sign of cultural symbiosis but rather as the self-presentation of a divided individual or group."[24] Mendelssohn's rendering of the Bible into German with Hebrew characters may have been touted as an effort to connect and rehabilitate his communities, but it had the destructive effect of erasing his own native language and that of his people.

---

22. Breuer, "Editor's Introduction," 232; Seidman, *Faithful Renderings*, 172. For a recent summary of contrasting scholarly opinions on Mendelssohn's project and relevance, see Elias Sacks, *Moses Mendelssohn's Living Script: Philosophy, Practice, History, Judaism* (Bloomington, IN: Indiana University Press, 2016), 7–9.

23. Seidman, *Faithful Renderings*, 155.

24. Seidman, *Faithful Renderings*, 159.

In the early modern German context, Yiddish was viewed by those who did not speak it as the secret language of the Jews—the vehicle for Jewish concealment. That it was familiar enough and still incomprehensible was used to mark those speaking and reading Yiddish untrustworthy, particularly in a political environment that valued cultural unity and transparency. Mendelssohn, as a concerned insider and outsider, did nothing to correct this perception and publicly characterized Yiddish as backward and superstitious and pursued its replacement in the name of integration. "I am afraid that this jargon has contributed not a little to the immorality of the common man and I expect some very good results from the use of the pure German way of speech that has been coming into vogue among my brethren for some time."[25] Yiddish Bibles, according to such a perspective, were morally corrupt. By replacing Yiddish Bibles with Hebrew/German Bibles, Mendelssohn professed to be replacing a grotesque hybrid with a civil interchange. However, according to Seidman, Mendelssohn's Bible amounted to little more than a performance of a more oppressive kind of hybridity. Despite his appeal to logic, he could not escape the most serious contradictions of German Enlightenment reasoning, namely, the professed belief in tolerance embedded in a colonizing discourse.

> For all Mendelssohn's desire to substitute a transparent, rational discourse for the opacity and "immorality" of Yiddish, Mendelssohn's translational project, with its German wrapped in Hebraic garb and Mendelssohn's Hebrew-German double-talk, retains the whiff of the colonial subject's speech. Mendelssohn's translation, despite its "purity," remains almost but not quite German.[26]

The standard accusation that Jews were hiding behind a veil—as it were, behind their language and their customs—found in this context is once again leveled against Mendelssohn in Seidman's analysis. Her characterization of translators as "double agents" with insider knowledge of two rival perspectives leaves us with questions regarding the intended consequences of Mendelssohn's translations and commentaries. Was his civilizing mission more of a help or a hindrance to its intended audience? Was he reinforcing a discourse about Jewish duplicitousness, or confronting and negating such a discourse?

---

25. As quoted Seidman, *Faithful Renderings*, 168.
26. Seidman, *Faithful Renderings*, 175.

84   JEWISH ALLEGORY IN EIGHTEENTH-CENTURY CHRISTIAN IMAGINATION

Jeffrey Librett, in his *The Rhetoric of Cultural Dialogue*, provides another view of Mendelssohn's contribution to Bible scholarship and interpretation by considering the rhetorical conditions of his Jewish-Christian context. Librett explores the ways dialogue posits *self* and *other* in terms of the literal and the figurative.[27] In a dialogue, the other becomes the figurative expression of the truth of the self. This is especially true in the context of post-Reformation German Christians, who "posit themselves unilaterally as the literal truth of the Jews' figure." This *configuration* was the source of significant anxiety on the part of German Christianity, which was confronted with its reliance on the (Jewish) figure for the sake of truth's final revelation or the "desire to rid itself—either by absorption or by expulsion or by extermination—of the material figurality of language, the rhetoric of sophistry of non-self-comprehending speech that is associated with the Jew."[28] Librett posits that Mendelssohn entered the scene just as these anxieties were reaching their climax and Enlightenment thinkers were exposing and expelling the perceived figurative-Judaic elements of their own Protestant heritage. Mendelssohn was, therefore, a fascination to Christians who were troubled by the Jewishness of their own religion. His response was a bold rebuttal suggesting a kind of reverse critique that Judaism was especially well suited to the overcoming of Protestant literalism. In challenging the Christian discourse concerning Jews and Christians, literalism and nonliteralism, Mendelssohn strategically positioned Judaism as the religion of spirit/life and Christianity as the religion of the letter/law. According to Librett's reading, Mendelssohn depicts a Christianity that codifies the spirit through revealed doctrine, while Judaism celebrates the movement and flexibility of God's providence through prescribed action, through ceremony (living spirit) rather than creed (dead letter).[29]

---

27. Librett defines dialogue as "the symmetrical exchange of expressions of intention between dyadic partners, to the end of mutual and nonviolent understanding." But his study of Jewish-Christian dialogue starts from the position of its impossibility, given the structures of violence and misunderstanding always at play. See Jeffrey S. Librett, *The Rhetoric of Cultural Dialogue: Jews and Germans from Moses Mendelssohn to Richard Wagner and Beyond* (Stanford: Stanford University Press, 2000), xvii.

28. Librett, *Rhetoric of Cultural Dialogue*, xix.

29. Librett, *Rhetoric of Cultural Dialogue*, 46. Librett casts the letter/spirit binary broadly over a wide range of Enlightenment-era dualisms. Letter is to spirit as realism is to empiricism, state is to religion, Catholicism is to Protestantism, female is to male, and symbol is to allegory. Librett uses Eric Auerbach's framing of allegory and symbol, in which allegory emphasizes the abstraction over the figure and symbolism

3. UNMASKING PLURALITY: MOSES MENDELSSOHN

In briefly considering these two scholarly analyses of Mendelssohn's work, we see how the philosopher himself has become something of an allegory with a range of possible significations. While Seidman's Mendelssohn engaged in double-speak in an unwitting corroboration with the colonizing efforts made against Jewish difference, Librett's Mendelssohn engaged in an "ontorhetorical" reversal between self and other, reclaiming for Judaism the right to interpret itself as something other than the prefiguration of Christian truth. Perhaps both Mendelssohns and both layers of intentionality can be simultaneously true. Mendelssohn's ability to reinterpret both the interplay between Jews and Christians and the interplay between the literal and the figurative was nevertheless constrained by the terms set by the dominant discourse of the Enlightenment. A study of his theories on the twin topics of history and language from his German writing will shed further light on this multifaceted figure.

Type and Telos

Christian views on human religious history have tended to employ a developmental model mapped on to a chronological interpretation of the Christian Bible.[30] The Venerable Bede at the turn of the eighth century, for instance, proposed an eight-stage progression of ages. The first five ages corresponded to the narratives of the Old Testament. For instance, the infancy of humanity was represented by the biblical narrative from Adam to Noah; childhood was represented by the chapters on Noah to Abraham; and old age marked finally with the Babylonian exile. The sixth age was the current Christian era, which was to be followed, according to apocalyptic descriptions, by a second reign of Christ and a final judgment day. The twelfth-century Italian theologian and mystic Joachim of Fiore presented a similar history in a Trinitarian outline, with the Old Testament representing the historical age of the Father, the New Testament the age of Christ, and the Apocalypse the age of the Spirit to come.[31] We find in the

---

emphasizes the concrete over the abstraction. Such a distinction between allegory and symbol, which was favored by Romantic authors, presents methodological difficulties that will be explored in chapter 5.

30. See Wilhelm Schmidt-Biggemann, "Epochs and Eras," in *Philosophia Perennis: Historical Outlines of Western Spirituality in Ancient, Medieval and Early Modern Thought* (Dordrecht: Springer, 2004): 369–408.

31. This threefold historical outline was, in large part, a Christian borrowing of

86 JEWISH ALLEGORY IN EIGHTEENTH-CENTURY CHRISTIAN IMAGINATION

work of Joachim and Bede, as well as many others, that Christian views of history are often accompanied by typological interpretations of the Bible. The relationship between the Old and New Testaments is one of type and antitype, coding and decipherment. Time is moved along by the process of decryption; the new Jerusalem is brought down from heaven by the realization of the Bible's previously veiled secrets.

Joachim's Trinitarian view of history, bolstered by the developmental model conceived by Bede and others, became especially popular in the eighteenth and nineteenth centuries when philosophers and sectarians alike anticipated the maturation of humankind and the long-awaited arrival of the age of the Holy Spirit. Lessing epitomized this phenomenon in his 1778 "The Education of the Human Race." Here we find Joachim's model of the three epochs restated. In Lessing's version, Judaism was the childhood of the human race and was provided the Old Testament as a developmentally appropriate textbook for that age, teaching the unity of God. Christianity, as the boyhood of humanity, was provided a new textbook with a more advanced message for that age: the immortality of the soul. Finally, the "everlasting Gospel" promised in the book of Revelation would usher in a third age of mature adulthood: "It will assuredly come!" he writes "the time of a new eternal Gospel, which is promised us in the Primer of the New Testament itself!"[32] Therefore, the early modern infantilization of Jews and their role in the unfolding of history is related, as it was in earlier times, to a typological and teleological hermeneutic.

Mendelssohn openly opposed his dear friend Lessing on very few matters, but the evolutionary view of history in Lessing's "Education of the Human Race" was one of them.[33] In fact, it provided the opportunity for Mendelssohn to elaborate an alternative view of human history, one that did not consign particular religious traditions to particular stages along a developmental continuum. In a letter to August von Hennings in 1782,

---

a similar notion from b. Sanh. 97a, known as the *Vaticinium Eliae*: "The school of Eliyahu taught: Six thousand years is the duration of the world. Two thousand of the six thousand years are characterized by chaos; two thousand years are characterized by Torah, from the era of the Patriarchs until the end of the mishnaic period; and two thousand years are the period of the coming of the Messiah" (trans. Berman).

32. Gotthold Ephraim Lessing, "The Education of the Human Race," in *Literary and Philosophical Essays: French, German and Italian*, trans. F. W. Robertson (New York: Collier, 1910), 86.

33. Another related, disagreement between Mendelssohn and Lessing was the question of the permanence of hell.

3. UNMASKING PLURALITY: MOSES MENDELSSOHN 87

Mendelssohn directly addressed the question of the progress of mankind versus the progress of the individual. Here he boldly states: "nature does not intend the perfection of mankind; its goal is the perfection of man, of the individual."[34] In order to provide the necessary environment for the advancement of the individual, this world must always remain imperfect, he argues. Growth can only occur when a person endures struggle and tribulation; happiness itself is the result of the overcoming of hardship. Without the occasional regression, on the part of the species as a whole, "what, then, would be left for our children to do?" Rather than comparing the progression of history to the developmental stages of a human being, from infancy to maturity, he preferred the model of a station by a post route. "The postilion, to be sure, must make the same trip over and over again. But he represents merely the means by which successively arriving travelers are enabled to continue on their way."[35]

In *Jerusalem*, Mendelssohn elaborates his position, this time more directly in response to Lessing. Rejecting a linear progression, he here uses language of "cycles," "oscillations," and "orbits" to describe the epochs of human history. "In reality, the human race is—if the metaphor is appropriate—in almost every century, child, adult, and old man at the same time, though in different places and regions of the world."[36] In rejecting a historiography that infantilizes Judaism, his arrangement is relativistic and cyclical. Societies around the globe have varying degrees of sophistication, which Mendelssohn measures in terms of their use of language. Some use language "stammeringly," while in another place they are "aided by science and art, shining brightly thought words, images, and metaphors, by which the perceptions of the inner sense are transformed into a clear knowledge of signs and established as such." While some use language plainly and others symbolically, one type of society is not innately more moral or devout than another, and a given society will experience periods of regression as well as development. Every age has its rewards and its challenges. And in direct contradiction to Christian soteriology he writes: "all the inhabitants of the earth are destined to felicity."[37] The idea that God would limit human perfection and salvation to those living at a particular time

---

34. Moses Mendelssohn, "Letter to August von Hennings," in *Moses Mendelssohn: Selections from His Writings*, ed. and trans. Eva Jospe (New York: Viking, 1975), 168.

35. Mendelssohn, "Letter to August von Hennings," 169.

36. Mendelssohn, *Jerusalem*, 96.

37. Mendelssohn, *Jerusalem*, 94. Mendelssohn gives an expanded argument

88   JEWISH ALLEGORY IN EIGHTEENTH-CENTURY CHRISTIAN IMAGINATION

and with access to a particular form of revelation is irrational and suggests an unjust God.

An example from his commentary on Gen 2 demonstrates Mendelssohn's views on progressivism and their implications for biblical interpretation. He here describes the events of the biblical narrative as a kind of encoded prediction of what happens to every human.

> The entire account of creation and everything that Scripture related with regard to Adam and Eve and Cain and Abel is without doubt completely and unfailingly true. What is told about those individuals actually happened to them. Notwithstanding this, they contain an allusion to and serve as an archetype for the human species in its entirety. What befell Adam and his sons and what happened to them in particular is what befalls humanity as a whole. This is why Scripture went to some length in relating their details, and the intelligent individual would understand the story of humankind from their creation until the end of the generations.[38]

At first glance, this appears to be the kind of typological and teleological reading of human history that we find so often in Christian sources. However, as we continue reading in this commentary, one key difference between Mendelssohn's model and a standard Christian model becomes apparent. The development represented by Adam and his children happens on an individual level only. This development involves the human task of achieving balance between two complementary faculties: comprehension and desire. When Adam ate of the tree of knowledge of good and evil, he became like the angels. But an angelic balance of these faculties is not appropriate for humans and desire inevitably overpowered his comprehension. Like Adam then, each individual's character is determined by the ability to bring the two faculties back into a harmonious relationship. A person's disposition emerges in accordance with an "individual's apprehension and ability to distinguish between good and evil, and by his facility to desire to do good and to prevent evil."[39] Mendelssohn describes here the perfection of the individual only as a rational independent being;

---

against Christian soteriology in "Counter-Reflections to Bonnet's Palingenesis." See Gottlieb, *Moses Mendelssohn*, 16–30.

38. Moses Mendelssohn, *Sefer Netivot ha-Shalom*, in Breuer, *Moses Mendelssohn's Hebrew Writings*, 313–14.

39. Mendelssohn, *Sefer Netivot ha-Shalom*, 314.

the collective advancement of the human species is not discussed. He thereby articulates a relationship between levels of meaning that is neither teleological nor supersessionist. One level does not advance on or displace another. The relationship between sign and signifier is more synchronic than diachronic; it relates to a view of human religious history that is cyclical rather than progressive, even though the spiritual journey of Adam is one to which every human should relate.

Mendelssohn's rejection of the developmental model of history was a point of contention among his readers, many of whom relied on a teleological understanding of the present age of Enlightenment. Kant would compare Mendelssohn's views to the myth of Sisyphus, whose eternal punishment involved pushing a great stone up a hill only to watch it roll back down again.[40] In his 1793 *Religion within the Limits of Reason Alone* Kant presents a progressive view of religious history and traces the gradual coming of the kingdom of God in the form of pure religion. Unlike his premodern predecessors, however, he removes Judaism entirely from the outline. Judaism, he maintains, is no religion at all but a purely political movement.[41] This was, at least in part a reaction to Mendelsshon's efforts to recast Judaism as a religion, rather than a political entity, in the eyes of his fellow countrymen.[42] Kant rejected the notion that Judaism was a religion and suggested that the advancement of humanity toward the pure religious faith began anew with Christianity, whose foundation in Judaism is nothing more than accidental. Some three decades later Hegel would likewise remove Judaism as a significant stage in the perfection and education of humanity. Hegel traces the movement of the spirit through four world-historical kingdoms: Oriental, Greek, Roman, and Germanic.[43] The spirit clings only to those nations whose success can nurture it along in its course from infancy to adulthood and passes over those, such as the Jewish nation, which are in decline. He writes

---

40. Immanuel Kant, "On the Common Saying: 'This May Be True in Theory, but It Does Not Apply in Practice,'" in *Kant: Political Writings*, ed. Hans Reiss, trans. H. B. Nisbet (Cambridge: Cambridge University Press, 1991), 88.

41. Immanuel Kant, *Religion within the Limits of Reason Alone*, trans. Theodore M. Greene and Hoyt H. Hudson (Chicago: Open Court, 1934), 116.

42. Leora Batnitzky, *How Judaism Became a Religion: An Introduction to Modern Jewish Thought* (Princeton: Princeton University Press, 2011), 13–31.

43. G. W. F. Hegel, *Philosophy of Right*, trans. S. W. Dyde (Kitchener, Ont.: Batoche, 2001), 269–70.

90 JEWISH ALLEGORY IN EIGHTEENTH-CENTURY CHRISTIAN IMAGINATION

that the Jewish people are the "type" for regressive movement, in which the "spirit is pressed back into itself, and finds itself in the extreme of absolute negativity."[44] Perhaps in response to Mendessohn, Hegel writes of those who reject the progress of humanity, "spirit has remained an empty word and history a superficial play of accidental and so-called mere human strife and passion."[45] Kant and Hegel both retain the developmental models of history from premodern Christian sources but reimagine Judaism as regressive or irrelevant rather than childlike. More will be said on this in the following chapter.

Judaism, in Mendelssohn's presentation, was not a moment in the past or an infantile stage of human development, but was a living tradition with resources uniquely suited for the problems of modernity. In countering the standard narrative, however, he recycled notions of primitivism while attempting to dissociate Judaism from the pagan cultures of antiquity. For instance, he posits that while pagans believed in a self-serving and malicious pantheon, the God of Judaism is loving and merciful. Mendelssohn retells the exodus story in contrast with Homer to show the goodness and lovingkindness manifested in God's interactions with Moses.[46] Such a distinction responds to accusations, from Cranz and others, that the God of the Jews and the Old Testament was a cruel and punishing tyrant. It has the unfortunate effect, however, of slipping very near an evolutionary perspective with precisely the kinds of pitfalls his approach set out to avoid. It is a tension point, between resisting evolutionary historicism and borrowing its terms, that he approaches several times in attempting to highlight the unique contributions of Judaism in the unfolding of history. Despite the occasional indication of self-reflexivity in this regard, this tension will arise again as he surveys the significance of the Hebrew language and Jewish ceremonial law.[47]

---

44. Hegel, *Philosophy of Right*, 271.
45. Hegel, *Philosophy of Right*, 267.
46. Mendelssohn, *Jerusalem*, 120–21.
47. In one such moment he writes: "In judging the religious ideas of a nation that is otherwise still unknown, one must ... take care not to regard everything from one's own *parochial* point of view, lest one should call idolatry what, in reality, is only *script*." Quote from Mendelssohn, *Jerusalem*, 113.

Hebrew: The "Living Script"

With the work of John Spencer, Ralph Cudworth, William Warburton, Gottfried Leibniz, and others, the seventeenth and eighteenth centuries saw a fervent interest in the study of hieroglyphics and an accompanying speculation on the role of various languages in revealing or concealing divine truth. Mendelssohn's interest in this trend inspired a sustained theory of the Hebrew language and the Jewish people in history.[48] In *Jerusalem*, he posits that the Hebrew language was the bridge between a pictographic system and an alphabetical system, each of which have their advantages and disadvantages. The earlier hieroglyphic writing enabled the preservation of ideas in symbols but over time led to superstition and idolatry. Mendelssohn believed abstract signs were necessary for the movement away from hieroglyphics and for the development of human reason, as they contained and communicated knowledge while encouraging the mind to look for meaning beyond a simple picture. "Wise Providence has placed within its [the soul's] immediate reach a means which it can use at all times. It attaches, either by a natural or an arbitrary association of ideas, the abstracted characteristic to a perceptible sign which, as often as its impression is renewed, at once recalls and illuminates this characteristic, pure and unalloyed."[49] The later alphabetic systems had their own problems, however, making humans too speculative, sparing them "the effort of penetrating and searching, and [creating] too wide a division between doctrine and life."[50] Hebrew, according to Mendelssohn, provided a middle way between these two dangers: it solved the problem of idolatry inherent in hieroglyphics but provided a more direct connection to the concrete reality of things than a fully conventional system. It did this by preserving some resemblances: the Hebrew letter *bet* looks like a *bayit* (house), the *gimel* like a *gamal* (camel) and so on.[51] These likenesses provide some

---

48. On the interest in Egyptology and hieroglyphics in the seventeenth and eighteenth centuries, including the work of Mendelssohn's interlocutor Warburton, see Jan Assmann, *Moses the Egyptian: The Memory of Egypt in Western Monotheism* (Cambridge: Harvard University Press, 1997), 55–143.

49. Mendelssohn, *Jerusalem*, 105.

50. Mendelssohn, *Jerusalem*, 118.

51. Mendelssohn, *Jerusalem*, 110n. See also Gideon Freudenthal's discussion in *No Religion without Idolatry: Mendelssohn's Jewish Enlightenment* (Notre Dame: University of Notre Dame, 2012), 105–34.

92   JEWISH ALLEGORY IN EIGHTEENTH-CENTURY CHRISTIAN IMAGINATION

grounding, but there is also enough abstraction to avoid idolatry. Hebrew was, therefore, a superior technology, making units of writing more abstract and human knowledge more refined while retaining a connection to the created world. The sacred language is a kind of archeological artifact documenting the shift in human knowledge that abstraction made possible. However, the threat of idolatry still remained, Mendelssohn cautioned. The value of Jewish tradition is not just the Hebrew script, but the "living script" that constitutes ceremonial law.

Mendelssohn postulated that even text that is made abstract, avoiding the pitfalls of hieroglyphics, can become an idol. Anything that is fixed in time and space can become the object of misdirected devotion. Even the Pythagoreans, who attempted to avoid idolatry by seeking the divine in numbers alone, eventually failed and put mathematics before God. This is why, according to tradition, Moses was permitted to write down only the bare minimum of the revelation he received, Mendelssohn posited. The rest was transmitted orally. Furthermore, the revelation that was committed to writing was primarily instruction for ceremonial law—a living script that could adapt to the unique needs and customs of every generation. Speech (Oral Torah) and action (fulfillment of the law) are superior symbols because of their flexibility and transparency. What written text conceals, ritual action reveals. As Gideon Freudenthal writes: "Mendelssohn's idea is this: a good symbol is 'transparent.' We look 'through' it to what it stands for."[52] Mendelssohn laments the invention of the printing press for precisely this reason: it fixed the words and fixed our attention on books rather than the oral teaching and embodied enactment of Torah. The words of the Torah, in this view, are revelatory to the extent that they point to a holy expression in action.

The emphasis on ceremonial law over written text seems to contradict his earlier emphasis on the shape of the Hebrew letters. Combined, however, these notions present a picture of Jewish life and language as sophisticated, rational, adaptable, moral, and transparent, all qualities that countered popular stereotypes. In particular, Mendelssohn's assertion that ceremonial law is the primary emphasis of the Torah responded to the accusation that Jewish customs were backwards and outdated. Here we have a description of Jewish law and ceremony as a living connection to God. Mendelssohn viewed Jewish ritual as a manifestation of revelation in

---

52. Freudenthal, *No Religion without Idolatry*, 107.

transparent signs, but it is by no means universal or absolute. It is its very particularity that becomes a model for other religions and other nations, whose knowledge of revelation may be quite different.

It is his reformulation of the relationship between the universal and the particular, and the role that divine revelation plays in this relationship, that will take us finally to Mendelssohn's most radical challenge to his Christian readers: the particularity of the Bible itself. According to Mendelssohn, we can discern three kinds of truth: two are generalizable to all people while one is not generalizable but is relative or particular to a given community. The first two, borrowed from his reading of Leibniz, are necessary truth and contingent truth. Each of these is universal and absolute. The third category, historical truth, is provided by providence to suit the unique needs of a given community and is not generalizable to humanity as a whole. Revealed truth comes under this third category, suggesting biblical revelation was targeted to a specific group. Mendelssohn further asserts that the content of historical truth (i.e., revelation) does not concern matters of salvation or redemption. Human reason and observation alone are capable of accessing necessary and contingent truth, which can provide the guidance needed for an individual to achieve their potential for perfection; any other arrangement would be cruel given that not everyone has equal access to the Bible. The historical truth revealed in scripture, he writes, is about action and not belief. The Torah is exceptional not because it is the only source of universal truth, but for its ability to steer its audience away from idolatrous forms of religious expression and toward a sanctified way of life in the world.

Despite his lament of the fixation on books in religious life and his celebration of the living script, Mendelssohn also returns at times in *Jerusalem* to a familiar framing of textual interpretation. He writes that the relationship between the ceremonial laws in the Bible and universalizable "eternal truths of reason" is like that of the body and the soul. Drawing on a familiar zoharic depiction of the Torah as a beautiful maiden unveiling herself for her lover, he writes:

> Although the divine book that we received through Moses is, strictly speaking, meant to be a book of laws containing ordinances, rules of life and prescriptions, it also includes, as is well known, an inexhaustible treasure of rational truths and religious doctrines which are so intimately connected with the laws that they form but one entity. All laws refer to, or are based upon, eternal truths of reason, or remind us of them, and rouse us to ponder them. Hence, our rabbis rightly say:

94 JEWISH ALLEGORY IN EIGHTEENTH-CENTURY CHRISTIAN IMAGINATION

the laws and doctrines are related to each other, like body and soul. ...
The more you search in it, the more you will be astounded at the depths
of insight which lie concealed in it. At first glance, to be sure, the truth
presents itself therein in its simplest attire and, as it were, free of any pre-
tensions. Yet the more closely you approach it, and the purer, the more
innocent, the more loving and longing is the glance with which you look
upon it, the more it will unfold before you its divine beauty, veiled lightly,
in order not to be profaned by vulgar and unholy eyes.[53]

Here the *book* is the site of access to worlds without and within, to layers of
meaning that range from the intellectual to the passionate to the embodied. This interpretive layering is grounded in rabbinic reading. Where the
cited ancestral rabbis might oppose Mendelssohn's formulation of the
body-soul metaphor, however, is in his implication that the inner, essential
doctrines of Torah are not unique to the Bible or to Judaism. The soul of the
text constitutes a kind of truth; an eternal truth that is accessible to all. It is
the outer layers—the ritual prescriptions and guidance for daily life—that
are revealed to Jews alone. These are the aspects revealed to a particular
community for a particular purpose. Their contents do not describe universal or exclusive mechanisms of salvation, but rather a path prepared for
a given community to lead them away from idolatrous forms of religious
expression. Such a line of reasoning openly challenged several fundamentals of Christianity, including the nature of revelation, the role of faith,
and the promise of salvation through Christ. Despite the implicitly con-
frontational aspects of this perspective, it is presented as a solution for the
coexistence of Jews and Christians in society. His views allow that a given
community can hold fast to its historical truth as divine revelation without
imposing its claims on those of other traditions, and that all humans can
access the inner, universal truths through reason. Furthermore, the multivocality in the Bible itself mirrors the possibility of a religiously diverse
society. The Torah is a living script, adaptable to changing contexts, and
also a layered text, making accessible various strata of meaning depending
on the capacity of the reader. It is a dizzying combination of truth claims
responding to the competing positions of his audiences, Jewish and Christian, and to competing narratives about the Bible, salvation, and history.

In many ways Mendelssohn's views on the particularity of written
revelation were made possible by Spinoza's influential and iconoclas-

---

53. Mendelssohn, *Jerusalem*, 99.

3. UNMASKING PLURALITY: MOSES MENDELSSOHN

tic *Theologico-Political Treatise* (1670), which provided a philosophical endorsement for historical criticism of the Bible and inspired such sentiments as Lessing's oft quoted statement: "The letter is not the spirit and the Bible is not religion. Hence, objections to the letter and to the Bible are not likewise objections to the spirit and to religion."[54] At the same time, Mendelssohn's body of work also provided a defense of rabbinic truth claims and methods backed by medieval-style arguments from tradition and from the purported observations of Jews present with Moses at Mount Sinai. His work marked a transition between the thought patterns of the Middle Ages and those of modernity. As such, it drove a vision for pluralism where Jew and Christian, traditionalist and critic, could occupy the same thought space, even if it also provided plenty to object to from the perspectives of both orthodoxy and secularism. In his *Jerusalem*, Mendelssohn suggests that by viewing revealed truth as historical, contextualized truth, Judaism provides a model for religious coexistence. Multiple types of historical truth, multiple histories, can thrive side by side. His last lines "Love truth! Love Peace" are a quotation from the eighth chapter of Zechariah, where Jews bring together the nations of the world. It is difficult to see this utopian vision as anything other than eschatological. But Mendelssohn's *Jerusalem* does not herald the messianic age. It points to the realizable harmony between citizens of different faith traditions and suggests that Germany's Jewish minority, rather than a mere remnant of a forgotten past, might have something to contribute to the health of the state.

Mendelssohn's response to the charge that Jews tended to hide their true intentions behind a mask, in imitation of Moses, was an audacious one. In return, he lodged a critique of creedal language, against its coercive, restrictive, and ultimately idolatrous effects. He affirmed the complexity of human speech and the layered, accommodating quality of divine speech by putting forward a theory that language always has the capacity to carry multiple meanings. Mendelssohn thereby recast Jewish allegorizing in light of the political, historical, and theological concerns of his day and for the sake of Jewish integration. His assertion that the text of the Bible, as

---

54. Gotthold Ephraim Lessing, "Editorial Commentary on the 'Fragments' of Reimarus, 1777," in *Lessing: Philosophical and Theological Writings*, ed. and trans. H. B. Nisbet (Cambridge: Cambridge University Press, 2005), 63. On Spinoza's influence on Lessing and Mendelssohn see Allan Arkush, *Moses Mendelssohn and the Enlightenment* (Albany: State University of New York Press, 1994), 133–66.

language, could mean more than one thing reflected a political affirmation that communities, diverse even in their truth claims, could live together amicably. The textual polyphony of the rabbinic tradition uniquely positioned Mendelssohn to envision an alternative to the triumphalism of the Christian understanding of history and of text. If anything, Christian literalism in his configuration, not Jewish allegory, stood in the way of providence. The following chapter will take up the case of Immanuel Kant, whose notions of allegory and of Judaism would be part of a sharp rebuttal to Mendelssohn's philosophy of religion, and who, despite his admiration of Mendelssohn and his personal relationships to other *Maskilim*, would declare Judaism no religion at all.

4

KANT AND SWEDENBORG:
ANTI-JUDAISM AND INTERPRETATION AT THE
BORDERS OF METAPHYSICS

Immanuel Kant, who shaped the course of both theoretical and practical philosophy for centuries to follow, is less well known for his principles of scripture interpretation. A study of these principles in the context of his unsettled relationship to metaphysics, however, reveals key ambivalences that are by now familiar to us regarding allegory and Judaism. In Kant's case, these ambivalences would have significant consequences regarding what and who qualified for inclusion in the areas of epistemology, religion, and state, especially given his commanding presence on the stage of Western philosophy. And while he was impacted deeply by Mendelssohn's views on both the Bible and metaphysics, he would ultimately reach different conclusions from those of Mendelssohn. Here we will trace the development of Kant's thinking in these areas alongside another contemporary with whom he had a complex relationship: the philosopher, scientist, and mystic, Emanuel Swedenborg, whose spiritual-sense commentaries of the Old Testament, Kant asserted, made "the mistake of including Judaism."[1]

This chapter will explore Kant's approach to biblical interpretation and his anti-Judaism relative to his work as a philosopher, demonstrating that his desire to remove metaphysics from philosophy mirrored his desire to remove Judaism from religion and allegory from the Bible. His admitted attraction to and reliance on both speculative metaphysics and Jewish sources reveals various anxieties of influence at play, anxieties that manifest most urgently in his interfacing with Swedenborg, as we will see. That his harshest attack on Swedenborg comes in a chapter titled "Antikabbalah"

---

1. Kant, *Conflict of the Faculties*, 65.

-97-

98   JEWISH ALLEGORY IN EIGHTEENTH-CENTURY CHRISTIAN IMAGINATION

provides the opportunity to evaluate attitudes and ideas about Jewish mysticism available for Kant's exploitation. It will allow us to investigate a web of associations around mysticism, religious identity, allegory, and corporeality, and the implications of these associations on ideas about which individuals, traditions, and schools of thought were qualified to comment on the true nature of things. In the end, anti-Judaism is written into the border walls of Kant's metaphysical boundaries in ways that would have a lasting impact on his readers over the following centuries.

Kant in the Garden of Eden

Kant interprets the story of the garden of Eden in his 1786 essay *Mutmaßlicher Anfang der Menschengeschichte* (Conjectural Beginning of Human History). Here, as with Mendelssohn, the development of every human being is compared to the journey of the first human. Kant offers an interpretation of Gen 3, in which he traces Adam's transition through four stages of reason. For instance, the desire to eat of the fruit of the tree describes the first stage, in which a person's discernment is determined by their senses rather than their intellect. The eating of forbidden fruit signifies the animal-like instincts of someone who choses food solely on the basis of taste and smell.[2] In later stages these instincts are replaced by the faculty of reason. The story as a whole, then, refers to the "transition from the brutishness of a merely animal creature to humanity, from the leading reins of instinct to the direction of reason, in a word, from the guardianship of nature into the state of freedom."[3] Adam's story is the story of every human who progresses through the stages Kant describes in order to achieve moral agency. Unlike Mendelssohn, however, he retains the impulse, with roots in patristic exegesis, to extend these developmental stages to the collective story of humanity. According to Kant, early humans, like the young Adam, were driven by natural

---

2. Immanuel Kant, "Conjectural Beginning of Human History," in *Toward Perpetual Peace and Other Writings on Politics, Peace, and History,* ed. Pauline Kleingeld, trans. David L. Colclasure (New Haven: Yale University Press, 2006), 26.

3. Kant, "Conjectural Beginning," 29. On comparison with Maimonides's interpretation of Genesis 3, and the difference between Kant and Maimonides with respect to their view of nature and morality, see Heidi Ravven, "Maimonides' Non-Kantian Moral Psychology: Maimonides and Kant on the Garden of Eden and the Genealogy of Morals," *Journal of Jewish Thought and Philosophy* 20.2 (2012): 199–216.

4. KANT AND SWEDENBORG

instinct. Collectively, however, we eventually arrived at a phase in which reason guided and liberated us.

In this example, we see Kant's general approach to biblical interpretation. The text is interpreted in the interest of what is useful to the moral progress of humankind or, in Kant's terms, in the interest of practical reason. Once this is done, everything else about the text may be discarded. The historicity of the events described in the Bible is of no concern to Kant. In his view, debates about the truth of the story of Adam's creation are a vexing distraction on the part of biblical theologians, preventing people from accessing things belonging to pure religion. Kant makes no apology for his suggestion that some stories recorded in the Bible are demonstrably false for depicting God as acting in a way contrary to moral law. Such is the case with the account of God instructing Abraham to sacrifice his son.[4] For Kant, a concern for, or faith in, the literal sense of the Bible mistakes the essence of religion for its vehicle. The vehicle is not religion, but a tool for arriving at religion properly understood.[5]

In his *Der Streit der Fakultaten* (*The Conflict of the Faculties*, 1798), the conflict between theologians and philosophers, specifically around biblical interpretation, demonstrates the kinds of interdisciplinary arguments that interest Kant when it comes to the meaning of scripture. The biblical theologian bases their interpretation on ecclesiastical faith, which Kant describes as "laws proceeding from another person's act of choice." The rational theologian, on the other hand, bases their interpretation on "inner laws that can be developed from every man's own reason."[6] With this distinction in hand, Kant presents the principles of interpretation that should guide a philosophical approach to sacred texts. These principles oppose ecclesiastical tradition in the strongest terms and center on the notion that there is but one true religion: morality.[7] The doctrines of the

---

4. Kant, *Conflict of the Faculties*, 115n.

5. This distinction has parallels with Maimonides, who, in book 3, chapter 28 of his *Guide for the Perplexed* distinguishes between rational/true beliefs, and necessary/traditional beliefs. When applied to the Bible, references to anthropomorphic traits of God in the text are interpreted as necessary rather than true. The reliance of both Kant and Maimonides on Aristotle's semiotics may account for this similarity. On Kant and Maimonides, see Michael Zank and Hartwig Wiedebach, "The Kant-Maimonides Constellation," *Journal of Jewish Thought and Philosophy* 20.2 (2012): 135–45.

6. Kant, *Conflict of the Faculties*, 61.

7. This appeal to a moral interpretive methodology resembles Augustine's approach. In discussing when to read literally and when to read figuratively, Augustine

100 JEWISH ALLEGORY IN EIGHTEENTH-CENTURY CHRISTIAN IMAGINATION

Trinity, resurrection, and the dual nature of Christ are all things that have no practical relevance at all until they are interpreted with a moral end in mind, and in many cases this requires a nonliteral reading.

He considers the bodily resurrection of Christ as an example and rejects outright the belief in the immortality of the body. "For who is so fond of his body that he would want to drag it around with him for eternity, if he cannot get along without it?" Such an assertion strains reason, according to Kant. The apostles, who spoke of a bodily resurrection "must have meant only that we have reason to believe Christ is still alive and that our faith would be in vain if even so perfect a man did not continue to live after (bodily) death. This belief, which reason suggested to him (as to all men), moved him to historical belief in a public event."[8] Christ's death, according to Kant's interpretation, inspired in his followers a sense of longing for immortality, or a conviction that he must still be alive spiritually. This intuition was then expressed in terms available to the apostles in that time, and we are required to translate their words to the standards of our day, independent of ecclesiastical tradition and according to reason.[9] To the extent that one can retrieve the moral religion that inspired the biblical authors in ancient times, the text retains its relevance. But like the body after death, everything extraneous is left behind to decay.[10]

Kant anticipates the objection from theologians and philosophers alike that this is nothing more than allegory. But, he argues, this could not be further from the truth. For the theologian, who mistakes the husk for

---

also appealed to morality: "anything not related to good morals or true faith is figurative." Kant goes further than Augustine in rejecting the narrative of the Bible in favor of an ethical kernel, but there is a similarity of emphasis. See Augustine of Hippo, *On Christian Teaching*, trans. R. P. H. Green (Oxford: Oxford University Press, 2008), 75.

8. Kant, *Conflict of the Faculties*, 69.

9. It is noteworthy that here Kant associates a "moral purpose" with a sense of the immortality of the soul, as morality and belief in an afterlife are a troublesome pair for the philosopher—appearing elsewhere in his writing to be mutually exclusive. For instance, in his Metaphysics lectures: "In general we still allege *that it is not at all suitable here to our vocation to worry much over the future world; rather we must complete the circle to which we are here determined, and wait for how it will be with respect to the future world.* The main point is that we conduct ourselves well at this post, righteously and morally, and attempt to make ourselves worthy of future happiness" (Immanuel Kant, *Lectures on Metaphysics*, trans. and ed. Karl Ameriks and Steve Naragon [Cambridge: Cambridge University Press, 2001], 106).

10. See also Kant, *Religion within the Limits*, 102.

the thing itself, *he* is the one who is forced to use allegory. To the accusation that his biblical interpretation is allegorical, Kant writes:

> My reply is that the exact opposite is true. If the biblical theologian mistakes the husk of religion for religion itself, [it is he who must interpret the scriptures allegorically;] he must explain the entire Old Testament, for example, as a continuous allegory (of prototypes and symbols) of the religious state still to come—or else admit that true religion (which cannot be truer than true) had already appeared then, making the New Testament superfluous.[11]

Here, in his explicit rejection of allegory, Kant associates the husk with the Old Testament and with Judaism. The theologian is compelled to connect the Old Testament and the New Testament by means of typology, but in doing so binds himself to outdated Jewish tenets that "can well make us moan," in Kant's words.[12] Allegory, he writes, is a crutch only required for those who insist on burdening Christianity with the scriptures of the Jews. This is a different project all together, he will insist, from distinguishing a true moral sense of scripture.

In this same essay, defending himself against accusations of allegorizing, Kant counters the related charge that his interpretation is mystical. To do so, he denies having been influenced by Swedenborg, whose allegorical Bible commentaries and experiences of realms beyond the natural world had publicly occupied his attention earlier in his career. Kant distinguishes his methods from Swedenborg's, that is, a rational interpretation from a mystical one:

> As for the charge that rational interpretation of Scriptures is mystical, the sole means of avoiding mysticism (such as Swedenborg's) is for philosophy to be on the lookout for moral meaning in scriptural texts and even to impose it on them. For unless the supersensible (the thought of which is essential to anything called religion) is anchored to determinate concepts of reason, such as those of morality, fantasy inevitably gets lost in the transcendent, where religious matters are concerned, and leads to an Illuminism in which everyone has his private, inner revelations, and there is no longer any public touchstone of truth.[13]

---

11. Kant, *Conflict of the Faculties*, 79.
12. Kant, *Conflict of the Faculties*, 65.
13. Kant, *Conflict of the Faculties*, 80–81.

102 JEWISH ALLEGORY IN EIGHTEENTH-CENTURY CHRISTIAN IMAGINATION

The winds of mysticism are barred by the stronghold of practical morality, Kant is saying. Swedenborg is associated with a kind of mystical and typological reading that runs counter to reason. However, the hitch in Kant's dissociation here is that Swedenborg's "doctrine of correspondences" produces an interpretation of Genesis that has much in common with Kant's own, wherein Adam and Eve become aspects of the individual self, and of humanity as a whole, on a journey of moral progress.[14] Kant was well aware of the obstacles created by this exegetical similarity and, as we will see, the resulting anxiety of influence is evident in many places in his work.

Swedenborg was a bothersome figure for Kant, in that he represented so much of what Kant rejected with his critical philosophy while also producing concepts and interpretations that had a great deal in common with his own. Like Kant, Swedenborg held that moral action and usefulness replaces faith as the factor determining the quality of one's religiosity. Furthermore, Swedenborg, like Kant, rejected certain creedal traditions such as the Trinity, the bodily resurrection, and a future judgment day.[15] Swedenborg's offense, in Kant's estimation, was neither his appeal to the immortality of the soul, nor his rejection of ecclesiastical faith, nor even his hermeneutics. For despite his dismissal of Swedenborg's allegories as *schwärmende Auslegungen* (raving interpretations), Kant held that the biblical narrative points to a deeper truth by means of symbols.[16] Swedenborg's offence, in terms of Kant's principles, was twofold: (1) his logical appeal to "things seen and heard" in worlds beyond the natural, and (2) his stubborn reliance on the Old Testament. These two areas are more connected than they first appear. Both rely on a doctrine of correspondences or a conviction that worlds, natural and spiritual, mirror one another the same way that the body mirrors the soul, the New Testament mirrors

---

14. See Emanuel Swedenborg, *Arcana Caelestia: Principally a Revelation of the Inner or Spiritual Meaning of Genesis and Exodus*, trans. John Elliott (London: Swedenborg Society, 1983–1999), 72–313. The Elliott translation adopts the spelling *Caelestia*, which follows the spelling that accompanied the first English translation of the commentary. I will use the spelling *Coelesita*, which follows the spelling of the first Latin editions and the majority of other subsequent editions and translations. Following convention, I will cite Swedenborg's theological works using paragraph numbers rather than page numbers.

15. In Swedenborg's view, while Christ's body did rise to heaven, the bodies of humans do not.

16. Immanuel Kant, *Träume eines Geistersehers, erläutert durch Träume der Metaphysik* (Leipzig: Reclam jun, 1880), 52.

4. KANT AND SWEDENBORG

the Old, and Christianity mirrors Judaism. Kant was both repulsed and attracted to such notions and ultimately used them to redraw the borders of metaphysics and religion all at once.

Allegories and Angels

Swedenborg is a useful case to consider in the context of early modern biblical interpretation and Jewish-Christian relations. His biblical commentary, the multivolume *Arcana Coelestia* (*Heavenly Secrets*, 1749–1754) presents an intricate, multilayered reading of Genesis and most of Exodus. He opens the commentary with the following line: "The Word of the Old Testament contains heavenly arcana [secrets], with every single detail focusing on the Lord, His heaven, the Church, faith, and what belongs to faith; but no human being grasps this from the letter."[17] The commentary unfolds three senses—the natural, the spiritual, and the celestial—and works its way meticulously through a verse-by-verse account of these meanings. The commentary responds, by means of allegory, to the epistemological challenges of the day. Prior to writing *Arcana Coelestia*, Swedenborg had a career in natural philosophy, publishing prolifically in areas such as anatomy, astronomy, metallurgy, and biology, in a manner complimentary to the taxonomic work of his cousin Carl Linnaeus. Swedenborg was deeply concerned with uncovering the order of the natural world, but also troubled by the impact of scientific discoveries on the foundations of Christian faith. In his late forties, Swedenborg became especially focused on proving the existence of the human soul and set to work determining the location and biological substance of the soul in the human body. *Regnum Animal* (*The Soul's Domain*, 1744) treats, among other things, the functioning of the cerebral cortex and the nervous system in an attempt to trace the movement of the soul in the brain. The goal was left unfulfilled as Swedenborg realized that if the soul did in fact exist, it was not detectable with scientific instruments. This work on the soul coincided with the beginning of his otherworldly visions, including encounters with Christ and sustained visions of angels and spirits, which he recorded in detail in his diaries. The combination of these experiences and his failure to detect the effects of the human soul in the body triggered a crisis of

---

17. Swedenborg, *Arcana Caelestia*, 1.

104   JEWISH ALLEGORY IN EIGHTEENTH-CENTURY CHRISTIAN IMAGINATION

faith. His turn to the Bible and its interpretation for the next ten years of his life was, in some sense, a response to this frustrated attempt to establish a connection between physical and spiritual bodies. In demonstrating an ontological connection between what can be seen in the text and what is hidden within it, a resolution to his scientific crisis emerged: "as to the letter alone [the Word] is like the body without a soul."[18] *Arcana Coelestia*, in addition to the extensive biblical indexes he prepared alongside the commentary, reveals Swedenborg's biblically based response to the challenges of materialism. The word of God is like a human being: its soul is detected not via contiguity with the body but through correspondence. Like an image reflected in the mirror, the human body and the whole of the natural world correspond to spiritual realities on other discrete planes of existence. In contrast to Whiston, therefore, whose scientific efforts produced a literal interpretation of the Bible, Swedenborg's scientific efforts produced biblical allegory: the natural world and the literal sense of scripture were alike in pointing to spiritual counterparts via correspondences.

Finally, we find in Swedenborg's work certain contradictions regarding his perception of Jews relevant to our study of allegory. Swedenborg borrows the old trope of Jerome, Augustine, Luther, and others that the Jews are literalists limited to the "external sense" of the Bible. Against the background of a rising preference for literalism in many circles, and also a growing association between Jews and allegory, Swedenborg's use of the old trope in the context of his allegorical commentary could be simply characterized as antiquated. Yet, as many of his readers have noticed, the parallels to kabbalah in his commentaries are hard to ignore. This is especially true given the contexts of his intellectual and relational orbits, contexts that were heavily indebted to kabbalistic thought. Swedenborg was a student at Uppsala University while Kemper was lecturing there, and Kemper's promoter, Benzelius, was Swedenborg's brother-in-law, with whom he lived for a period of time.[19] Readers, then and now, detect the influence of kabbalah especially in his emphasis on the unique capacity of the Hebrew language and Hebrew storytelling to engender correspondences to other worlds. Johann Adam Möhler would write of Swedenborg

---

18. Swedenborg, *Arcana Caelestia*, 3.

19. While Benzelius is an obvious factor connecting Swedenborg to Kemper, there is no evidence that Swedenborg studied directly with Kemper, as many have speculated.

in his 1832 *Symbolik*: "He insists, that it was only by a special revelation he was made attentive to it, or at all events favoured with the true key for its right use. But what is his distinction between the various senses of Holy Writ, other than Sod (body), the Derusch (soul), and the Phaschut (spirit) of the Cabala—senses which themselves correspond to [those] of Philo."[20] The absence of reference to kabbalah in Swedenborg's vast and all-encompassing corpus of writing is especially curious given his context and shared horizon with kabbalistic exegetical themes and suggests either a conscious or unconscious erasure is at play. Swedenborg's use of the outdated trope of Jewish literalism may have been an attempt to counter accusations of Judaizing, a defensive maneuver used by those before him like Jerome, whose reliance on Jewish exegetical authority also brought such accusations.

Swedenborg's *Arcana Coelestia* is not just a biblical commentary. Each chapter in this eight-volume opus begins and ends with a section on "The Marvels—things seen in the world of spirits and in the angelic heaven."[21] These accounts, which detail such things as the nature of heaven and hell, the speech of angels, and the experience of waking up after death, bookend each episode of biblical commentary and are unrelated thematically to the exegetical material. Many of the *memorabilia*, or "memorable relations" as they are often referred to in English, continue between chapters as episodes or installments of a larger essay. The layering of two modes, or genres, of writing had repercussions for how *Arcana Coelestia* was received: religious followers tended to emphasize and preach on the exegetical material, while artists, novelists, and poets, such as John Flaxman, Honoré de Balzac, and William Blake, responded to the visions. Kant focused more explicitly on Swedenborg's memorable relations, as we will see, but his open dismissal of Swedenborg's exegetical work is itself revealing. Swedenborg's particular iteration of Neoplatonic themes is one that Kant wrestled with intimately as he attempted to reform the field of metaphysics, and subsequent to this deep engagement Kant expended no small amount of energy distinguishing his views from those of the Swedish mystic.

In their chapter "The Battle of Reason with Imagination," Hartmut Böhme and Gernot Böhme are among those who make the case that

---

20. Johann Adam Möhler, *Symbolism: Exposition of the Doctrinal Differences between Catholics and Protestants as Evidenced by Their Symbolical Writings*, trans. James Burton Robertson (New York: Crossroad, 1997), 468.

21. Swedenborg, "Author's Introductory Note," in *Arcana Caelestia*.

106   JEWISH ALLEGORY IN EIGHTEENTH-CENTURY CHRISTIAN IMAGINATION

Kant's critical turn is in large part due to his engagement with Sweden-borg.[22] They write: "We presume that in Swedenborg Kant perceived a sort of twin brother, a counterpart, from whom he found it vitally important to distance himself."[23] The example they use from Swedenborg to make this argument is his presentation of the language of angels. Swedenborg's angels communicate thought in speech, but it is an unmediated speech—a way of presenting ideas without social convention or pretense. A single uttered sound communicates pure thought without any rhetorical elements, and nothing can be withheld or hidden. Kant would have been attracted to this concept, concerned as he was with *pure reason* and *pure religion*, but he ultimately sided with the usefulness of "civilizing external gloss," as Böhme and Böhme put it. A representational theory of language "essentially contains the possibility of deception and falsification," but civilized behavior and civilized speech are nevertheless art forms indispensable to good human relations and good education, Kant concluded.[24] This attraction to, and then rejection of, Swedenborg's descriptions of worlds beyond our own would become a pattern for the philosopher.

For Kant, especially later in his career, the idea of angelic speech is ultimately wrapped up in a set of concepts that must remain unverifiable. The philosopher no longer orbits a spiritual sun but a natural one. His is the "Copernican revolution for philosophy," as Wouter Hanegraaff puts it.[25]

---

22. Helmut Böhme and Gernot Böhme, "The Battle of Reason with Imagination," in *What Is Enlightenment? Eighteenth-Century Answers and Twentieth-Century Questions*, ed. James Schmidt (Berkeley: University of California Press, 1996), 426–52. A similar argument is made in Constantin Rauer, *Wahn und Wahrheit: Kants Auseinandersetzung mit dem Irrationalen* (Berlin: Akademie Verlag, 2007). Friedemann Stengel (*Enlightenment All the Way to Heaven: Emanuel Swedenborg in the Context of Eighteenth-Century Theology and Philosophy*, trans. Suzanne Schwarz Zuber [West Chester, PA: Swedenborg Foundation, 2023], 731–32) criticizes Böhme and Böhme for their emphasis on Kant's negative response to Swedenborg, though he agrees with their assessment of Swedenborg's importance for the development of Kant's critical theories. See also Jason Ānanda Josephson-Storm, *The Myth of Disenchantment: Magic, Modernity, and the Birth of the Human Sciences* (Chicago: University of Chicago Press, 2017), 184–90.

23. Böhme and Böhme, "Battle of Reason," 437–38.

24. Quote from Böhme and Böhme, "Battle of Reason," 449. See the section "On Permissible Moral Semblance," in Immanuel Kant, *Anthropology from a Pragmatic Point of View*, trans. Mary J. Gregor (The Hague: Nijhoff, 1974), 30–32.

25. Wouter Hanegraaff, *Swedenborg, Oetinger, Kant: Three Perspectives on the Secrets of Heaven* (West Chester, PA: Swedenborg Foundation, 2007), 97.

4. KANT AND SWEDENBORG 107

His public rejection of Swedenborg marked a larger moment in the history of science. That Swedenborg himself would be used as a tool in finally separating religion from science, metaphysics from physics, is tragic given his own efforts to keep them intertwined.[26] An overview of Kant's interest in Swedenborg, including his book about Swedenborg written at the time of his critical turn, will illuminate how the "something else" signaled by allegory related to notions about realities within or beyond language, scripture, and the body. Ambivalences regarding allegory were reflected in Kant's redefinition of metaphysics itself.

Kant's Interest in Swedenborg

Swedenborg's brief representation in the deliberations of eighteenth-century German philosophy can be explained on the one hand by his own indebtedness to Leibniz and Christian Wolff. More than that, however, it was his visions of the world of the dead that seemed to capture the imagination of Kant, Friedrich Schelling, and others and was deemed relevant to discussions on the limits of science and reason.[27] Swedenborg's doctrine of correspondences, with its familiar Leibnizian tenor and its application to

---

26. Swedenborg's contributions to science were neither insignificant nor irrelevant to Kant's own pursuits. Swedenborg's version of the Nebular Hypothesis (i.e., that the planets originated in the sun), for instance, predated that of Kant and LaPlace. See Sten Lindroth, *Swedish Men of Science 1650–1950* (Stockholm: Swedish Institute, 1952), 54–55.

27. On Swedenborg's reception among German intellectuals, including Johann Goerg Hamann, Johann Caspar Lavatar, and Johann Wolfgang Goethe, see Hanegraaff, *Swedenborg, Oetinger, Kant*, 109–13; Ernst Benz, *Swedenborg in Deutschland: F. C. Oetingers und Immanuel Kants Auseinandersetzung mit der Person und Lehre Emanuel Swedenborgs, nach neuen Quellen bearbeitet* (Frankfurt am Main: Klostermann, 1947); Benz, "Swedenborg as a Spiritual Pathfinder of German Idealism and Romanticism," trans. George Dole. In two parts: *Studia Swedenborgiana* 11.4 (2000): 61–76 and *Studia Swedenborgiana* 12.1 (2000): 15–35. Max Morris, "Swedenborg im Faust," *Euphorion* 6 (1899): 491–501; Rolf Christian Zimmermann, "Goethes Verhältnis zur Naturmystik am Beispiel seiner Farbenlehre," in *Epochen der Naturmystik: Hermetische Tradition im wissenschaftlichen Fortschritt*, ed. Antoine Faivre and Rolf Christian Zimmermann (Berlin: Schmidt, 1979), 333–63; Michael Heinrichs, *Emanuel Swedenborg in Deutschland: Eine kritische Darstellung der Rezeption des schwedischen Visionärs im 18. und 19. Jahrhundert* (Frankfurt am Main: Lang, 1979); Ulrich Gaier, "Könnt'ich Magie von meinem Pfad entfernen: Swedenborg im magischen Diskurs von Goethes *Faust*," in *Emanuel Swedenborg 1688–1772: Naturforscher und Kundiger*

108   JEWISH ALLEGORY IN EIGHTEENTH-CENTURY CHRISTIAN IMAGINATION

science, life after death, and biblical hermeneutics, resonated in thinkers such as these, though not without triggering the anxieties of an Enlightenment age fixated on reason and certainty.

Kant read and responded to *Arcana Coelestia* at a turbulent time for German metaphysics. Frederick Beiser describes the tumultuous context:

> [The] problem arose when the old Aristotelian metaphysics, which had dominated German intellectual life in the seventeenth century, was thrown back on the defensive by the growth of the new sciences. The geometrical method of Cartesian physics, and the inductive-mathematical method of Newton, had undermined both the concepts and methods of the old Aristotelianism. The scholastic forms had been banished from physics as so many occult qualities and the deductive method of syllogistic reasoning was dismissed as fruitless. Metaphysics, it therefore seemed, was doomed to extinction, the legacy of a moribund scholasticism.[28]

Opposing responses to this crisis, from Leibniz and Wolff on one hand and the Pietists on the other, further muddied the waters. Kant's own equivocation on matters related to knowledge of God, providence, and the immortality of the soul arises, therefore, amid contexts that were very much in flux on these matters. Kant engaged with and responded to Swedenborg, both positively and negatively, during various stages in the development of his thought, and his public criticism of Swedenborg is in many places autobiographical, revealing his own attraction to the kinds of worlds and ideas Swedenborg traveled in, even if he ultimately rejected them.

Kant was concerned with the limits of what we can know through the use of reason. This question required, for Kant, the bracketing of areas of metaphysics that considered the existence and nature of spiritual realities and centered on what our senses and mental faculties could reasonably demonstrate with certainty. His aim was practical and sensible, even if his style was notoriously opaque. However, as with his principles of biblical interpretation, his conclusions reveal more of a reframing of problematic categories rather than their outright rejection.

---

der Überwelt, ed. Horst Bergmann and Eberhard Zwink (Stuttgart: Württembergische Landesbibliothek, 1988), 129–39.

28. Frederick Beiser, "Kant's Intellectual Development: 1746–1781," in *Cambridge Companion to Kant*, ed. Paul Guyer (Cambridge: Cambridge University Press, 1992), 27.

He rejected Swedenborg's allegorical methods, but his alternative of a "moral sense" involved a familiar uncovering of wisdom hidden within the text and amounted to a reformulated *geheimen Sinn*. Similarly, his continued interest in the *intelligible world* and the *community of spirits*, despite his demarcation of reason's limits within the sensible world, was accompanied in several places with abridgments of Swedenborgian thought, as we will see.

Through his private correspondences, his university lectures, and his published writings we learn of Kant's fascination with Swedenborg. In a letter to Charlotte von Knobloch, written early in his career, Kant describes his skepticism of tales of miracles and clairvoyance, but writes that his position changed when he heard the stories coming from Sweden.[29] Kant summarizes, at the request of von Knobloch, the findings of an investigation he organized into the facts surrounding three incidents: two involving Swedenborg's communication with people who had died (one being the brother of Sweden's Queen Louisa Ulrika at her request), and a third involving Swedenborg's knowledge of a distant fire in Stockholm. Kant sent a friend to investigate the events, interview witnesses, and speak directly with Swedenborg, and reported on the collected evidence in positive terms, noting "Swedenborg's extraordinary gift beyond all possibility of doubt."[30] He mentions his frustrated attempts to correspond directly with the Swede and that he awaited, with longing, the publication of a forthcoming book by Swedenborg out of London.[31] This enthusiasm on Kant's part is not sustained, or if it is, his public rhetoric about Swedenborg takes a very different tone.

---

29. Immanuel Kant, "Letter to Charlotte von Knobloch," in *Documents concerning the Life and Character of Emanuel Swedenborg*, ed. R. L. Tafel, (London: Swedenborg Society, 1875), 2:625–28. The dating of this letter is unclear. See the discussion in Tafel, *Documents*, 2:620–25, where it is argued that the letter was written after *Träume eines Geistersehers* in 1768. Gregory Johnson puts it at 1763 before the publication of *Träume*, see *Kant on Swedenborg: Dreams of a Spirit-Seer and Other Writings*, ed. Gregory R. Johnson, trans. Gregory R. Johnson and Glenn Alexander Magee (London: Swedenborg Foundation, 2002), 183n2.

30. Tafel, *Documents*, 2:628.

31. Rather than respond to Kant's inquiries directly, Swedenborg had indicated that the answers to all of Kant's questions would be answered in the book. "I have made every provision for receiving it as soon as it leaves the press," writes Kant. Tafel suggests the book was *De Commercio Animæ & Corporis* (*Interaction of the Soul and the Body*, 1769). See Tafel, *Documents*, 2:624.

110   JEWISH ALLEGORY IN EIGHTEENTH-CENTURY CHRISTIAN IMAGINATION

Kant also discusses Swedenborg in his university lectures, the notes from which we have from his students, including Johann Gottfried Herder. Swedenborg's name arises in the lectures when Kant is discussing the possibility of communication with spirits, and he encourages his students to neither outright reject nor accept naively Swedenborg's visions. For "to dismiss all, must deny soul or state after death—phantoms have fooled us 99 times out of 100. Thus one inclines not to believe the probability of the majority of cases; but do not dismiss all of them summarily! Do not call liar, but rather *non liquet* [not proved]."[32] And elsewhere on Swedenborg: "[his] sensations indeed on the whole could be true, but are in part never certain."[33]

In his *Anthropology from a Pragmatic Point of View*, the last of his major works that he edited himself, Kant is careful to dissect a nuanced difference between Swedenborg's doctrine of correspondences and his own view of the relationship between true religion and religious symbols:

To say, with Swedenborg, that the real phenomena of the world present to the senses are merely a *symbol* of an intelligible world hidden in reserve is *fanaticism*. But in exhibiting the concepts that are the essence of all religion—concepts (called Ideas) that belong to morality and so to pure reason—it is *enlightenment* to distinguish the symbolic from the intellectual (public worship from religion), the temporarily useful and necessary husk from the thing itself. Otherwise we exchange an *Ideal* (of pure practical reason) for an *idol*, and miss the final end. It is an indisputable fact that all peoples on earth have begun by making this mistake and that, when it came to the question of what their teachers themselves really meant in composing their sacred writings, the interpretation had to be *literal* and not symbolic; for it would be dishonest to twist the teacher's words. But when it is a question not merely of the *truthfulness* of the teacher but also, and indeed essentially, of the *truth* of his teaching, then we can and should interpret these writings as a merely symbolic form of representation, in which established formalities and customs accompany those practical Ideas. For otherwise the intellectual meaning, which is the final end, would be lost.[34]

---

32. Johann Gottfried Herder, "Excerpts from Herder Metaphysics and Herder Supplements (1763–1764)," as translated by Johnson and Magee, *Kant on Swedenborg*, 74.

33. Herder, "Excerpts," 75.

34. Kant, *Anthropology*, 65. This section of the book considers various cognitive powers, such as making associations, having foresight, having imagination, and dreaming. For each of these powers he considers the range of their expression from

4. KANT AND SWEDENBORG

Here Kant begins with a distinction between enthusiasm and enlightenment, in which Swedenborg's idea of the relationship between spiritual and natural things through correspondences is rejected in favor of a more conventional view of symbols. However, as we read on, the true culprit for misreading symbols is identified not with the fanatic Swedenborg, but with biblical literalists. Those who make an idol out of pure ideas are readers who miss the true teaching of scripture and focus instead on the ways these ideas are represented in forms of culture and language. In this instance, Kant does not address Swedenborg's exegetical methods as much as his view of a dualistic universe, and where he does address biblical interpretation he seems to side with a nonliteral reading that rejects the husk for the kernel within.

His lectures and letters therefore reveal a certain equivocation and curiosity, centering on communication with spirits, the connection between physical and spiritual realities, and the ability of symbols and language to mediate these connections. The fact that Kant went on to write an entire book on Swedenborg, however, challenges the perception that this was a fleeting or peripheral interest of his.

Kant's most famous and controversial engagement with Swedenborg comes in his short work, anonymously published, *Träume eines Geistersehers, erläutert durch Träume der Metaphysik* (*Dreams of a Spirit-Seer, Elucidated by Dreams of Metaphysics*, 1766). This work was the first introduction to Swedenborg for many European intellectuals and in many cases the last word on his relevance, or irrelevance, to the concerns of the day. If we limit ourselves strictly to the field of philosophy, or to those who would place themselves and their work in that category, the reception of *Arcana Coelestia*, and of Swedenborg's work in general, more or less begins and ends with Kant's *Träume*. Kant had the last word on Swedenborg in certain circles, for while his assessment was far from unequivocal, it was enough to discourage further investigation among his followers. Furthermore, the location of *Träume* in the development of Kant's critical philosophy, at a time when his views on the role of metaphysics and the limits of reason were radically shifting, makes it relevant to the present study, and it will be necessary to spend some time here unraveling it.

---

those that are favorable (using reason, inner sense, and experience) and those that are fanatical or arise from madness or self-deception. The section also considers the power of using signs.

112 JEWISH ALLEGORY IN EIGHTEENTH-CENTURY CHRISTIAN IMAGINATION

Dreams of a Spirit Seer

Any analysis of Kant's *Träume* must grapple with its many inconsistencies in both content and style. That readers, from the time of its publication to today, cannot seem to agree on whether the greater part of Kant's estimation of Swedenborg in this book stems from admiration or ridicule is perhaps because Kant himself was conflicted and, at least some of the time, intentionally vague and contradictory in this regard. In the same year of its publication, Mendelssohn wrote "The joking pensiveness with which this little work is written leaves the reader sometimes in doubt as to whether Herr Kant intends to make metaphysics laughable or spirit-seeing credible."[35] Kant responded to Mendelssohn in a letter: "it was difficult for me to devise the right way to clothe my thoughts so as not to expose myself to mockery. It seemed to me most advisable to forestall others by first of all mocking myself, a completely honest procedure since my own mind was conflicted on this."[36] Johann Georg Heinrich Feder, likewise, wrote in his review of *Träume*, "After reading through these pages, we have become doubtful whether they were written in jest or in earnest; at any rate both are almost always together."[37] And in a letter to Swedenborg about Kant's book, theologian Friedrich Christoph Oetinger writes that "the author lifts you on high with praises, as much as he pushes you down with accusations lest he be regarded as a fanatic."[38] We do not know whether Swedenborg read the book or how he reacted to it. But the confusion it generated about his own work would certainly create immediate obstacles for his readership. In his review, Herder advised those who were curious about Swedenborg to read Kant's book in place of *Arcana Coelestia*: "which is here amusing when it could have cost effort."[39]

---

35. Moses Mendelssohn, "Review of Dreams of a Spirit-Seer: 1767," as translated by Johnson and Magee, *Kant on Swedenborg*, 123.

36. Immanuel Kant, "Letter to Moses Mendelssohn, April 8, 1766," as translated by Johnson and Magee, *Kant on Swedenborg*, 83–84.

37. Johann Georg Heinrich Feder, "Review of Dreams of a Spirit-Seer: September 23, 1766," as translated in Johnson and Magee, *Kant on Swedenborg*, 120.

38. Friedrich Christoph Oetinger, "Letter to Emanuel Swedenborg: December 4, 1766," as translated by Alfred Acton in *Letters and Memorials of Swedenborg* (Bryn Athyn, PA: Swedenborg Scientific Association, 1955), 630.

39. Johann Gottfried Herder, "Review of Dreams of a Spirit-Seer: March 3, 1766," as translated by Johnson and Magee, *Kant on Swedenborg*, 115.

4. KANT AND SWEDENBORG

Kant's book is divided into two parts. The first, "Which Is Dogmatic," and the second, "Which Is Historical," deal respectively with universal questions of metaphysics and the particular case of Swedenborg. In an introductory "Preliminary Report Promising Very Little before the Actual Treatise" Kant wonders at the proliferation and success of otherworldly tales, of "Hypochondriac emanations, fairy tales and convent miracles."[40] Should a philosopher admit even one of these tales? Or should such things be rejected categorically? Kant, seeking to balance dogmatism with skepticism, answers that it is just as foolish to discount them all as to believe without discernment and admits to his own credulity on such matters.[41]

The first chapter of *Träume* sets up a series of questions about the connection between the body and the spirit and about the nature, substance, and location of spiritual realities. Throughout, Kant repeats his general opinion that while he is "inclined to affirm the existence of immaterial beings in the universe" including his own soul, definitive answers to such questions are beyond the reach of our understanding.[42] Thus, while he "cannot say whether or not spirits exists" or what "spirit" even means, he can compare the experiences different people report concerning spiritual realities, and by observing which of these reports align with his own imperfect perceptions and which run counter to them, something can be clarified.[43]

With this methodology in place, Kant moves on in the second chapter, titled "A Fragment of Occult Philosophy to Reveal Our Community with the Spirit World," and presents a description of the spirit world very much resembling Swedenborg's reports, though he does not yet name Swedenborg. He considers a reality where the human soul is simultaneously linked to two worlds, the physical world and the spiritual world, and the human individual thereby stands in relationship to two communities. When a person dies, relationships of the natural world cease, but

---

40. Immanuel Kant, *Dreams of a Spirit Seer*, trans. John Manolesco (New York: Vantage, 1969), 29.

41. "[The] author of this treatise tried to avoid the former prejudice and thus allowed himself to be somehow led astray by the latter. Thus he admits with a certain humility that he was naive enough to undertake an investigation into the alleged truth of some of the stories of the kind mentioned. He found, as is the case when one has nothing to look for, he found ... nothing" (Kant, *Dreams of a Spirit Seer*, 30).

42. Kant, *Dreams of a Spirit Seer*, 30.

43. Kant, *Dreams of a Spirit Seer*, 33.

114 JEWISH ALLEGORY IN EIGHTEENTH-CENTURY CHRISTIAN IMAGINATION

the individual continues their spiritual relationships, which are formed in accordance with the moral life developed while living in the body. It is through community with spirits that a person is able to receive influx from the spiritual world and, on occasion, to have insight into this process. Such a view aligns seamlessly with descriptions in *Arcana Coelestia*, where we read for example: "Without communication by means of spirits with the world of spirits, and by means of angels with heaven, and thus through heaven with the Lord, man could not live at all; his life entirely depends on this conjunction, so that if the spirits and angels were to withdraw, he would instantly perish."[44]

Kant's descriptions of influx from spirits align with Swedenborg's correspondences. Insights from the spiritual world come in the form of symbols or representations, which take on different configurations with different people according to their "different constitution." The heterogeneity of representations is an obstacle for us in understanding spiritual realities, but not too great an obstacle. "In this way it is not improbable that spiritual impressions could penetrate into our consciousness if they were to stimulate images in our imagination which are somehow co-related to them. In this way, ideas communicated under the influence of spirits tend to take concrete shapes in the signs of language which is customarily spoken."[45] The symbolic nature of language is explained as a kind of crystallization of ideas coming into the mind from the spiritual world.

With this more or less positive summary of a dualistic and symbolic universe looking very much Swedenborgian in place, Kant's third chapter takes on a radically different tone and reduces spirit seeing to malfunctioning of the brain. The chapter is titled "Antikabbalah: A Fragment of Common Philosophy Dissolving the Community with the Spirit World." Drawing on Descartes, he points to the internal activity in the brain that occurs when one is engaged in a fantasy or waking dream. In a person who is mad, there is confusion of nerve activity and objects of fantasy are perceived as objectively real. In this way, ghost stories and spirit-seeing can be explained as mental illness. The chapter ends by reflecting on one inconvenience brought about by these considerations: "they render superfluous the deeply-thoughtout conjectures in the previous chapter." In chapter 4, then, the two approaches so far laid out are weighed on a

---

44. Swedenborg, *Arcana Caelestia*, 50.
45. Kant, *Dreams of a Spirit Seer*, 55–56.

"scale of understanding." The credulous voice of chapter 2 is balanced against the skeptical voice of chapter 3, and Kant admits he is a believer. "This is a defect which truly speaking I cannot remove, nor do I want to remove it ever."[46] His bias in favor of the viewpoint of chapter 2 is destabilizing. He cannot shake his attraction to such things, and he utilizes skepticism to safeguard against imprudent naiveté. The two viewpoints, when combined, create a parallax effect; speculation balanced with hope is the only way of preventing optical illusion. "Nothing is more sacred to me, nothing more important right now than to find the path to truth in a calm, open-minded attitude, regardless of whether it will or will not confirm or rebut my previous judgements, regardless of whether it will leave me decided or undecided."[47] We sense the urgency with which he tests his credulity with criticism.

Kant's description of the scale of understanding is autobiographical, and he understands it to be so. Readers should make up their own minds, he writes, which brings him to the question of ultimate concern: What we can know scientifically? If belief is personal, epistemology is communal. Here the limits are more clearly delineated. Philosophy simply cannot answer questions about the nature of spirit, nor should it attempt to do so. Curiously, Kant ends part 1 of his book by washing his hands of spirit seers, even as part 2 delves more deeply into the particular case of Emanuel Swedenborg. "And now I lay aside this whole subject of spirits, a remote part of metaphysics; I treat it as finished and done with. In the future I shall display no further interest in it."[48] Perhaps, rather than putting the subject to bed, this statement marks the end of his personal confessions, for the thrust of the remainder of the book is to create a distance between his own ideas and those of Swedenborg, who he finally addresses by name.[49]

---

46. Kant, *Dreams of a Spirit Seer*, 68
47. Kant, *Dreams of a Spirit Seer*, 67.
48. Kant, *Dreams of a Spirit Seer*, 71.
49. Commentators have in the past described Kant's spelling of Swedenborg's name (Schwedenberg) as derogatory. However, Stengel demonstrates a wider use of this spelling, indicating a tendency among German writers to spell his name phonetically rather than a deliberate misspelling. The adoption of this spelling by Mendelssohn and Herder is in imitation of Kant. However, as Stengel shows, others independently produced creative versions of Swedenborg's name with no ill intent. Johann Georg Hamann writes of "Schwedenberg" as *Arcana Coelestia*'s author as early as 1764. Oetinger alternated between "Schwedenborg" and "Swedenborg," and occasionally even "Schwedenburg" or "Suedenborg," and Justus Christian Hennings noted in

116 JEWISH ALLEGORY IN EIGHTEENTH-CENTURY CHRISTIAN IMAGINATION

Kant begins part 2 with the three famous stories surrounding Swedenborg's clairvoyance. He presents these with an attitude of indifference unlike the tone of his letter to Charlotte von Knobloch that treated the same subject. Why should a philosopher report on stories about Swedenborg, "the arch-spirit seer of all spirit seers"? Kant's answer builds a comparison to metaphysicians, who weave fairy tales of a similar sort. Philosophy should either accept or reject both together.[50] But is Kant suggesting metaphysics in its present form has no place in philosophy, or that spirit-seeing does have a place? His answer in favor of rejecting them both unfolds in the last two chapters, though not without further contradictions.

Here Kant formally introduces *Arcana Coelestia* as "eight quarto volumes of sheer nonsense," a line Mendelssohn would repeat in his review.[51] Kant dismisses the allegorical content of Swedenborg's commentary outright: "His discoveries are often applied exegetically to clarify the secret meaning of the first two books of Moses, and similar new interpretations are devised for the whole of the Holy Scriptures."[52] Kant's interest lies instead, he writes, in the memorable relations and in descriptions of the interaction between physical and spiritual things. Yet the two areas, exegesis and metaphysics, have more in common than Kant here admits, and this becomes apparent as he considers Swedenborg's case more explicitly.

Chapter 2 of the second part pleads with the reader not to draw comparisons between Kant and Swedenborg. "I state as bluntly as possible: when it comes to such comparisons and insinuations I have no sense of humor."[53] Curiously, this petition is followed by a convincing and reasonable description of some of Swedenborg's key ideas that appear most similar to Kant's. For instance, Swedenborg claims that each individual has two memories: an internal memory and an external one. Likewise, each has two kinds of senses: outer senses and inner senses.[54] Time and space are perceived differently by the inner senses: proximity in this sense

---

1780 "that one sometimes writes Swedenborg, other times Schwedenborg." See Stengel, *Enlightenment*, 736. Kant uses the "Schwedenberg" spelling throughout *Träume*, though he did use the correct spelling in his letter to Charlotte von Knobloch. My quotations from *Träume* will follow translator John Manolesco's lead in spelling the name correctly.

50. Kant, *Dreams of a Spirit Seer*, 76.

51. Kant, *Dreams of a Spirit Seer*, 82

52. Kant, *Dreams of a Spirit Seer*, 82.

53. Kant, *Dreams of a Spirit Seer*, 81, see also 89.

54. Kant, *Dreams of a Spirit Seer*, 84.

4. KANT AND SWEDENBORG

117

is determined by likeness rather than physical location.[55] We are interiorly "close" to spirits who are like us, even if they are spirits whose bodies are from another continent.[56] Material beings exist by the power of the world of spirits. It is the totality of all spirits, or the community of spiritual beings to which a person interiorly belongs, that gives a person life.[57] Furthermore, the parts of the body are mutually related according to physical laws, but body parts also receive animating powers from the soul. This "inner meaning" is not known to man, but such is also true for everything in the visible world. Each thing has two meanings: a minor, material meaning and an inner meaning, the former being a mere symbol of the latter.[58]

Here Kant makes explicit the connection between these metaphysical ideas and their exegetical implications. The symbolic manner of communication between the spiritual and natural worlds, the accommodation of angels to images familiar to their earthly counterparts via symbols, is the same mechanism used in biblical language. He writes: "This is the reason why Swedenborg tried to give a new interpretation to the Bible. Their inner meaning, namely, all the symbolic references in the scriptures to the world of spirits, he claims, alone contains the essence of all values, whilst the remainder is a mere shell."[59] The discernment of the essence of values within the shell is precisely the language Kant uses in advocating for the principles of interpretation, as articulated in *The Conflict of the Faculties* summarized above.

As if anticipating the reader's comparison with his own interpretations of the Bible, Kant interrupts this summary with open ridicule of his subject. "I am tired of copying the wild vagaries of the words of all dreamers or of continuing with his descriptions of the state after death."[60] He worries that by giving Swedenborg so much attention, readers (especially, he writes, pregnant women or more poetically, those pregnant with idealism), will be misled.[61]

---

55. Kant, *Dreams of a Spirit Seer*, 85.

56. From Kant's first lecture in Metaphysics: "[a person] is already in this world in community with all righteous and well-meaning souls, be they in India or Arabia; only he does not yet see himself in this community, until he is freed from sensuous intuition" (as translated in Johnson and Magee, *Kant on Swedenborg*, 91–92).

57. Kant, *Dreams of a Spirit Seer*, 86.

58. Kant, *Dreams of a Spirit Seer*, 87.

59. Kant, *Dreams of a Spirit Seer*, 87.

60. Kant, *Dreams of a Spirit Seer*, 89.

61. Elsewhere he states that women are especially prone to believing these things; see Kant, *Dreams of a Spirit Seer*, 77

118   JEWISH ALLEGORY IN EIGHTEENTH-CENTURY CHRISTIAN IMAGINATION

If Kant's *Träume* expresses an internal struggle regarding his own credulity or the misunderstanding of his readers, this anxiety is then redirected at metaphysicians, whom Kant refers to as "brainless sophists who needlessly add to the bulk of our quarterly journals."[62] These "dreamers of reason" are not unlike the mystics or "dreamers of sense" in their lack of grounding and critical reason. By the end of the book, Kant has replaced a speculative metaphysics, "with whom my destiny made me fall in love hopelessly" with a critical metaphysics.[63] The first, which answers questions concerning the hidden nature of things, sets its sights too high and tends to disappoint. The second, which determines the problems that can be resolved with human reason and those that cannot, "becomes a true science tracing the limits of human understanding."[64] He therefore sets the course for a true philosophy aimed at determining these limits, a project that would motivate his subsequent work and most importantly his three critiques: *Kritik der reinen Vernunft* (1781), *Kritik der praktischen Vernunft* (1790), and *Kritik der Urteilskraft* (1790). And so it would appear that this has been the goal all along: to exclude from philosophy all activity that cannot be explained by physical laws or corroborated through mutual experience. "Human reason was not meant to try and part the highest clouds in heaven or lift from our eyes the curtains in order to reveal to us the secrets of other worlds."[65] With that, Swedenborg's *Secrets of Heaven* is decisively bracketed and removed from philosophical discourse. Or so it would seem. In actuality, Swedenborg's removal from Kant's thought and public discourse was not so absolute.

Kant's 1770 inaugural dissertation, *De mundi sensibilis atque intelligibilis forma et principiis* (*On the Form and Principles of the Sensible and Intelligible Worlds*), appears to backtrack on critical theories worked out in *Träume* by asserting the ability of reason to access knowledge of the intelligible world. Beiser explains this apparent contradiction by tracing the development of Kant's thought in the years between 1746 and 1781 through four phases of his "unhappy love affair" with metaphysics. Earlier "infatuation" turned to a period of disillusionment and skepticism, such as we see in *Träume*. However, his dissertation marks a subsequent phase of "partial reconciliation" in the 1770s before Kant entered the fourth and

---

62. Kant, *Dreams of a Spirit Seer*, 82–83, 90
63. Kant, *Dreams of a Spirit Seer*, 90
64. Kant, *Dreams of a Spirit Seer*, 91.
65. Kant, *Dreams of a Spirit Seer*, 98.

final phase of his "divorce" from metaphysics beginning in 1781. If Beiser's four phases are accurate, they explain Kant's more positive engagement with Swedenborg in his lectures on Metaphysics (L1) in the 1770s, where we read, for example: "The thought of Swedenborg is in this quite sublime."[66] Particular affinities with Swedenborgian thought in these lectures include: the subjectivity of space and time in the spiritual world; that a person's spirit is in community with other spirits now, even as the person is alive in their physical body; and that the makeup of this community is determined by the moral quality of a person's action in the world.[67] He concludes that however intuitively truthful such matters may be, providence has nevertheless closed the door to our soul's future life, and the chief matter before us is how to live righteously in the present.

Kant's thinking during this period was shifting and searching for new ground upon which to establish a new era of metaphysics, a project he eventually abandoned. His subsequent efforts to establish a perimeter, a border wall, within which philosophy should rightly be limited, paralleled his efforts to wall off pure religion from the vestiges of Judaism.

Antikabbalah

Kant's rejection of speculative metaphysics was a rejection of the ideas represented by Swedenborg's doctrine of correspondences: that every *thing* has both an appearance and a noumenon, the latter being the *Ding an sich* "the thing in itself." Kant's denunciation of Swedenborg is therefore related to the empirical limits that pronounced the unknowability of noumena and the related unknowability of a spiritual world. This parallels Kant's professed rejection of an allegorical, spiritual-sense reading of scripture, especially of the Old Testament, such as he found in Swedenborg's *Arcana Coelestia*. Kant also encouraged the liberation from reliance on the things of the natural world perceived with the senses (i.e., phenomena). In Kant's philosophical system both realms, noumenal and phenomenal, are replaced with a reliance on autonomous reason and its singular ability to guide the moral life. But it is the liberation from the external, natural world—the body and its material environment—that Kant presents in terms of a rejection of Jews and those aspects of Christianity deemed

---

66. Kant, *Lectures on Metaphysics*, 105. On the problem of dating these lectures, see the introduction by Karl Ameriks and Steve Naragon in Kant, *Lectures*, xxx–xxxiii.

67. Kant, *Lectures*, 103–6.

120   JEWISH ALLEGORY IN EIGHTEENTH-CENTURY CHRISTIAN IMAGINATION

Jewish. This notion of a purified Christianity is what lies behind his infamous advancement of the "euthanasia of Jewishness."[68] The remainder of this chapter will investigate Kant's anti-Judaism in light of the themes of biblical allegory and metaphysics.

In his 1793 *Die Religion innerhalb der Grenzen der bloßen Vernunft* (*Religion within the Limits of Reason Alone*), Kant lays out his argument that while Christianity is concerned with what is moral, Judaism is concerned merely with what is statutory. He writes that Judaism was originally no religion at all, but a political entity concerned with externalities, legalism, rewards, and punishments. In Kant's view, the relationship between the Jews and their God, Jehovah, laid out in the Old Testament concerns only the here and now and the immediate rewards for obedience rather than moral agency. According to Kant, places in the Hebrew scriptures that appear to have moral content, such as the Ten Commandments, do so only because of the moral religion imbued into it later by Christ-followers. Furthermore, Judaism is not the foundation of Christianity, as it is widely received to be, but merely the accidental context out of which Christianity, as an entirely new principle, grew: "it is evident that the Jewish faith stands in no essential connection whatever, *i.e.*, in no unity of concepts, with this ecclesiastical faith whose history we wish to consider, though the Jewish immediately preceded this (the Christian) church and provided the physical occasion for its establishment."[69] The laws and rites outlined in the Old Testament are of no consequence for Christians, and such externalized ceremonies are to be actively opposed. Elsewhere he depicts this opposition in imitation of Jesus, who brought about "in his own lifetime a public revolution (in religion), by overthrowing morally reprehensible ceremonial faith and the authority of its priests."[70]

For Kant, then, the rejection of Judaism would be a purging for the Christian church. If the first Christians found it necessary to ground themselves in Jewish texts, over time this has had the negative effect of

---

68. Immanuel Kant, *Religion and Rational Theology*, trans. and ed. Allen W. Wood and George Di Giovanni (Cambridge: Cambridge University Press, 1998), 276. For a discussion of Kant's anti-Semitism and his break with metaphysics, see Michael Mack, *German Idealism and the Jew: The Inner Anti-Semitism of Philosophy and German Jewish Responses* (Chicago: University of Chicago Press, 2003), 23–41.

69. Kant, *Religion within the Limits*, 116.

70. Kant, *Religion and Rational Theology*, 75.

4. KANT AND SWEDENBORG   121

magnifying the legalism of church councils and perpetuating the drive to "seek religion without and not within us."[71] In a couple of telling footnotes, Kant imagines Mendelssohn's reasons for not converting to Christianity and speaks on behalf of his Jewish counterpart in expressing a "clever" response. He paraphrases Mendelssohn's argument in *Jerusalem* that Christianity is founded on Judaism and to convert would be, in Kant's words, to "demolish the ground floor of a house in order to take up his abode in the second story."[72] Kant provides his parenthetical commentary to this notion, writing that "(Actually nothing would then be left but pure moral religion unencumbered by statutes.)" This sentiment is echoed in another footnote, where he puts words in Mendelssohn's mouth, replying to the suggestion that he should convert: "Christians, first get rid of the Judaism in your own faith, and then we will give up ours."[73] The books of the Jews should be preserved not for the benefit of religion but for the value of scholarship only. As a religion, Judaism contributes nothing in Kant's view.

One can see a perverse influence of Mendelssohn on Kant's thinking in this area, even if his conclusions, to exclude Judaism from public life, from the body politic, are antithetical to Mendelssohn's pluralistic vision for Germany.[74] As we saw in the last chapter, Mendelssohn emphasized the particularity of revelation and that ceremonial Judaism was not only revealed truth but also historical and particular for the Jewish people. Kant essentially agrees with Mendelssohn in viewing historical religion as the externalized form of natural religion. However, whereas Mendelssohn views the two as mutually sustaining for a given community, Kant views them as antithetical. Historical religion and ceremonial law should be opposed rather than embraced. Kant expresses an impatience with those who would preserve the external forms of devotion similar to his impatience with those who would preserve parts of the Bible opposed to moral law. One should discard those aspects of texts and traditions that distract

---

71. Kant, *Religion within the Limits*, 155.

72. Kant, *Religion within the Limits*, 154n. See Mendelssohn, *Jerusalem*, 87.

73. Kant, *Conflict of the Faculties*, 93n.

74. Spinoza's influence is perceptible here as well. Spinoza viewed the biblical laws as political in nature and their applicability limited to a historical moment in time. On Spinoza's influence, see Susan Meld Shell, "Kant and the Jewish Question," *Hebraic Political Studies* 2.1 (2007): 115; Wojciech Kozyra, "Kant on the Jews and their Religion," *Diametros* 17.65 (2020): 38–40; and Mack, *German Idealism*, 23, 34.

122   JEWISH ALLEGORY IN EIGHTEENTH-CENTURY CHRISTIAN IMAGINATION

from rather than encourage the morally useful life, and for Kant these are precisely the aspects that define Judaism.

Kant's relationship to Mendelssohn, his thought, and his legacy in the next generation of *Maskilim* would influence his views on Judaism in both positive and negative ways. In the same year of its publication, Kant sent Mendelssohn a copy of his *Träume* followed shortly by a letter concerning the state of metaphysics and suggesting that the two might work together on advancing the future of their field. This admiration, not to mention that it was tagged to Kant's book on Swedenborg and metaphysics, suggests Kant saw Mendelssohn, early on at least, as a potential ally in the work of keeping mysticism out of philosophy. Susan Meld Shell traces the relationship between the two philosophers and suggests a dialogue is detectable in their respective publications. "Indeed, in several respects Kant and Mendelssohn served as each other's negative amanuenses: Kant's *Dreams of a Spirit Seer* provoked Mendelssohn's *Phaedo*, which is answered in the 'Paralogism' section of the first *Critique*."[75]

Kant's earlier attraction to Mendelssohn would later be replaced with disapproval and attack. But his criticism comes, at least in part, out of an engagement with Mendelssohn's successors, the second generation of *Maskilim*, who had little regard for the orthodox members of their faith and who united with Kant in opposing Mendelssohn's views on religious life. The mutual admiration between Kant and these later German Jewish philosophers came with a shared distaste for halakic Judaism, which they viewed as superstitious and backward looking. They saw the Talmud and halakah as extraneous to pure religion and a hindrance to enlightened progress.[76] Marcus Hertz, a close friend and student of Kant's, wrote "without you I would still be like so many of my kinsmen pursuing a life chained to the wagon of prejudices, a life no better than that of any animal."[77] Kant, would, of course, continue to be influential for generations of Jewish philosophers, many of whom would be interested in discerning a moral essence to Judaism the way Kant did with Christianity. As Michael Mack writes concerning key forces in the development of Reform Judaism and neoorthodoxy, "post-Mendelssohn German Jewish thought in the nineteenth century attempted to cast Judaism into the conceptual mold of

---

75. Shell, "Kant and the Jewish Question," 104.
76. See Kozyra, "Kant on the Jews," 34–38, 50–51.
77. As quoted in Kozyra, "Kant on the Jews," 34.

Kant's rational theology and moral philosophy."[78] Furthermore, the oppositional stance toward Hasidic rabbis and their followers on the part of these *Maskilim* echoes Kant's rejection of Swedenborg. Both dismiss what they perceive to be a fanaticism that would find hidden worlds of meaning in the words of sacred texts and in the soul's mystical ascent to heaven and back.[79]

Various theories exist concerning the nature and trajectory of Kant's anti-Judaism. Shell traces Kant's views on Jews and Judaism through successive stages from a more positive stance early on to antagonism and finally to a constructive approach through his relationship to Jewish students who shared his revolutionary interests. Others suggest there is consistency in his conceptions regarding Jews and Judaism in his philosophical writings, even if his personal relationships evolve functionally over time.[80] His positive relationships aside, the contemporary reader finds it difficult to harmonize his passion for morality, freedom, and civic duty to one's compatriots with his open prejudices. It is not simply Kant's silence on the question of Jewish civil rights that stands out, but also his outright hostile characterization of Jews as fixed in their ways through every generation, forever foreigners, and an unproductive "nation of cheaters." [81] As Paul Lawrence Rose notes, it is the cool rationalism of Kant's style and his posture of objectivity that makes such statements so insidious. Kant's attacks amounted to "a new secularized form of Jew-hatred."[82] Rose also considers the ways Kant espoused a revolutionary anti-Semitism. The particular nationalist quality of anti-Semitism in Germany in the eighteenth century contributed to a prejudice against Jews as a nation apart, alien, and opposed to horizons of progress and freedom. Kant introduced a moralist hostility into the mix of German deliberations on the Jewish question that would shape the discourse for generations to come. Mack, for his part, deemphasizes Kant's innovations in this regard and stresses his reliance on

---

78. Mack, *German Idealism*, 12.

79. For a comparison of the mystical ascents and interpretive strategies of Swedenborg and the Baal Shem Tov, see Rebecca K. Esterson, "What Do the Angels Say? Alterity and the Ascents of Emanuel Swedenborg and the Baal Shem Tov," *Open Theology* 4.1 (2018): 414–21.

80. Kozyra, "Kant on the Jews," 41; Mack, *German Idealism*, 39–40.

81. Kant, *Anthropology*, 77.

82. Paul Lawrence Rose, *German Question/Jewish Question: Revolutionary Antisemitism in Germany from Kant to Wagner* (Princeton: Princeton University Press, 2014), 94.

124   JEWISH ALLEGORY IN EIGHTEENTH-CENTURY CHRISTIAN IMAGINATION

standard Christian doctrinal essentials and longstanding stereotypes: his pseudotheology put to the service of a pseudoscience. Like Rose, however, Mack sees Kant's legacy rooted in the introduction of Christian thought into the secularized modern state with "major implications for the debate about Jewish civil equality that became quite intense in German speaking culture at the end of the eighteenth century."[83] Despite a pretense of impartiality, Kant remained loyal to an inherited set of religious biases.

In addition to these insights into the nature of Kant's anti-Judaism, we would do well to consider Kant's rhetoric about Jewish interpretation and how it fits into his conflicted views concerning allegory and literalism. Kant's most explicit reference to Jewish exegesis is found in *Conflict of the Faculties*, where he suggests that the cleverness of Jewish interpretation is what allowed Judaism to survive and influence Christianity in its early days.

> The disciples of the Mosaic-messianic faith saw their hopes, based on God's covenant with Abraham, fail completely after Jesus' death (we had hoped that he would deliver Israel); for their Bible promised salvation only to the children of Abraham. Now it happened when the disciples were gathered at Pentecost, one of them hit upon the happy idea, in keeping with the subtle art of Jewish exegesis, that pagans (Greeks and Romans) could also be regarded as admitted into this covenant, if they believed in the sacrifice of his only son that Abraham was willing to offer to God (as the symbol of the world-savior's own sacrifice); for then they would be children of Abraham in faith.[84]

Jesus's disciples are here influenced by their Jewish "Mosaic-messianic faith," which he contrasts negatively against an "evangelical-messianic" faith of the gospel. As such, their expectations concerning the Messiah have been frustrated by the crucifixion, and they are in a state of despondency. Rather than credit the miracle described in the story of Pentecost for what happened next, Kant suggests that the events that followed were due to "the subtle art of Jewish exegesis." The Jewish disciples reinterpreted the covenant. The sacrifice of Isaac would become an allegory for the death of Christ on the cross; the covenant with Israel would be an allegory for a covenant with all humanity. For Kant, Christian typology is born of Jewish

---

83. Mack, *German Idealism*, 33.
84. Kant, *Conflict of the Faculties*, 121n.

cunning. He goes on to say that the requirement to believe in the work of the Holy Spirit with these early disciples is nothing but superstition. It is not clear whether he means belief in the miracle described in Acts is superstition, or belief in an interpretive connection between Judaism and Christianity is superstition. The two are somehow intertwined in his version of the story. As such, Kant's reinterpretation of Pentecost is deeply contradictory. One would expect him to celebrate the universalizing of the gospel message. Elsewhere he argues that the work of biblical scholars is precisely to draw out the moral aspects of the text that can be used by all people—biblical studies for the sake of the categorical imperative.[85] But this is not how he reads the story. Rather than view Pentecost as the universalization of the covenant with Israel, Kant sees it as the moment Judaism was inscribed into the already universalized moral religion embodied in the teachings of Jesus, and along with Judaism came superstition.

Against this origin story of Christian typology, we can better analyze Kant's irritation at Swedenborg's approach to the Bible. Swedenborg reproduced patristic allegory in the name of enlightenment and argued for its truth using both his experiences and his reason. He claimed both empirical and rational authority, and produced a reading of the text that prioritized ethics over creed. But in Kant's estimation, he also brought along the things most detrimental to pure religion, namely, fantasy and Judaism.

Kant's own principles of interpretation would, in his view, resist any recourse to typology with its Jewish origins and troublesome history in the church, and would instead utilize autonomous reason to sift the text, drawing out the essential truths embedded therein. When one attempts to summarize his method of interpretation from various places in his writing, one discerns an overall effort to sort out the Christian scriptures from the Jewish ones. The Old Testament and the New Testament are broadly categorized here in a mode of supersession, but the sifting itself, it seems, is equally applied to Old Testament texts such as the story of Adam in Genesis (keep but reinterpret) and the command to sacrifice of Isaac (discard as immoral and Jewish), as it is to New Testament texts, such as the resurrection of Christ (keep but reinterpret), and the descent of the Holy Spirit on Pentecost (discard as superstitious and Jewish). If one is stuck on a particularly difficult text such as Ps 59, which describes God seeking revenge, Kant suggests the following procedure: if it is at all possible to

---

85. Kant, *Religion within the Limits*, 102.

126 JEWISH ALLEGORY IN EIGHTEENTH-CENTURY CHRISTIAN IMAGINATION

find a New Testament text to use instead, do so. If it is possible to reinterpret the text, by whatever means, to a moral end, do so. One might, for example, interpret the invisible enemy in the Psalm as an enemy within, an evil inclination (this is precisely how Swedenborg interprets Ps 59).[86] If neither procedure produces the desired results, Kant writes, one should "rather have it that this passage is not to be understood in a moral sense at all but only as applying to the relation in which the Jews conceived themselves to stand to God as their political regent."[87] Kant's procedure, in short, suggests that if one's interpretation of a difficult verse cannot lead to a moral end, the verse in question should be understood in light of its Jewish origins and essentially dismissed.[88]

Kant associated Jews and, in turn, the Old Testament with the material, natural world and a political paradigm that hindered pure religion. And if Judaism was useful to Kant in negatively defining pure religion, kabbalah was useful in negatively defining practical reason. Like so much of his *Träume*, Kant's use of the term "Antikabbalah" to title his harshest critique of the spirit-seeing of Swedenborg is ambiguous. He does not explain the wording of this chapter title, and kabbalah is mentioned nowhere else in the book. The chapter appears, in part, to be criticizing the philosophy of the Leibniz-Wolffian school, which Kant interfaced with for his lectures on metaphysics. The "Antikabbalah" chapter draws a connection between "dreamers of reason" and "dreamers of sense," thereby ridiculing metaphysicians and mystics all at once. The discourse about kabbalah is, for Kant, less about Jewish esotericism and more about including certain forms of rational metaphysics in broad categories of fanaticism that can be wholly disqualified from commenting on scientific matters.[89] That Swedenborg

---

86. Swedenborg, *Arcana Caelestia*, 10481.

87. Kant, *Religion within the Limits*, 101n.

88. Mack argues that this move on Kant's part is a reversal of the spirit-letter opposition of Paul. He does so, building on the work of Daniel Boyarin, Peter Ochs, and Jacob Taubes, whose work suggests Paul did not intend a rejection of the letter, such as we find in Kant. See Mack, *German Idealism*, 37–38, and Mack, "Law, Charity and Taboo or Kant's Reversal of St. Paul's Spirit Letter Opposition and Its Theological Implications," *Modern Theology* 16.4 (2000): 417–41.

89. Stengel does not think Kant is referring to Swedenborg with the term "Antikabbalah" but argues from Häfner's *Macht der Willkür* that he may be alluding to the masonic order Elus Coëns, founded in 1754 by the Portuguese Christian kabbalist Jacques Martinès de Pasqually. See Stengel, Enlightenment, 766 n. 150.

4. KANT AND SWEDENBORG

and kabbalah also have in common a spiritualized interpretation of Jewish scriptures confirms Kant's ambivalence regarding Jews and allegory alike.

In both Kant's treatment of Judaism and of Swedenborg, something of the anxiety of influence can be discerned. As we have seen, Swedenborg's concepts of the spiritual world resonated with Kant's philosophical system and often in quite specific ways, such as the subjectivity of time and space. Some of his interpretations of the Bible appear remarkably similar to Swedenborg's, even as he openly and vehemently rejects Swedenborg's exegetical methods. And in the case of Judaism, some of his harshest criticisms are also in areas that overlap with his own thought. Sidney Axinn demonstrates this dynamic in arguing, for instance, that Kant asserts the impossibility of knowing concretely about the spiritual world or life after death but criticizes Jews for centering their ethical system on concerns for this life rather than the hereafter.[90] He denounces the Old Testament as lacking in moral substance, but also cites the Ten Commandments as essential to moral religion. And his anti-anthropomorphism is not unlike that found in formative Jewish philosophers.[91] Criticism, even in its harshest forms, does not imply lack of positive overlap. Both Kant and Swedenborg serve as examples of eighteenth-century Christian thinkers whose anti-Jewish rhetoric contradicts aspects of their own work, which either resemble or relied on aspects of Jewish hermeneutical traditions. Harold Bloom borrows the term *kenosis* from Paul's Epistles in his descriptions of the anxiety of influence. He compares the notion that Son *emptied* himself of the Father to notions that an author *empties* themself of the source of their inspiration. In Bloom's *kenosis*, however, an author does this defensively, even murderously, at times as an act of erasure.[92] As we have seen, when applied to Christian authors and their Jewish sources, the *kenosis* often takes on a perverse significance, whereby the emptying applies to Jesus's Jewishness rather than his divinity. Kant envisioned a pure Christianity and a pure philosophy that has "died away from" (*absterben*)

---

90. Kant writes, for instance: "Furthermore, since no religion can be conceived of which involves no belief in a future life, Judaism, which when taken in its purity is seen to lack this belief, is not a religious faith at all." From Kant, *Religion within the Limits*, 117.

91. Sidney Axinn, "Kant on Judaism," *JQR* 59.1 (1968): 11–17.

92. Harold Bloom, *Anxiety of Influence: A Theory of Poetry* (Oxford: Oxford University Press, 1997), 89–92; Bloom, *Kabbalah and Criticism* (New York: Continuum, 1983), 54.

128 JEWISH ALLEGORY IN EIGHTEENTH-CENTURY CHRISTIAN IMAGINATION

its Jewishness and left behind the mysticism of speculative metaphysics, while his own writing belies the possibility of such a purging.[93]

Returning to Swedenborg's conception of angelic language will permit some concluding considerations. Kant, in rejecting the idea of unmediated speech in heaven, sided with language's indispensable feature of masking inner thought with outer words. In doing so, he highlighted the very principle of interpretation that both he and Swedenborg utilized in reading the Bible. Sacred text, like human speech (and unlike Swedenborg's angelic speech), conceals its true meaning within the literal sense of the words. Yet, for Kant, the literal sense could also be a troubling distraction from the moral life or, even worse, its opposite. The interpretive question regarding the nature of language, written or spoken, gets at the heart of the social and epistemological conditions of the eighteenth century, whereby language is "by its very nature mediation, and the idea of unmediated language is an absurdity."[94] Tensions regarding the nature of biblical language are at play here. If the language of the Bible is true in its literal sense and immediately accessible, as so many biblical scholars and theologians insisted with increasing confidence at that time, it is then unique from other forms of language. It is like Swedenborg's angelic speech—wholly different and uniquely holy. Between Kant, Swedenborg, and the biblical literalists such as William Whiston, a common set of questions can be discerned: Is divine speech different from human speech, and is this difference marked by varying degrees of immediacy? Does the Bible, as holy word, mask its true meaning, or is its truth immediate? Both Kant and Swedenborg reacted negatively to the forms of biblical literalism of their time. Both sought an inner meaning concerned with morality or with right action over and above right belief, and both looked for wisdom hidden within the figures of speech.

But Swedenborg's angelic speech has a second quality besides immediacy that speaks to the interpretive questions of his day. According to Swedenborg, angelic language sounds like Hebrew and looks like Hebrew when written down. The Hebrew language therefore originates in the spiritual world. To angels, the full spectrum of its meaning is immediately known from the quality of its tone or the shape of its letters. But when this same speech or this same writing is "dropped down," as it were, to earth,

93. See the discussion of Kant's terms *absterben* and *euthanasie* in relation to Judaism in Mack, *German Idealism*, 32–35.

94. Böhme and Böhme, "Battle of Reason," 449.

4. KANT AND SWEDENBORG   129

it is obscured. The same sounds or texts appear to humans as coded language, a series of glyphs in need of translation.[95] Again, for Kant, as drawn as he might be to these kinds of speculations, such things are ultimately not within the disciplinary boundaries of philosophical inquiry. Yet the story of Hebrew's coded decent to earth reveals something of the shifting discourses about Jewish literalism and Jewish allegory that we find in the space between Kant and Swedenborg.

In Kant we see an important similarity to and an important distinction from Swedenborg's treatment of Judaism. For Swedenborg, the Old Testament and the Hebrew language are uniquely conducive to creating correspondential connections to spiritual realities. For Kant, the Old Testament is an outdated hindrance to true religion, and allegory is the troublesome result of trying to make it relevant. Yet, while their assessments of the value of Hebrew scriptures differ markedly, their characterizations of Jews themselves are alike in drawing on available stereotypes of Jews as materialistic. *Arcana Coelestia* therefore, while challenging Kant's prejudice against Old Testament religion, would have confirmed his prejudice against Jews. As Friedemann Stengel writes, for both men the stereotype is put to use in distinguishing true, *internal* religion from the empty, external symbols of religion:

> This tendentious construction of Judaism in Kant also pervades *Secrets of Heaven*, although of course one must add that Kant would also have had—particularly on this subject—recourse to an expansive tradition of literary anti-Semitism. However, the rationale that led Swedenborg to his view of Judaism does not diverge from Kant's. What makes it conspicuous is that it fulfills a similar function within his overall philosophy: in Swedenborg's work as well, the focus is on morality and on the relationship between external faith and one's internal—moral—disposition.[96]

Therefore, even as Swedenborg's biblical commentaries are faulted for "including Judaism" in Kant's estimation, they also similarly associated Judaism with external forms of religion. Swedenborg's reliance on old tropes of Jewish literalism combined with Christian kabbalistic notions of

---

95. Emanuel Swedenborg, *The Spiritual Diary*, trans. Johann Friedrich Immanuel Tafel, John Henry Smithson, and George Bush (New York: Bush, 1846–1850), 4671; Swedenborg, *Heaven and Its Wonders and Hell*, trans. John C. Ager (West Chester, PA: Swedenborg Foundation, 2009), 260.

96. Stengel, *Enlightenment*, 781–82.

130   JEWISH ALLEGORY IN EIGHTEENTH-CENTURY CHRISTIAN IMAGINATION

the Hebrew language. Like Kemper, Swedenborg imagined that the Jews had forgotten the meaning of their own language, the truth of their own scriptures. Jews were both the gatekeepers to the secrets of heaven and the least capable of turning the key. Kant, in bracketing the very question of a corresponding relationship between the noumenal and the phenomenal, brackets Swedenborg and the Jews alike as figures, respectively, for speculative metaphysics and the distractions of the body and material world. And yet, his "moral sense" interpretation of the Bible appears to be a reformulation of the biblical allegories he otherwise associates with both Jews and the mystic from Sweden.

We see in these various currents and countercurrents something of the anxieties about biblical language in the eighteenth century and questions regarding the Bible's relevance or irrelevance in the march of modernity. For Kant, the Bible is the landscape for his great epistemic sorting venture. With the use of reason alone, one can sort the useful from the useless, the essential truths of the Christian scriptures from their accidental originating context. For Kant, Jews are mere figures for an ancient people whose symbols are either entirely foreign or immoral, and the project of linking them to Christianity via typology should be abandoned. That his meaningful relationships with living Jewish contemporaries in the field of philosophy did not bring with them a more nuanced view is a tragedy with consequences far outlasting the immediate context of the *Aufklärung*.

5
POETRY AND PREJUDICE:
WILLIAM BLAKE'S ALLEGORIC GOD

England's celebrated poet and painter William Blake famously insisted on the distinction between vision and allegory in the opening of his commentary on the painting *A Vision of the Last Judgement*. Concerning the biblical book of Revelation, he wrote:

> The Last Judgment is not Fable or Allegory but Vision. Fable or Allegory are a totally distinct& inferior kind of Poetry. Vision or Imagination is a Representation of what Eternally Exists. Really & Unchangeably. Fable or Allegory is Formd by the Daughters of Memory. Imagination is Surrounded by the daughters of Inspiration who in the aggregate are calld Jerusalem.[1]

Blake's assertion that vision and allegory are "Two Distinct Things" has triggered numerous scholarly analyses from those interested in early Romantic symbolism. Some critics, such as William Butler Yeats, insist on the veracity and acumen of Blake's distinction, while others see it as reflecting the epistemologies of his time. Tracing the opinions of critics over the course of the twentieth century perhaps tells us more about allegory's plight since Blake's time than his own context. Some of these perspectives will be explored below. If there is a lack of consensus regarding Blake's categories, however, it is almost certainly because of Blake's own contradictions in terms. In the pages that follow this statement, for instance, he produces complex interpretations of biblical figures whose relationship to meaning strains any professed dissociation from allegory. "[It] ought to be understood that the Persons Moses & Abraham are not here meant but

---

1. Blake, "Vision of the Last Judgement," 554.

-131-

132   JEWISH ALLEGORY IN EIGHTEENTH-CENTURY CHRISTIAN IMAGINATION

the States Signified by those Names."[2] Every figure represented in Blake's painting has a corresponding significance determined by their role in the biblical narrative, their gender, and their placement in the painting. Those on the left side of the painting have a meaning distinct from those on the right, and those above and those below likewise communicate meanings relative to their position. We read, for instance that Noah and his two sons "represent Poetry Painting & Music the three powers <in Man> of conversing with Paradise which the flood did not sweep away," and further on that "Above the Head of Noah is Seth this State calld Seth is Male & Female in a higher state of Happiness & wisdom than Noah being nearer the State of Innocence beneath the feet of Seth two figures represent the two Seasons of Spring & Autumn." And "Between Seth & Elijah three Female Figures crownd with Garlands Represent Learning & Science which accompanied Adam out of Eden."[3]

The question of whether these mechanisms of representation utilize memory versus inspiration is not as straightforward as Blake contends given their reliance on familiar and contextually specific symbols. Straightforwardness, however, is not what Blake is after. When asked to explain his poetry and illuminated texts, he famously declined with the line "That which can be made explicit to the idiot is not worth my care." Blake's work triumphs in this spirit, defying attempts at systematic analysis or, as Harold Bloom puts it, the "irrelevant formal expectations" of critics.[4] We would do well, therefore, to avoid any attempt at formalizing Blake's use of vision and allegory as discrete techniques of writing or of representation. Instead, we will consider the oppositional function of allegory in Blake's poetic world—how it is employed to distinguish between two modes of being, one genuine and one artificial. The allegoric mode, rather than being a specific literary form, is any expression of religion that is dogmatic, mechanistic, repressive, or legalistic. The allegoric mode is what opposes the expression of the true, the spontaneous, the passionate, and the contradictory, all things that characterize genuine human experience. Things that we might otherwise call allegory, the representation of one thing through the image of another thing, can show up in Blake's poetry as well as his visual art where either mode is treated.

---

2. Blake, "Vision of the Last Judgement," 556.
3. Blake, "Vision of the Last Judgement," 559–61.
4. Harold Bloom, *Blake's Apocalypse: A Study in Poetic Argument* (Garden City, NY: Doubleday, 1963), 405.

5. POETRY AND PREJUDICE: WILLIAM BLAKE'S ALLEGORIC GOD 133

After a brief review of the scholarly literature on Blake and allegory, we will consider the function of the allegoric mode in Blake's poetic works. In the second half of this chapter we will take up the question of Blake's use of the figure of the Jew and his association between the allegoric mode and Old Testament religion, as he understood it. This will require a study of Blake's relationship to deism, whose rejection of the God of the Old Testament inspires Blake's neo-Marcion mythology, especially in the figure of Urizen, the disconnected and vengeful God of creation. Set against the figures from our previous chapters, we find that anti-Judaism reemerges in Blake as means for discarding what is unwanted from biblical religion. Like Kant then, a double ambivalence toward allegory and Judaism emerges despite a reliance on both Jewish sources and the multivocality of sacred texts.

The Reception of Blake's Vision/Allegory Distinction

In order to investigate the distinction between vision and allegory, as configured by Blake in the commentary quoted above, we will look at it from a number of different angles with the help of Blake's readers from various moments over the last 120 years.

Around the turn of the century, Yeats produced a series of essays, published together as *Ideas in Good and Evil*, containing his reflections on symbolism and poetry. In these essays he draws heavily on Blake's terminology, crediting Blake as the first to insist on this key differentiation. It is not without significance, however, that Yeats recasts Blake's distinction as that between *symbol* and *allegory* rather than *vision* and *allegory*, even though symbol is not a term Blake uses anywhere in his writing. The translation of vision as symbol puts Blake in line with subsequent Romantic poets such as Coleridge, who did contrast symbol and allegory, but it has the effect of moderating the experiential nature of Blake's visions.[5] Blake not only drew inspiration from the kinds of experiences we might today call mystical; he also claims to have written by "immediate Dictation" as a mere secretary recording the words of his "friends

---

5. Coleridge writes: "Now an allegory is but a translation of abstract notions into picture language, which is itself nothing but an abstraction from objects of senses," but the symbol "always partakes of the reality which it renders intelligible; and while it enunciates the whole, abides itself as a living part in that unity of which it is the representative." See Coleridge, "Statesman's Manual," 437.

134 JEWISH ALLEGORY IN EIGHTEENTH-CENTURY CHRISTIAN IMAGINATION

in Eternity."[6] His concept of the visionary carries a different conceptual load than that of the symbolic, suggesting a form of inspiration that depends on the whim of his muses. Yeats accounts for this by suggesting that people who have religious, mystical, or even drug-induced visions are seeing symbols in their essential form. The artist, however, sees them unencumbered by their particular religious and historical contexts; they differ "in having accepted all symbolisms."[7] Therefore, while one could argue that Yeats's translation of Blake's idea of *vision* into *symbol* neglects the aspect of inspired imagination so critical for Blake (vision and imagination are used synonymously by Blake), it could equally be argued that Yeats's conception of symbolism is itself expansive and imaginary.

As we have seen in other contexts, allegory is often associated with what is arbitrary or made up on the part of the interpreter. It is noteworthy, then, that Yeats insists that symbol, and not allegory, is what is made up and arbitrary and that this is what gives it spiritual potency. He writes that Blake "was a symbolist who had to invent his symbols; and his counties of England, with their correspondence to tribes of Israel, and his mountains and rivers, with their correspondence to parts of a man's body, are arbitrary.... He was a man crying out for a mythology, and trying to make one because he could not find one to his hand."[8] Rather than draw on established sets of allegorical images, Blake had to create his own new world, and this he did in the image of his Creator.

Yeats's view that creativity mimics divinity and that "the imaginative arts were therefore the greatest of Divine revelations" harmonizes with Blake's own view.[9] It is precisely when Blake inverts an expected use of symbols that he claims vision, and not allegory, is in play. For instance, he intentionally represents the three furies—states of misery from Greek mythology personified as winged female monsters—as men rather than their customary form as women. By demonstrating his mastery over the symbol and his ability to change it substantively, he is freed from the chains of allegory and taps into a more genuine, liberated connection. Blake writes "It is not because I think the Ancients

---

6. See the letter to Thomas Butts (April 25, 1803) in Erdman, *Complete Poetry*, 728–29.

7. W. B. Yeats, "Symbolism in Painting," in *Essays and Introductions* (New York: Collier, 1961), 149.

8. W. B. Yeats, "William Blake and the Imagination," in *Essays and Introductions*, 114.

9. Yeats, "William Blake and the Imagination," 112.

5. POETRY AND PREJUDICE: WILLIAM BLAKE'S ALLEGORIC GOD 135

wrong, but they will be pleas'd to remember that mine is Vision & not Fable."[10] Blake's ability to change the symbol at will proves his genius and infuses the old image with new life.

Returning to Yeats, we find confusion in a subsequent essay regarding the idiosyncratic nature of symbolism as opposed to allegory. Here he insists the contrary is true, that symbol is "the only possible expression of some invisible essence" while allegory can take on a variety of forms, representing some embodied or familiar thing. A symbol in this formulation is less flexible because its real connection to a deeper truth is stable, whereas an allegory is unmoored: "the one is a revelation, the other an amusement."[11] This contradiction also reflects Blake, who insists that "Vision or Imagination is a Representation of what Eternally Exists. Really & Unchangeably." Both poets seem to want it both ways—that the preferred mode of representation (symbol for Yeats, vision for Blake) corresponds to a reality that is unchanging, but is best tapped in a spirit of liberation from fixed or dogmatic symbol sets. This, one could argue, raises questions about the reliability of said underlying and stable essences of meaning, anticipating Paul de Man's deconstructionist understanding of allegory in the latter half of the twentieth century.[12]

The celebrated Canadian literary critic Northrop Frye also found inspiration in Blake's particular formulations of allegory and vision, but this time with a more positive framing of allegory. Frye was troubled by the prejudice against allegory that had infiltrated his discipline. "As ignorance of the methods and techniques of allegorical poetry is still almost universal, the explicitly allegorical writers have for the most part not received in modern times much criticism which is based directly on what they were trying to do."[13] He saw in Blake a new kind of poetic thought that served a needed pedagogical function. Blake was a "reliable teacher of a poetic language which most contemporary readers do not understand."[14] Through Blake, the reader is trained in a grammar

---

10. Blake, "Vision of the Last Judgment," 557.

11. W. B. Yeats, "William Blake and His Illustrations to the Divine Comedy," in *Essays and Introductions*, 116.

12. See Jeremy Tambling, *Allegory* (New York: Routledge, 2009), 128–51.

13. Northrop Frye, *Fearful Symmetry: A Study of William Blake* (Princeton: Princeton University Press, 1947), 10–11.

14. Frye, *Fearful Symmetry*, 11.

136   JEWISH ALLEGORY IN EIGHTEENTH-CENTURY CHRISTIAN IMAGINATION

of an imaginative iconography, which provides a key to reading other allegorical works such as those of Spenser, Langland, or Hawthorne, according to Frye.[15]

To make his case, Frye points to Blake's singular positive reference to allegory found in an 1803 letter to Thomas Butts, in which he writes that his own work will

> speak to future generations by a Sublime Allegory which is now perfectly completed into a Grand Poem[.] I may praise it since I dare not pretend to be any other than the Secretary the Authors are in Eternity I consider it as the Grandest Poem that This World Contains. Allegory addressd to the Intellectual powers while it is altogether hidden from the Corporeal Understanding is My Definition of the Most Sublime Poetry.[16]

Following this distinction, Frye asserts that there are right and wrong ways to read allegory. To read according to one's "corporeal understanding" is to read with the expectation that the text can be decoded, that one can explain or, even worse, translate, a poem with the aid of dictionaries and charts.[17] In Frye's view, this deductive way of reading allegorical works is what led to the modern prejudice against allegory. On the other hand, allegory addressed to the "intellectual powers" allows for the immediate impact of the poem to penetrate more interior levels of perception. This superior way of reading allegory understands the work, in its final form, to be a whole imaginative world, that is, as a "literary language with its own idioms and its own syntactical arrangement of ideas."[18]

Key to understanding the difference between wrong reading and right reading, according to Frye's interpretation of Blake, is the artistic imagination. True allegory is art that resists the question of what lies beyond itself. Faulty allegory, "what is usually called allegory, that is, art the meaning of which points away from itself toward something else which is not art, is a profane abomination."[19] However, Frye's assertion that this inferior

---

15. Frye, *Fearful Symmetry*,10.

16. Blake, July 6, 1803 letter to Thomas Butts, in Erdman, *Complete Poetry*, 730.

17. For an alternative reading of Blake's "Corporeal Understanding," see Theresa M. Kelley, *Reinventing Allegory* (Cambridge: Cambridge University Press, 2010), 97–98. She suggests the phrasing is an "ironic negation" given Blake's general celebration of the embodied and incarnated.

18. Frye, *Fearful Symmetry*, 10.

19. Frye, *Fearful Symmetry*, 115–16.

5. POETRY AND PREJUDICE: WILLIAM BLAKE'S ALLEGORIC GOD   137

form of allegory is nowhere found in Blake is hard to defend against, for instance, Blake's own explanations of the figures in his *A Vision of the Last Judgement* with their abstract referents such as learning, science, innocence, and the seasonal states of spring and autumn.

Frye's tendency to describe Blake's poetry and commentary with idealized notions of allegory is evident in his related treatment of Blake's syncretism. Blake's use of non-Christian mythology serves as "contrapuntal symbolism" to supplement but also to universalize, according to Frye. This, added to Blake's assertion that there was originally one religion, compels us to a mode of return, to a more primitive way of reading wherein we discover a shared iconography of the imagination.[20] Frye then, in ways not unlike Yeats, heralds Blake's poetic genius as at once embodied and ideal, personal and universal, exposing a tension point (or, alternatively, a productive paradox) common to notions about allegory itself.

If we move from a poetic and literary perspective on Blake to a historical one, or from an emic to an etic perspective, we encounter scholars who are less concerned with what allegory is, fundamentally, than what allegory as a concept does for Blake. This shift in perspective also pushes us into the later parts of the twentieth century. One trend in contemporary scholarship relevant for our purposes is to view Blake's allegories as imitating the allegories of the Bible. In this vein, Leslie Tannenbaum argues that trends in biblical criticism in the eighteenth century are reflected in Blake's prophetic works, and that we will better understand Blake's relationship to the Bible if we understand the state of biblical studies around him.[21] Tannenbaum first highlights how the impact of deists and freethinkers was greater at this time than that of higher criticism. Learned interpretation of the Bible was directed at countering perceived attacks, particularly regarding the integrity of the prophetic books, such as we saw in chapter 1. Tannenbaum demonstrates how Blake's prophecies reflect views about the nature of biblical literature from the work of scholars such as Robert Lowth, Thomas Howes, and William Warburton, to name just a few. As such, Blake embraces a kind of primitivism or rhetorical style that reveals truth through forms that are nonlinear, nonrational, and pictural in nature. He adopts a living, gothic form rather than a mathematical one.

---

20. Frye, *Fearful Symmetry*, 115–16.

21. See also the work of Christopher Rowland, who compares Blake's use of allegory to that of Paul and Augustine in *Blake and the Bible* (New Haven: Yale University Press, 2010), 9–11.

138   JEWISH ALLEGORY IN EIGHTEENTH-CENTURY CHRISTIAN IMAGINATION

Like the Bible described by Blake's contemporaries, his prophecies depict multiple perspectives simultaneously, use multiple styles and genres, and contain contradictions and digressions, expressing a kind of genius believed to have been forgotten in the halls of rationalism and enlightenment. "He found in the Bible a concept of art that is visual, dramatic, and rhetorical, that combines spectacle and confrontation, that acts upon the reader and enjoins the reader to act in response to it."[22] Typology in particular, according to Tannenbaum, was a method celebrated by Blake and his contemporaries as essentially biblical and most effective at delivering the language of the divine, whose truths look backward and forward in time.

Against this backdrop, wherein Blake is read against the wisdom of his day regarding the aesthetics of biblical literature, Tannenbaum parses Blake's allegory/vision distinction. Vision expresses a view of history and time that is *kairos* rather than *chronos*. It produces eternal images that recur in the poetry of every age. The visionary, however, is always vulnerable to corruption, especially at the hands of those professing orthodoxy. Visions can become allegories when they are possessed and fixed by priests and authorities. They can also be redeemed by the artist who liberates them and returns them to their prophetic functions through the poetic imagination. "By forcing his readers to recognize all of those types as products of the imagination, he is snatching those myths out of the hands of the priests, the tyrants, and the bigots and is returning them to their rightful home, the human breast, wherein all deities reside."[23] In this, Blake responds to deist attacks on the Bible by essentially agreeing with them. The prophecies do originate in the human imagination. Where the deists are mistaken is in assuming that this imaginative quality reduces their status as revelation. Blake's allegory/vision distinction, in Tannenbaum's portrayal, responds to a set of historical circumstances in ways that may be unexpected, but in terms that are not unfamiliar to his context.

Finally, scholars who study the history of allegory, such as Theresa Kelley and Jon Whitman, point to early Romanticism as a turning point when allegory is redefined and repackaged into new forms, ensuring its survival into modernity despite the professed ambivalence toward the allegories of earlier generations. Kelley, in particular, points to the need to understand what Blake meant by allegory when he expresses an aversion to it, even

---

22. Leslie Tannenbaum, *Biblical Tradition in Blake's Early Prophecies: The Great Code of Art* (Princeton: Princeton University Press, 1982), 53–54.

23. Tannenbaum, *Biblical Tradition*, 111.

5. POETRY AND PREJUDICE: WILLIAM BLAKE'S ALLEGORIC GOD 139

if he himself "consistently exercises a formal commitment to emblematic or allegorical structures of meaning."[24] Allegory, negatively framed, is the neoclassical model wherein a one-to-one relationship between an abstract notion and an image is secured, such as in the personifications of Music, Despair, Hope, and Revenge in William Collins's "The Passions: An Ode For Music." Against these restricted forms of allegory, Blake and the early Romantics professed their disapproval, but in practice they built on and expanded earlier notions of allegory. One thinks of the Irish painter James Barry, whose work impacted Blake's and whose embrace of allegory is on display in the figures of his mural series "The Progress of Human Knowledge and Culture" located in the Great Room of the Royal Society of Arts in London. Blake's allegories are perhaps not as obvious as those in Barry's figured history, but they have in common the use of human forms and relationships to depict various kinds of events and ideas. Blake's allegories build on and respond to those who came before him. As Whitman writes: "In the midst of a sustained polemic against allegory Romantic Writers put allegorical emblems to uses unsanctioned by Neoclassical arguments."[25] The presence of allegory in Blake's poetry and painting is undeniable. But the rhetorical function of allegory as a mode of being, which can either be rejected or embraced, is a key component of Blake's legacy.

The Allegoric Mode

The remainder of this chapter will build on the perspectives summarized above, considering the question of how allegory functions in Blake's writing as a discursive mode. To do so, we start again with his commentary on *A Vision of the Last Judgment* and his distinction between allegory and vision, especially where he writes: "Fable or Allegory is Formd by the Daughters of Memory. Imagination is Surrounded by the daughters of Inspiration who in the aggregate are calld Jerusalem." What previous studies on this topic have overlooked is Blake's formula "the Daughters of Memory," which shows up elsewhere in his work, always contrasted with the Daughters of Inspiration.[26]

---

24. Kelley, *Reinventing Allegory*, 96.

25. Kelley, *Reinventing Allegory*, 94. See also Whitman, "From the Textual"; Tambling, *Allegory*, 62–76.

26. William Blake, *Milton*, plate 1 [i] and plate 14 [15], in Erdman, *Complete Poetry*, 95 and 108.

140   JEWISH ALLEGORY IN EIGHTEENTH-CENTURY CHRISTIAN IMAGINATION

The source of this binary configuration—memory versus inspiration—likely comes from Swedenborg, who was a known source of theological inspiration for Blake, even if he was also, like other major sources of influence for Blake, a conceptual sparring partner. In books that Blake possessed and carefully annotated, Swedenborg similarly presents memory as the weaker side of a fundamental binary. For instance, in *Divine Love and Wisdom*, Swedenborg writes concerning two kinds of people: the more intuitive, heart-centered "celestial" people and the more reason-driven "spiritual" people:

> [Those] who are in celestial love have wisdom inscribed on their life, and not on the memory, for which reason they do not talk about Divine truths, but do them; while those who are in spiritual love have wisdom inscribed on their memory, therefore they talk about Divine truths, and do them from principles in the memory. Because those who are in celestial love have wisdom inscribed on their life, they perceive instantly whether whatever they hear is true or not.[27]

Swedenborg's binary anticipates Blake's. Those who are "celestial" perceive divine realities immediately and experientially. Those who perceive with the use of the memory, on the other hand, are compelled to merely talk about these realities before acting on them. The intellectual and verbal activity required introduces a delay and a degree of separation from the divine. Early translations of Swedenborg into English rendered his frequently used term *scientia* as "memory-knowledges" because of this principle. *Scientia*, for Swedenborg, is figured in the biblical Egypt as, again, a secondary spiritual state characterized by separation from the divine and the pursuit of intellectual knowledge through worldly, scientific, education. These two modes of being—one that connects via immediate perception and one that connects mediated through reason or verbal signification—recur frequently in Blake, as we will see. It is this secondary mode, described by Swedenborg as wisdom inscribed on the memory, which Blake calls "allegoric." In what follows we will explore Blake's allegoric mode in some detail to further illustrate what the Daughters of Memory reveal.

---

27. Emanuel Swedenborg, *Divine Love and Wisdom*, trans. John C. Ager (West Chester, PA: Swedenborg Foundation, 1995), 427. See also Swedenborg, *Arcana Caelestia*, 27; Swedenborg, *Heaven and Hell*, trans. John C. Ager (West Chester, PA: Swedenborg Foundation, 2009), 517.

5. POETRY AND PREJUDICE: WILLIAM BLAKE'S ALLEGORIC GOD   141

Blake himself uses the terms "allegoric" and "allegory" an almost equal number of times in his surviving poetry, commentaries, and letters. Taking our cue from the poet then, we will consider the implication of this adjectival form of the word, that the allegoric is one of two antithetical modes of being. And while we do have the more positive reference to allegory in his letter to Thomas Butts, which was key to Frye's interpretation, the term allegoric is strongly and consistently negative. The following are a few instances of Blake's use of this term.

In his marginalia for Robert Thornton's *The Lord's Prayer, Newly Translated*, Blake presents a parody of a scholarly translation of the Lord's prayer: "For thine is the Kingship <or Allegoric Godship> & the Power or War & the Glory or Law Ages after Ages in thy Descendents <for God is only an Allegory of Kings & nothing Else> Amen."[28] Blake presents his own translation in rebellion against notions that readers should approach the Bible through the commentaries of learned scholars. He writes of his adversary's translation efforts: "This is Saying the Lords Prayer Backwards which they say Raises the Devil." Here, the scholarly rendition misses the true sense of the prayer and reaches an inverted, allegoric God only.

In the epic poem *The Song of Los*, those who labor are promised "allegoric riches" as they are tossed into poverty.[29] Elsewhere, things associated with the hegemonic rise of priestly legalism and authoritarianism, sometimes through the figure of the Druid or the tabernacle, are described as allegoric. This is the case in Blake's epic poem *Jerusalem: The Emanation of The Giant Albion*, where the "Covering Cherub" (elsewhere referred to as the angelic guard who stands in the way of a return to Eden) is associated with the curtains of the tabernacle, which conceal and restrain the glory of Jerusalem in "allegoric delusion & woe."[30] The covering is described as follows:

> Twelvefold in Allegoric pomp in selfish holiness
> The Pharisaion, the Grammateis, the Presbuterion,
> The Archiereus, the Iereus, the Saddusaion, double
> Each withoutside of the other, covering eastern heaven[31]

---

28. William Blake, "Annotations to Thornton's *The Lord's Prayer, Newly Translated*," in Erdman, *Complete Poetry*, 669.

29. William Blake, *The Song of Los*, plate 6:18, in Erdman, *Complete Poetry*, 68.

30. William Blake, *Jerusalem: The Emanation of the Giant Albion*, plate 89:43–47 in Erdman, *Complete Poetry*, 249.

31. Blake, *Jerusalem*, plate 89:4–8 in Erdman, *Complete Poetry*, 248.

142   JEWISH ALLEGORY IN EIGHTEENTH-CENTURY CHRISTIAN IMAGINATION

These covering forces are figured via a series of Greek New Testament terms for priestly and legal authorities: the scribes and the Pharisees. The figure of the Druids is employed elsewhere for similar purposes. In Blake's mythology they are a priestly class who overtook England in ancient times and brought about its fall: "The Atlantic Mountains where Giants dwelt in Intellect / Now given to stony Druids, and Allegoric Generation."[32] Elsewhere, in his *Descriptive Catalogue*, Blake writes "Adam was a Druid, and Noah; also Abraham was called to succeed the Druidical age, which began to turn allegoric and mental signification into corporeal command, whereby human sacrifice would have depopulated the earth."[33] Each of these symbols for the priestly or scribal classes of antiquity describes a primordial separation and evokes the dogmatic and repressive allegoric mode.

The binary implied by Blake's allegoric mode is a regular feature in the poetry that spans his career. In one of his final poems, *The Everlasting Gospel*, which was sketched into the few available margins in his personal notebook, we find two Christs, two Bibles, and two heavens described: one invented by those who seek to oppress and the other that liberates. "The Vision of Christ that thou dost see / Is my Visions Greatest Enemy."[34] "Thy Heavens doors are my Hells Gates."[35] "Both read the Bible day & night / But thou readst black where I read white."[36] The poem's title comes from the book of Revelation, where the everlasting gospel is preached to "every nation, and kindred, and tongue, and people" on earth (Rev 14:6) while an alternative song is given to the one hundred and forty-four thousand from among the tribes of Israel. This smaller assembly, selected from among God's chosen people, are described as being without flaw, perfect in their sexual and verbal purity (Rev 14:4–5), all qualities associated with Blake's allegoric mode with its "dark pretense to Chastity" and "sneaking submission."[37] Blake's association of Judaism with the allegoric gospel is made most explicit in a line that accompanies those quoted above, contrasting the "I" of genuine religion with the "thou" of pretense: "Thine

---

32. Blake, *Jerusalem*, plate 50:1–2 in Erdman, *Complete Poetry*, 199.

33. William Blake, *Descriptive Catalogue*, plate 41 in Erdman, *Complete Poetry*, 542–43.

34. William Blake, *The Everlasting Gospel*, plate e:1–2 in Erdman, *Complete Poetry*, 524.

35. Blake, *Everlasting Gospel*, plate e:8 in Erdman, *Complete Poetry*, 524.

36. Blake, *Everlasting Gospel*, plate e:13–14 in Erdman, *Complete Poetry*, 524.

37. Blake, *Everlasting Gospel*, plate k:30 in Erdman, *Complete Poetry*, 519.

5. POETRY AND PREJUDICE: WILLIAM BLAKE'S ALLEGORIC GOD 143

has a great hook nose like thine / Mine has a snub nose like to mine."[38] Blake's flagrant anti-Judaism and its affiliation with his allegoric mode will be taken up in detail below. A consideration of these themes in another poem, *The Marriage of Heaven and Hell*, will enable a further clarification of these points.

The Marriage of Heaven and Hell, is a lengthy and elaborately illustrated poetic satire on Swedenborg's *Heaven and Hell*. Specifically, we can trace Blake's inspiration for the poem to number 588 in Swedenborg's work, in which we find the following line: "In regard to the number of the hells, there are as many of them as there are angelic societies in the heavens, since there is for every heavenly society a corresponding infernal society as its opposite."[39] Blake was enamored with the concept of a corresponding heaven and hell, and annotated this number with the following interpretation of it: "under every Good is a hell, i.e. hell is the outward or external of heaven & is the body of the lord, for nothing is destroy'd."[40] While this reading strays from Swedenborg's intention, Blake was nevertheless inspired subsequently to explore a type and antitype relationship between good and evil, or as he framed them, banal passivity and productive energy. And it is the undervalued half of this union that the poem celebrates.

In *The Marriage of Heaven and Hell*, angel and devil take on untraditional personae. The angels are rule makers and enforcers, spoilers of pleasure and free expression under the pretext of reason, virtue, and humility: "Prisons are built with stones of Law, Brothels with bricks of Religion."[41] The devil is the story's hero, replacing the errors of the Bible with the proverbs of hell and preaching that true love of God consists in "honoring his gifts in other men each according to his genius" rather than vain devotion to God alone.[42]

The poem earns its title both from the image on the cover page, in which a resident of heaven and a resident of hell embrace in the nude, and in the poem's last lines: "Note: This Angel, who is now become a Devil, is my particular friend; we often read the Bible together in its infernal or

---

38. Blake, *Everlasting Gospel*, plate e:3–4 in Erdman, *Complete Poetry*, 524.

39. Swedenborg, *Heaven and Hell*, 588.

40. William Blake, annotation on Swedenborg's *Heaven and Hell*, in Erdman, *Complete Poetry*, 602.

41. William Blake, *The Marriage of Heaven and Hell*, plate 8:1 in Erdman, *Complete Poetry*, 36.

42. Blake, *Marriage*, plate 22 in Erdman, *Complete Poetry*, 43.

144 JEWISH ALLEGORY IN EIGHTEENTH-CENTURY CHRISTIAN IMAGINATION

diabolical sense, which the world shall have if they behave well. I have also the Bible of Hell, which the world shall have whether they will or no."[43] The two Bibles then, one heavenly and one hellish, document this extraordinary union. Reading the Bible according to an "infernal sense" (a play on Swedenborg's "internal sense") Blake presents the Bible of hell, which boasts a kind of open access and immediacy, like that of his everlasting gospel that has been lost or forgotten in the history of human religion.

The piece is punctuated with a series of "Memorable Fancies," or descriptions of encounters with places and beings in heaven and hell.[44] In one of these, Blake is led by an angel to his eternal resting place in hell, which first appears as a dark and gruesome cave infested with spiders and monsters. When the angel parts from him, however, he sees the landscape in its true light, as a moonlit river with a harpist on its banks producing sublime melodies. He accuses the angel of deceit and says: "All that we saw was owing to your metaphysics." This tale illustrates Blake's overarching message: a religion that condemns a person for living according to their nature is a religion that conceals and reverses the truth. It is allegoric religion.

Blake points back in time to the moment when he believes this confusion in the history of religions occurred. He suggests that the true fall of humankind, our original sin, occurred when the essences were confused with their names or with their allegories:

The ancient Poets animated all sensible objects with Gods or Geniuses calling them by the names and adorning them with the properties of woods, rivers, mountains, lakes, cities, nations, and whatever their enlarged & numerous senses could perceive.

And particularly they studied the genius of each city & country. placing it under its mental deity.

Till a system was formed, which some took advantage of & enslav'd the vulgar by attempting to realize or abstract the mental deities from their objects: thus began Priesthood.

---

43. Blake, *Marriage*, plate 24 in Erdman, *Complete Poetry*, 44.

44. Blake's memorable fancies imitate Swedenborg's "memorable relations" first published as part of *Arcana Coelestia*. This one, for example, responds to Swedenborg's notion that residents of hell appear beautiful to themselves and appear to reside amid splendid surroundings until exposed as wretched by the light of heaven. Blake's story mischievously suggests that Swedenborg misunderstood what he witnessed in hell and that heaven's light was in fact the false light.

5. POETRY AND PREJUDICE: WILLIAM BLAKE'S ALLEGORIC GOD 145

Choosing forms of worship from poetic tales.
And at length they pronounced that the Gods had orderd such things.
Thus men forgot that All deities reside in the human breast.[45]

In Blake's view, humans forgot the true nature of things when the priesthood took possession of the tools for decoding. God was hidden away behind inaccessible versions of the story and behind incomprehensible rituals. Priesthood initiated forgetting through the calcification of religious symbols.

Priesthood, for Blake, stands in contrast with prophecy. Prophecy is described in the next plate of the poem in another "Memorable Fancy" in terms similar to the "ancient Poets" cited above, with their prelapsarian connection to geniuses and deities. Blake describes himself dining with the biblical prophets Isaiah and Ezekiel and asking them how they dared to make their claims and if they feared being misunderstood. The prophets, in turn, describe their own experiences and their immediate perceptions of the "infinite in everything." But Ezekiel goes on, and describes a deviation that happened among his people over time, an impulse to be singular and to dominate, persuade, and conquer and govern other kingdoms so that "all nations believe the Jews code and worship the Jews god, and what greater subjection can be."[46] The Old Testament here becomes the site of confusion and contrast. The fall occurs somewhere between prophecy and priesthood. And the religion that emerges from this history, Judaism, is like the lying angel in Blake's hell-heaven, who shifts the light of perception. The angel and the Jew alike obscure the truth and replace it with coded allegory.

Blake's Anti-Judaism

An understanding of Blake's association between allegoric religion and Judaism requires first a study of the anti-Jewish elements of his work more broadly. A full discussion of Blake's anti-Judaism is difficult to find in the vast corpus of literature about Blake from the last 120 years. Many scholars do not mention it at all. Some focus on a more positive relationship with kabbalistic influences, though the evidence for this is murky and, as we have seen from chapter 2, Christian kabbalah often thrived in anti-Jewish

---

45. Blake, *Marriage*, plate 11 in Erdman, *Complete Poetry*, 38.
46. Blake, *Marriage*, plate 12 in Erdman, *Complete Poetry*, 38–39.

146 JEWISH ALLEGORY IN EIGHTEENTH-CENTURY CHRISTIAN IMAGINATION

climates.[47] Some warn of misinterpreting Blake in this regard, as in Christopher Rowland's cautioning: "Care is needed here to avoid assuming anti-semitism on Blake's part. The language is unfortunate, but the 'Jewish imposture' is less an ethnic or religious categorisation than a hermeneutical one, in which the term stands for any kind of religion based on divine fiat (he often criticises Christians on the same grounds)."[48] That Christians have utilized just such a "hermeneutical Jew" repeatedly in many contexts, often as a means of intra-religious critique, is indisputable. But it is disingenuous to suggest that this kind of activity is not also anti-Jewish or anti-Semitic. For other scholars, this issue is raised only as a momentary expression of regret, such as Harold Bloom's lament of his otherwise beloved poet: "Though he caught the prophetic spirit of Amos and Isaiah so precisely in most respects, he was incapable of freeing himself from the traditional Christian misinterpretations of Pharisaic religion, and adopted the absurd and simplistic dialectic which opposes the supposed legalism of the Jews to the presumably greater spirituality of their offspring and rivals."[49] We will return to precisely this "simplistic dialectic" below, arguing that it is best framed as part of the neo-Marcion impulse that arose in

---

47. A case study on the coexistence of Christian kabbalah and anti-Judaism can be found in Kocku von Stuckrad, "Christian Kabbalah and Anti-Jewish Polemics: Pico in Context," in *Polemical Encounters: Esoteric Discourse and Its Others*, ed. Olav Hammer and Kocku von Stuckrad (Leiden: Brill, 2007), 1–23. Blake's anti-Judaism intermingles with similarities in content with some forms of kabbalah. His knowledge of kabbalah is evident from his *Jerusalem*, in which we find the line referencing Adam Kadmon addressed "To the Jews": "You have a tradition, that Man anciently contain'd in his mighty limbs all things in Heaven & Earth." Readers of Blake find plenty to compare with kabbalah in the cosmic themes of his mythic poetry and prose, though it is difficult to prove definitively when his sources are kabbalistic in nature. Sheila Spector, for instance, elaborates an intricate kabbalism in Blake's work not only in his choice of words, symbols, and narratives, but in the very structuring principle of his modality. Her analysis is itself poetic but contributes little to what we know about Blake's direct engagement with kabbalistic sources, Christian or Jewish. The most we can say from his work, such as in *Jerusalem*, is that he marries concepts that are useful to him from kabbalah with satirical attacks on the people who produced it, a move entirely consistent with his use of biblical themes. See Sheila A. Spector, *Wonders Divine: The Development of Blake's Kabbalistic Myth* (Lewisburg, PA: Bucknell University Press, 2001). For more on Blake's esoteric sources, see Kathleen Raine, *Blake and the New Age* (New York: Routledge, 2013).

48. Rowland, *Blake and the Bible*, 8.

49. Bloom, *Blake's Apocalypse*, 433–34.

5. POETRY AND PREJUDICE: WILLIAM BLAKE'S ALLEGORIC GOD   147

modernity alongside deism and Christian liberalism. It will be helpful to first summarize the argument of one scholar who does give full treatment to this topic.

Karen Shabetai, who considers "The Question of Blake's Hostility toward the Jews," points to Blake's failure to live up to his own humanitarian standards. She explains the lack of scholarly attention to this topic as resulting, in part, from the fact that Blake's most hostile remarks are found in his unpublished works, his private annotations, and his notebook. In public, "he is more subtle, or at least more obscure, which might explain how Blake's seeming anti-Semitism has managed to fly under the critical radar."[50] Shabetai catalogues the instances of Blake's references to Jews and divides them into three categories. First are those instances which express religious tolerance or invite Jews to conversion in welcoming tones. An example of this is found in Blake's *Jerusalem*, in the section titled "To the Jews," where he writes: "The Return of Israel is a Return to Mental Sacrifice & War. Take up the Cross O Israel & follow Jesus."[51] The second category includes attacks on Judaism used to critique some other group, such as legalistic or repressive tendencies in Christianity. In his commentary on *A Vision of the Last Judgement*, for instance, he writes that the images of the children of Abraham "Represent Religion or Civilized Life such as it is in the Christian Church who are the Offspring of the Hebrew."[52] Finally, the more gratuitous incidents make up the third category, which "are in excess of the rhetoric required to level the attack on his ostensible target."[53] This includes the use of stereotypes such as the Jews "leave counting gold!"[54] or references to spindle noses found in his notebook: "I always thought that Jesus Christ was a Snubby or I should not have worshipd him if I had thought he had been one of those long spindle nosed rascals."[55] To those who would defend Blake as simply drawing on anti-Jewish symbols available to him, Shabetai points to examples from publications of his day that critique hostile depictions of Jews and Judaism, concluding that Blake's

---

50. Karen Shabetai, "The Question of Blake's Hostility toward the Jews," *English Literary History* 63.1 (1996): 139.

51. Blake, *Jerusalem*, plate 27 in Erdman, *Complete Poetry*, 174.

52. Blake, "Vision of the Last Judgement," 559.

53. Shabetai, "Question," 141.

54. Blake, *Marriage*, plate 26 in Erdman, *Complete Poetry*, 44.

55. Blake, *Marriage*, plate 26 in Erdman, *Complete Poetry*, 44; Blake, *Notebook*, 64 in Erdman, *Complete Poetry*, 695.

148 JEWISH ALLEGORY IN EIGHTEENTH-CENTURY CHRISTIAN IMAGINATION

rhetoric exceeds what is "necessary to make his more positive argument about a redeemed Christianity."[56]

Where Shabetai's analysis misses the mark, however, is in her assertion that Blake's anti-Judaism is more medieval in nature than modern. She points to his association between Judaism and Satan and its parallels to premodern notions, which, in the words of historian Normon Cohn, view "Jews as a league of sorcerers employed by Satan for the spiritual and physical ruination of Christendom."[57] Blake's use of the "Synagogue of Satan" image from the book of Revelation is unambiguously negative where it appears.[58] However, Shabetai glosses over the more positive or ironic uses of the figure of Satan and the devil, such those found in *The Marriage of Heaven and Hell* discussed above. Satan is an unstable figure for Blake, more of a rupture from medieval ideas than a continuation of them. Furthermore, Blake's depictions of Jews demonstrate key features of modern anti-Judaism even beyond his racialized references to Jewish noses. It is Blake's neo-Marcionism—the view that the God of the Jews is a separate, nefarious, trickster God—that puts him most in line with the anti-Judaism of modernity.

In 1925 the German-Jewish philosopher Franz Rosenzweig wrote a letter to his friend and collaborator Martin Buber expressing his fears that neo-Marcionism was encroaching on Christian biblical studies. This was in response to the trending scholarly fascination with Marcion, the second-century heretic who believed that the Bible told the story of two Gods: the lesser, jealous, demiurge of the Old Testament who created and ruled over a troubled creation, and the higher, loving, and transcendent God of the New Testament. Adolf von Harnack's *Das Evangelium von dem fremdem Gott*, for instance, presented Marcion's theology favorably, raising questions about the relevance of the God of the Jews for Christianity. Alarmed by the implications of this move in liberal Christian theology and

---

56. Shabetai, "Question," 139.

57. Shabetai, "Question," 145, quoting Normon Cohn, *Warrant for Genocide: The Myth of Jewish World Conspiracy and the Protocols of the Elders of Zion* (New York: Harper and Row, 1967) 15–16.

58. Although, as Shabetai demonstrates, the term "Synagogue of Satan" appears in pamphlets and writings of Blake's context with anti-Semitic tones, there is evidence to suggest that its original use in Revelation may have referred to those who left behind their Jewish practice and identity, meaning they were not Jewish enough. See David Frankfurter, "Jews or Not? Reconstructing the 'Other' in Rev 2:9 and 3:9," *HTR* 94.4 (2001): 403–25.

5. POETRY AND PREJUDICE: WILLIAM BLAKE'S ALLEGORIC GOD   149

other neo-gnostic influences that swept Germany in the years leading up to World War II, Rosenzweig and Buber dedicated themselves to biblical translation and the publication of philosophical works that would resurrect not just the theology of the Hebrew Bible but also the biblical concept of creation. Contrary to Marcionism, they argued, this world is not to be overcome but to be made sacred.[59]

While noticed and named at this time, neo-Marcionism did not originate in early twentieth-century German biblical criticism. In one sense this theology, often characterized as gnostic, has never been entirely absent from Christianity but has persisted, as Benjamin Lazier puts it, as "a primordial heresy, one that could—and would—return intermittently to haunt it, if always in modified form."[60] Early modern proponents of the heresy, however, laid the ground for its particular success into the following centuries. The biblical theology that so alarmed Rosenzweig and Buber, whereby the reasonableness, morality, and legitimacy of the God of the Old Testament is put on trial against Enlightenment ideals, has its roots in the philosophical controversies of the eighteenth century, such as we find in the challenges to biblical religion made by the English deists and by Kant and his followers. However, Marcionism acquired its most vivid expression in modernity in the poetry and illustrations of Blake, whose own mythical demiurge, Urizen, appears regularly as the embodiment of Blake's allegoric mode.

We know of Blake's explicit engagement with this "doctrine of the Gnostics," as he called it, from conversations recorded in the diary of his friend Henry Crabb Robinson. Here we find two Gods described: harsh Elohim is associated with the creator God of Genesis, and loving Jehovah is associated with Jesus.[61] Importantly, Blake's characterization of the God of the Old Testament, which we will explore in detail below, was heavily informed by deism and especially the work of Thomas Paine.[62] While deism shows up in

---

59. Paul Mendes-Flohr, "Gnostic Anxieties: Jewish Intellectuals and Weimar Neo-Marcionism," *Modern Theology* 35.1 (2019): 71–80.

60. Benjamin Lazier, *God Interrupted: Heresy and the European Imagination between the World Wars* (Princeton: Princeton University Press, 2010), 27.

61. See conversations recorded in Henry Crabb Robinson, "Extracts from the Diary, Letters, and Reminiscences of Henry Crabb Robinson," in Arthur Symons, *William Blake* (New York: Dutton, 1907), 263 and 298. Robinson here refers to the origins of this idea as the "Manichæan doctrine or that of the two principles."

62. For more on the relationship between the thought of Blake and Paine, see

150 JEWISH ALLEGORY IN EIGHTEENTH-CENTURY CHRISTIAN IMAGINATION

his poetry characterized negatively, Blake was also deeply shaped by its discourse, especially concerning the characterization of the Jewish scriptures as opaque, immoral, and allegorical. As Shabetai notes, Blake is "indebted to deist arguments specifically at moments when he is criticizing Judaism."[63]

Our most reliable source for Blake's engagement with deistic discourses on the Bible, and the relationship of this engagement with Blake's anti-Judaism, comes from his annotations to Richard Watson's *An Apology for the Bible*, which was itself a response to Paine's *The Age of Reason*. Blake engages the thought of both men in his annotations, blasting Watson for his defense of tradition with "Daggers and Poison" and praising Paine's bold arguments concerning outdated assumptions about biblical authorship and authority. Blake is not without criticism for many of Paine's own conclusions but asserts that "Paine has not Attacked Christianity. Watson has defended Antichrist."[64]

Energized by the debate between the Methodist bishop and the deist revolutionary, Blake expands on Paine's attacks against biblical traditionalism and carries the thread to anti-Jewish extremes not found in *The Age of Reason*. In response to the debate concerning God's command to conquer and destroy entire peoples, in which Paine found evidence of the Bible's depravity, Blake goes a step further and writes concerning the Jews:

> To me who believe the Bible & profess myself a Christian a defence of the Wickedness of the Israelites in murdering so many thousands under pretence of a command from God is altogether Abominable & Blasphemous. Wherefore did Christ come was it not to abolish the Jewish Imposture Was not Christ murderd because he taught that God loved all Men & was their father & forbad all contention for Worldly prosperity in opposition to the Jewish Scriptures which are only an Example of the wickedness & deceit of the Jews & were written as an Example of the possibility of Human Beastliness in all its branches.[65]

This is followed by a comparison between Paine and Christ, that the former strove against Christendom and the latter against the Jews. While

---

Robert N. Essick, "William Blake, Thomas Paine, and Biblical Revolution," *Studies in Romanticism* 30.2 (1991): 189–212.

63. Shabetai, "Question," 145.

64. William Blake, Annotations to *An Apology for the Bible* by R. Watson, in Erdman, *Complete Poetry*, 612.

65. Blake, Annotations, 614.

5. POETRY AND PREJUDICE: WILLIAM BLAKE'S ALLEGORIC GOD   151

Paine himself was critical of New Testament as well as Old Testament biblicism, Blake draws a sharp distinction characterizing the authors of the one as distinctly opposed to the other in the harshest of terms. The Jews, in Blake's rendering, are impostures and deceivers, falsifiers of the truth for the sake of their own material gain:

> That God does & always did converse with honest Men Paine never denies. he only denies that God conversd with Murderers & Revengers such as the Jews were. & of course he holds that the Jews conversed with their own [self will] <State Religion>which they calld God & so were liars as Christ says.[66]

And further:

> All Penal Laws court Transgression & therefore are cruelty & Murder[.] The laws of the Jews were (both ceremonial & real) the basest& most oppressive of human codes. & being like all other codes given under pretence of divine command were what Christ pronouncd them The Abomination that maketh desolate. i.e State Religion which is the Source of all Cruelty.[67]

These instances of explicit anti-Judaism found in Blake's private annotations are reflected in more muted tones in his public-facing poetry. For instance, the idea that Christ came "in opposition to the Jewish Scriptures" is reflected in *The Marriage of Heaven and Hell*, where angel and devil debate the relationship between the two Testaments. The angel opens in defense of the Bible's unity, while the protagonist devil preaches the disharmony of the Old and New Testaments:

> Thou Idolater, is not God One? & is not he visible in Jesus Christ? and has not Jesus Christ given his sanction to the law of ten commandments and are not all other men fools, sinners, & nothings?
> The Devil answer'd; bray a fool in a morter with wheat. yet shall not his folly be beaten out of him: if Jesus Christ is the greatest man, you ought to love him in the greatest degree; now hear how he has given his sanction to the law of ten commandments: did he not mock at the sabbath, and so mock the sabbaths God? murder those who were murderd

---

66. Blake, Annotations, 615.
67. Blake, Annotations, 618.

152   JEWISH ALLEGORY IN EIGHTEENTH-CENTURY CHRISTIAN IMAGINATION

because of him? turn away the law from the woman taken in adultery? steal the labor of others to support him? bear false witness when he omitted making a defence before Pilate? covet when he pray'd for his disciples, and when he bid them shake off the dust of their feet against such as refused to lodge them? I tell you, no virtue can exist without breaking these ten commandments: Jesus was all virtue, and acted from impulse: not from rules.[68]

The devil quotes Prov 27:22 for his illustration, with subtle changes from the King James Version, which reads "Though thou shouldest bray a fool in a mortar among wheat with a pestle, yet will not his foolishness depart from him." Blake adds the verb to "be beaten," which, when introduced to the Bible's metaphor, evokes a threshing floor. An adversarial relationship is celebrated here, as the Bible is turned against itself. Jesus's "impulse" is contrasted with the Decalogue's "rules" like the binary discussed above, which contrasts the immediacy of "Daughters of Inspiration" with the mediated "Daughters of Memory." Whatever restrictions the Ten Commandments impose, Blake contends, Christ overthrows and thereby liberates and paves the way for direct experience. And while this resonates, in many respects, with Luther's theology of the cross, which contrasted the legalism of the Old Testament with the grace of the New, Blake's version is more severe. His version vehemently rejects the allegedly repressive parts of the Bible and adopts the dramatic imagery of Marcionism by figuring the God of the Old Testament as a distinct deity, who both hides from and curses his own creation. And it is precisely the posture of hiding and cursing that characterizes the allegoric mode, all figured in Blake's Urizen.

Urizen, God of the Allegoric Mode

Blake's character Urizen appears in many of Blake's poems but is most prominently featured in his own prophetic work, *The Book of Urizen*, which is illuminated with images of a bearded and brooding God. Urizen sits upon and among his scriptures, eyes closed and face downcast, as one sitting in a graveyard. His name is most often interpreted to mean "your reason," echoing the accusatory "thou" employed in *The Everlasting Gospel* summarized above. *The Book of Urizen* is formatted to mimic the King James Bible, with chapter headings and double columns of text. Printed

---

68. Blake, *Marriage*, plate 23 in Erdman, *Complete Poetry*, 43.

5. POETRY AND PREJUDICE: WILLIAM BLAKE'S ALLEGORIC GOD 153

copies of the book vary in their layout and content, perhaps in imitation of the manuscript variations that so fascinated biblical scholars at the time. Such variations were also viewed as evidence of instability by the Bible's critics of the day, as we have seen. Blake's book embraces instability and provocation, presenting a distorted retelling of the book of Genesis in which the world is formed out of sin and rage and the first humans lament their own creation. The opening lines of its first chapter set the tone for Urizen's Genesis.

> Lo, a shadow of horror is risen
> In Eternity! Unknown, unprolific!
> Self-closd, all-repelling: what Demon
> Hath form'd this abominable void
> This soul-shudd'ring vacuum?—Some said
> "It is Urizen", But unknown, abstracted
> Brooding secret, the dark power hid.[69]

Abstracted and secret, then, *The Book of Urizen* recites the biblical stories in the allegoric mode. The poem traces the origin story of Urizen, the eternal priest, and Los, the eternal prophet. Los figures as a shadow-Christ, whose purpose is to grieve. The poem is punctuated with the phrase "Los wept" in imitation of Jesus in John 11:35. Urizen, then, is the shadow-Elohim, creator God and primordial lawgiver. But in Blake's version, the world emerges not in the rhythm of evening and morning "and it was good," but over the course of seven gruesome ages, each age concluding with the refrain "And a [first] Age passed over: / And a state of dismal woe."

The world is formed of the womb Urizen creates around himself, miserable and raging, as he attempts to hide from eternity. His body materializes part by part in the earth-womb he forms for his own occultation. The poem is saturated with images of nature in its most violent forms, swirling around his embryonic clod: fire storms, torrents, whirlwinds, sulfurous smoke, and oceans of void. These phenomenon project Urizen's tumultuous state of being and also his wickedness, formed as they are by "terrible monsters Sin-bred."[70] In addition to creating a world of misery and sin, Urizen produces laws made of iron using tools of measurement and division. His scriptures are both repressive and secret, containing

---

69. William Blake, *The Book of Urizen*, plate 3:1–7 in Erdman, *Complete Poetry*, 70.
70. Blake, *Book of Urizen*, plate 4:28 in Erdman, *Complete Poetry*, 72.

154   JEWISH ALLEGORY IN EIGHTEENTH-CENTURY CHRISTIAN IMAGINATION

rules and mysteries. "Here alone I in books formd of metals / Have written the secrets of wisdom / The secrets of dark contemplation." When Urizen finally emerges from his earth-womb, he finds his children have been unable to keep his iron laws and curses them. In despair he wanders away from them and forms a "Net of Religion" to torment the inhabitants of his world. Those of his children who remain at the poem's end leave the world of his creation in terms evoking the exodus: "They called it Egypt, & left it."[71] Egypt here parallels Swedenborg's Egypt with its correspondence to *scientia*, the mental activity associated with memory and separation.

In Blake we see the influence of the likes of Kant and Paine, who describe the God of the Old Testament as a legalistic, immoral, and vengeful God. The demiurge who had been banished by Marcion's accusers is resurrected in the name of revolution. Blake incarnates this God in Urizen, manifesting anxieties about the God of the Jews that originated in the second century. That he does so while also denouncing the sources of this critique in modernity—Enlightenment philosophy, deism and rationalism—is a move characteristic of Blake, whose sources of influence are also adversaries. The Bible itself is both object of ridicule and provider of powerful symbols and visions for Blake. By reading the Bible against itself and by drawing out a heretical, even diabolical, interpretation he attempts a fuller relevance and genius, but in the process discloses his alliance to an ancient and deep-seated prejudice. While professing liberation from the God of judgment, he nevertheless exposes himself as bound by inherited chains of bigotry.

As we have seen, Blake associates Judaism with the oppressive potential of religion. Judaism becomes an unfortunate symbol for everything he loathes in his own religion: legalism, moral superiority, hypocrisy, and the abuse of religious authority. Blake's discursive use of the figure of the Jew stands on the shoulders of countless Christians before him, but nevertheless stands out against the backdrop of his own emphasis on liberation. His anti-Judaism in the name of emancipation foreshadows the lamentable neo-Marcion trends of the years leading up to the World War II and, arguably, inclinations tucked into corners of Christian liberalism even today.[72]

---

71. Blake, *Book of Urizen*, plate 28:22 in Erdman, *Complete Poetry*, 83.

72. For a discussion of anti-Judaism in Christian feminism and liberation theology, as they relate to the discourse about the God of the Old Testament, see Amy-Jill Levine, *The Misunderstood Jew: The Church and the Scandal of the Jewish Jesus* (New York: HarperCollins, 2006), 167–90.

Blake's portrait of Judaism imitates his portrait of allegory. What one signifies for religion, the other signifies for poetry: they both stand in for a mode of repression, rules, and artificiality. Urizen, then, is Blake's Jewish, allegoric God. He is the God of codes in two senses: legal codes and cryptic codes. Decoding is what liberates. In depicting the God of the Jews this way, Blake exposes a discourse about Jews and allegory characteristic of the eighteenth century, even if his modality is conspicuously countercultural. The thread we have traced in cases from theological and philosophical contexts regarding the discursive connection between Jews and allegory is reflected again in the context of early Romanticism despite its counter-Enlightenment impulse.

Conclusion

This book has endeavored to highlight a feature of early modern Jewish-Christian relations that has thus far been overlooked, a feature that is significant for what it reveals about discursive constructions of the religious other during the Enlightenment era. We find in this period the reversal of the long-standing Christian trope of Jewish literalism in noteworthy instances of eighteenth-century public discourse, whereby Christians were recast as literalists and Jews as keepers of the Bible's allegories. This new framing of Jewish exegetical tendencies was constructed in both positive and negative terms. Jewish allegory was condemned by some and used as a negative foil in identifying a scientifically, philosophically, or historically legitimated Christian exegetical strategy. The allegories of the Jews, so conceived, were also appropriated by others for their utility in solving the problems of reading an ancient text in modernity. Not infrequently, these negative and positive framings were combined, and we find even in the work of a single individual both appropriation and condemnation. Examples from England, Sweden, and Germany have highlighted various facets of this phenomenon. The invented connection between Jews and allegory manifested in eighteenth-century ideas about biblical prophecy, conversion, eschatology, the semiotics of ancient languages and cultures, Old Testament religion, and even the borderlines of science and philosophy. Imagining Jewish allegory, therefore, was a project shared across disciplines, and we find evidence of its effects not just in formal biblical exegesis but also in theology, philosophy, and the arts. While this way of characterizing Judaism was a Christian innovation and responded primarily to intra-Christian debates about the Bible or religion more broadly, at least one noteworthy Jewish response, from Moses Mendelssohn, made use of the new paradigm to exhibit the multivocality made possible by a Jewish philosophy of language. Mendelssohn deemed inadequate Christian creedalism and the idea that religious language was singular and determined in its meaning. Combined, these examples not only tell the story

-157-

158   JEWISH ALLEGORY IN EIGHTEENTH-CENTURY CHRISTIAN IMAGINATION

of a sweeping ambivalence toward Judaism and allegory in the eighteenth century but also offer counternarratives of allegory's ultimate demise. Its entanglement with Christian and Jewish religious identity resulted in the continued presence of biblical allegory, even in contexts that professed to have left it behind with other premodern superstitions. Many of the figures surveyed in this study, even those who distanced their own methods from allegory, interpreted the biblical text against its most obvious sense or, rather, read the Bible to be saying *something else*.

Several factors have been identified in the preceding pages to explain the ambivalence toward allegory that characterized this age. Even while religious commitments remained intact for many Enlightenment thinkers, the effects of their critical impulse challenged traditional reliance on revealed truth. Empiricism and rationalism, in many ways rival siblings, formed an alliance in displacing long-held assumptions about the nature of God, God's world, and God's word. Truth was sought in human reason and in the experimental sciences with unprecedented confidence. Following late seventeenth-century philosophical meditations on the subject, such as John Toland's *Christianity Not Mysterious* (1696) and John Locke's *Reasonableness of Christianity* (1695), defenders of the faith were tasked with demonstrating the integrity of the Christian Bible and the logical sophistication of its message. English deists raised questions about biblical ethics, the accuracy of biblical prophecy, and the recourse to allegory on the part of apologists. In the German context, we find a new criticism of metaphysics, which paralleled the rejection of typological or spiritual-sense hermeneutical enterprises and resulted in the construction of philosophical or pragmatic alternatives, such as Kant's "moral sense." The Bible would survive the Enlightenment, it seemed to many, to the extent that it could produce meaning in accordance with the Enlightenment values of transparency and translatability.

Alongside efforts to fashion biblical religion as reasonable and moral, we find the impulse to divide the Bible into portions suitable for a modern Christianity and portions that should be rejected. William Whiston attempted to do this by identifying the parts of the Bible he believed to have been corrupted by allegorizing Jews and thereby sought to reconstruct an original, timeless text that made perfect, literal, sense. The simplest way to divide up the biblical texts, however, was to tear along the perforated lines between the Old and New Testaments. We find this impulse in Christian theological discourses and other disciplinary spaces as well. Kant and Blake, in many ways radically opposed aesthetically and

CONCLUSION   159

methodologically, were aligned in their characterization of the Old Testament as oppressive and corrupting. Judaism, in such a construction, came to stand in for those aspects of Christianity that had to be rejected going forward, and we find precisely in these constructions the rhetorical use of allegory. For Blake, the God of the Old Testament represented the allegoric mode of religious expression: contrived, vengeful, and pretentious. For Kant, allegory was viewed as the unfortunate consequence of needing to hold onto the Old Testament at all. Kant named typology "the subtle art of Jewish exegesis," and blamed it for enabling the troublesome retention of Jewishness in Christian thought and practice. We find therefore that despite their modernizing efforts, some eighteenth-century thinkers resurrected the ancient heresies of Marcion, whose negative characterization of the Old Testament was known for its rejection of biblical allegory.[1] Aligned with the deceiving, punishing God of the Old Testament, allegory was once again viewed as a sinister method for sanctifying the morally questionable parts of the Bible.

Efforts to convert Jews to Christianity, which accelerated in this era, can also be understood against the backdrop of this kind of characterization of the Old Testament and of allegorizing. Conversion came to be seen as a mirror process to reading the Bible cover to cover. The convert was imagined as the embodiment of a new covenant prefigured in the Hebrew language of their childhood. Such a narrative was often central to the convert's own self-identity, as we see in the case of Kemper, who understood his past life as a Jew to be an allegory for his Christian life in the present. This construction did not result so much in the elimination of the Old Testament but in its decoding. Such a view of conversion had a great deal in common with premodern notions, which emphasized the fulfillment of prophecy in efforts to convert as well as interpret scripture. However, it was Kemper's reliance on a matrix of kabbalistic symbols and talmudic metaphors to tell the story of his conversion that marks his case as unique to this context. It was precisely the allegories of his Jewish past that enabled the decoding of his journey as well as the decoding of the Bible for his Hebrew-language commentaries. The combination of his reliance on and at times harsh condemnation of Jewish sources reflected the Christian spaces he moved in, wherein Judaism was alter-

---

1. See Adolf Harnack, *Marcion: The Gospel of the Alien God*, trans. John E. Steely and Lyle D. Bierma (Eugene, OR: Wipf & Stock, 1990), 46–47.

160   JEWISH ALLEGORY IN EIGHTEENTH-CENTURY CHRISTIAN IMAGINATION

nately painted as foundational and adversarial and Jewish allegorizing as revelatory and deceiving.

The eighteenth century was a time of revolutions. Nearly every discipline and discourse of this century expressed a spirit of emancipation in one way or another. When it came to the Bible, some interpreters sought to leave behind conventional meanings and methods, shackled as they were to the orthodoxies of the past, in favor of some more immediate, liberative meaning. The preference for the plain sense of scripture that we find articulated by many in this era was not simply a preference for the scientific, historical, or linguistic tools associated with modernity; it was also an expression of liberation from aspects of religion perceived to be oppressive or backward looking. The spirit of emancipation that concerned the Bible was therefore directed at those things within Christendom that were associated with authoritarianism and false piety, and it was also directed at Jews and Judaism. The association between Jews and slavery, which began with the third-century interpretations of Paul's Epistle to the Galatians, was regurgitated in the eighteenth century, though in terms containing an inverse logic. Rather than slaves to the letter or the law, Jews represented enslavement to allegory, that is, to contrived or constricting ways of reading the Bible. According to this logic, reading the Bible Jewishly required strained decipherment. Reading the Bible plainly was the promise of Christian deliverance.

That this negative view of Jewish allegory could live alongside more positive formulations, whereby zoharic symbolism and early rabbinic story telling were probed for their potential to unlock the secrets of the cosmos or the relationship between the Old and New Testaments, is indicative of the sweeping ambivalences of this time. Sutcliffe writes that for certain Enlightenment thinkers "Judaism was powerfully associated both with obstinate particularism and with utopian universalism."[2] This ambivalence extended to biblical allegory itself, which was condemned as outdated, irrational, or contrived even by those whose own interpretations evoked the allegories of their ancestors under a different name. It was therefore a constellation of contrasting and contradictory ideas that occasioned the imagining of Jewish allegory and fostered its presence across disciplinary spaces.

---

2. Sutcliffe, *Judaism and Enlightenment*, 164.

CONCLUSION   161

While it is not within the scope of the present study to explore how
these ambivalences extended into the nineteenth and twentieth centuries,
a few suggestions for further inquiry can be made. How did the narrative of the rise of biblical literalism in Christianity shape the discourse
about Jews and Judaism going forward? The historical-critical impulses
of the nineteenth century were born of the dynamics summarized above.
We find in centers of learning during this time even more impassioned
efforts to determine the meaning of the Bible's original, historical sense,
setting aside notions of any divinely intended second meaning. And we
also find persistent notions concerning the divisibility of the Bible into
parts evincing Jewish corruption and parts deemed genuine. The anti-
Jewish foundations of Wellhausen's Documentary Hypothesis are by now
fully chronicled.[3] His suggestion that the parts of the Torah written last in
the Second Temple period imposed a rigid and legalistic "Priestly" overlay
replacing or perverting the innocent and ethical forms of earlier expressions exposed his own biases. His expressed desire to return, as it were, to
an earlier, pre-Jewish Bible by means of source criticism echoes the efforts
of Whiston 150 years earlier and belies notions that his was a historically
or scientifically objective enterprise.

It is difficult to overstate the influence of Wellhausen on perceptions
of what the Bible is and how it should be read over the last century and a
half. A brief look at one striking example of source criticism in a context
far removed from Wellhausen's own demonstrates not only its prevalence
but its functional relationship to anti-Judaism. In the trailblazing 1895 *The
Woman's Bible* we find yet another instance of dividing biblical material
between sources deemed genuine and sourced believed to have been corrupted by Jews. Organized under the leadership of the suffragist Elizabeth
Cady Stanton, *The Women's Bible* provided commentary on parts of the
Bible that either feature or conspicuously exclude women. In an entry on
the first three chapters of Genesis, contributor Ellen Battelle Dietrick uses
the tools of source criticism to divide the creation story into the "Elohistic"
account and the "Iahoistic" account, which she arranges in two columns

---

3. Jon Levenson, "The Hebrew Bible, the Old Testament, and Historical Criticism," in *The Hebrew Bible, the Old Testament, and Historical Criticism: Jews and
Christians in Biblical Studies* (Louisville: Westminster John Knox, 1993), 1–32. For a
summary of the scholarship on this matter and a critique of Wellhausen's reception in
professional biblical studies today, see Stacy Davis, "Unapologetic Apologetics: Julius
Wellhausen, Anti-Judaism, and Hebrew Bible Scholarship," *Religions* 12 (2021): 560.

162   JEWISH ALLEGORY IN EIGHTEENTH-CENTURY CHRISTIAN IMAGINATION

for the sake of their comparison. Under the first column she lists all the aspects of the Genesis story that affirm the equality of the sexes, including the creation of male and female simultaneously, descriptions of their freedom, and their joint dominion over the earth. In the second column she lists all the aspects that emphasize the primacy of the creation of Adam over Eve, a punishing God, or the subjugation of women generally. She then pronounces:

> Now as it is manifest that both of these stories cannot be true; intelligent women, who feel bound to give the preference to either, may decide according to their own judgement of which is more worthy of an intelligent woman's acceptance. ... My own opinion is that the second story was manipulated by some Jew, in an endeavor to give "heavenly authority" for requiring a woman to obey the man she married.[4]

Dietrick goes into some detail describing the process of textual distortion she imagines on the part of the Jewish scribes who reconstructed the texts of the Bible after the originals were lost by fire. She describes their efforts as careless and uncritical, prone to mistakes, but also as cunning and determined. Somehow the Bible emerges, in her reconstruction, completely divisible, such that the discerning reader can separate the corrupted portions from the original and thereby move into an enlightened and egalitarian Christian future purged of Judaized distortions.

We are left with the following questions for consideration: Do the examples of Wellhausen and Dietrick, which do not explicitly use allegory to characterize Judaism, nevertheless build on ideas about Jewish allegorizing from earlier generations in suggesting that Judaized language was imposed on the Bible with the effect of disfiguring the divinely intended, plain sense of scripture? Is there a line to be drawn between these developments and the rise of neo-Marcionism among German theologians that so alarmed Rosenzweig and Buber in the 1920s? Can we trace the more positive constructions of Jewish allegory on the part of Christian Hebraists and Christian kabbalists past the eighteenth century? How did the emergence of Jewish studies as an academic discipline shape Christian and Jewish ideas about the Bible's meaning and relevance? The greatest irony of the Bible's reception in the eighteenth century was that the pro-

---

4. Ellen Battelle Dietrick, "Comments on Genesis," in *The Woman's Bible* (New York: European, 1895), 18.

CONCLUSION   163

fessed preference for the plain sense of scripture was what revealed its own contradictions. The appeal to universal principles in scripture was made more cumbersome when interpretation was bound to the particularities of the letter. Has the present-day shift to contextual theology and contextual exegesis resolved this tension point? What are today's greatest ambivalences regarding language, scripture, history, and religious identity, and what do they owe to the rhetorical formulations of our ancestors, who coupled their perceptions of the religious other to the Bible's other sense?

Bibliography

Arkush, Allan. *Moses Mendelssohn and the Enlightenment*. Albany: State University of New York Press, 1994.

Assmann, Jan. *Moses the Egyptian: The Memory of Egypt in Western Monotheism*. Cambridge: Harvard University Press, 1997.

Augustine of Hippo. *On Christian Teaching*. Translated by R. P. H. Green. Oxford: Oxford University Press, 2008.

Axinn, Sidney. "Kant on Judaism." *JQR* 59.1 (1968): 9–23.

Batnitzky, Leora. *How Judaism Became a Religion: An Introduction to Modern Jewish Thought*. Princeton: Princeton University Press, 2011.

Beiser, Frederick. "Kant's Intellectual Development: 1746–1781." Pages 26–61 in *Cambridge Companion to Kant*. Edited by Paul Guyer. Cambridge: Cambridge University Press, 1992.

Benz, Ernst. "Swedenborg as a Spiritual Pathfinder of German Idealism and Romanticism." Translated by George Dole. *Studia Swedenborgiana* 11.4 (2000): 61–76; and *Studia Swedenborgiana* 12.1 (2000): 15–35.

———. *Swedenborg in Deutschland: F. C. Oetingers und Immanuel Kants Auseinandersetzung mit der Person und Lehre Emanuel Swedenborgs, nach neuen Quellen bearbeitet*. Frankfurt am Main: Klostermann, 1947.

Berman, David. "Anthony Collins and the Question of Atheism in the Early Part of the Eighteenth Century." *Proceedings of the Royal Irish Academy* 75.C (1975): 85–102.

Berman, Israel V., trans. and ed. *The Talmud: The Steinsaltz Edition*. 21 vols. New York: Random House, 1989–1999.

Berti, Silvia. "At the Roots of Unbelief." *Journal of the History of Ideas* 56.4 (1995): 555–75.

Blake, William. *The Complete Poetry and Prose of William Blake*. Edited by David Erdman. Rev. ed. Berkeley: University of California Press, 2008.

Bloom, Harold. *The Anxiety of Influence: A Theory of Poetry*. Oxford: Oxford University Press, 1997.

166 JEWISH ALLEGORY IN EIGHTEENTH-CENTURY CHRISTIAN IMAGINATION

———. *Blake's Apocalypse: A Study in Poetic Argument*. Garden City, NY: Doubleday, 1963.

Böhme, Helmut, and Gernot Böhme. "The Battle of Reason with Imagination." Pages 426–52 in *What Is Enlightenment? Eighteenth-Century Answers and Twentieth-Century Questions*. Edited by James Schmidt. Berkeley: University of California Press, 1996.

Boyarin, Daniel. *Border Lines: The Partition of Judaeo-Christianity*. Philadelphia: University of Pennsylvania Press, 2004.

Breuer, Edward. *The Limits of Enlightenment: Jews, Germans, and the Eighteenth-Century Study of Scripture*. Cambridge: Harvard University Press, 1996.

Breuer, Edward, ed. *Moses Mendelssohn's Hebrew Writings*. New Haven: Yale University Press, 2018.

Brown, Dennis. *Vir Trilinguis: A Study in the Biblical Exegesis of Saint Jerome*. Kampen: Kok, 1992.

Burnett, Stephen G. *Christian Hebraism in the Reformation Era (1500–1660): Authors, Books, and the Transmission of Jewish Learning*. Leiden: Brill, 2012.

Buchwald, Jed Z., and Mordechai Feingold. *Newton and the Origin of Civilization*. Princeton: Princeton University Press, 2013.

Carlebach, Elisheva. *Divided Souls: Converts from Judaism in Germany, 1500–1750*. New Haven: Yale University Press, 2008.

Cavendish, Margaret. *The Blazing World*. Edited by Sylvia Bowerbank and Sara Mendelson. Peterborough, Ont.: Broadview, 2000.

Chandler, Edward. *A Defence of Christianity from Prophecies of the Old Testament; Wherein Are Considered All the Objections against This Kind of Proof, Advanced in a Late Discourse of the Grounds and Reasons of the Christian Religion*. London: Knapton, 1725.

Chandler, Samuel. *A Vindication of the Christian Religion*. London: Chandler, 1725.

Coleridge, Samuel Taylor. *On the Constitution of the Church and State*. Edited by John Colmer. London: Routledge, 1976.

———. "The Statesman's Manual." Pages 417–54 in *Complete Works: With an Introductory Essay upon His Philosophical and Theological Opinions*. Edited by W. G. T. Shedd. New York: Harper and Brothers, 1853.

Colie, Rosalie L. "Spinoza in England, 1665–1730." *Proceedings of the American Philosophical Society* 107.3 (1963): 183–219.

Collins, Anthony. *A Discourse of the Grounds and Reasons of the Christian Religion*. London: 1724.

BIBLIOGRAPHY

———. *The Scheme of Literal Prophecy Considered; in a View of the Controversy, Occasion'd by a Late Book, Intitled, A Discourse of the Grounds and Reasons of the Christian Religion*. London: T. J., 1726.

Coudert, Allison P. "Leibniz, Locke, Newton and the Kabbalah." Pages 149–80 in *The Christian Kabbalah: Jewish Mystical Books and Their Christian Interpreters*. Edited by Joseph Dan. Cambridge: Harvard University Press, 1997.

Curteis, Thomas. *A Dissertation on the Unreasonableness, Folly, and Danger of Infidelity; Occasion'd by a late Virulent Book, Intitul'd A Discourse on the Grounds and Reasons of the Christian Religion*. London: Willkin, 1725.

Davis, Stacy. "Unapologetic Apologetics: Julius Wellhausen, Anti-Judaism, and Hebrew Bible Scholarship." *Religions* 12 (2021): 560.

Dawson, John David. *Christian Figural Reading and the Fashioning of Identity*. Berkeley: University of California Press, 2002.

Dwek, Yaacob. *The Scandal of Kabbalah*. Princeton: Princeton University Press, 2011.

Efron, Noah J. *Judaism and Science: A Historical Introduction*. London: Greenwood, 2007.

Efron, Noah J., and Menaḥem Fisch. "Astronomical Exegesis: An Early Modern Jewish Interpretation of the Heavens." *Osiris* 16 (2001): 72–87.

Eggerz, Niels. "Johan Kemper's (Moses Aaron's) Humble Account: A Rabbi between Sabbateanism and Christianity." *Continuity and Change in the Jewish Communities of the Early Eighteenth Century*. Vol. 12 of *Early Modern Workshop: Jewish History Resources*. Ohio State University. August 17–19, 2015.

Eskhult, Josef, "Andreas Norrelius' Latin Translation of Johan Kemper's Hebrew Commentary on Matthew: Edited with Introduction and Philological Commentary." PhD diss., Uppsala University, 2007.

Eskhult, Mats. "Rabbi Kemper's Case for Christianity in his Matthew Commentary, with Reference to Exegesis." Pages 148–64 in *Religious Polemics in Context: Papers Presented to the Second International Conference of the Leiden Institute for the Study of Religions*. Edited by Arie van der Kooij and T. L. Hettema. Assen: Van Gorcum, 2004.

Essick, Robert N. "William Blake, Thomas Paine, and Biblical Revolution." *Studies in Romanticism* 30.2 (1991): 189–212.

Esterson, Rebecca K. "Allegory and Religious Pluralism: Biblical Interpretation in the Eighteenth Century." *JBRec* 5 (2018): 111–39.

168 JEWISH ALLEGORY IN EIGHTEENTH-CENTURY CHRISTIAN IMAGINATION

——. "What Do the Angels Say? Alterity and the Ascents of Emanuel Swedenborg and the Baal Shem Tov." *Open Theology* 4.1 (2018): 414–21.

Favret-Saada, Jeanne. "A Fuzzy Distinction: Anti-Judaism and Anti-Semitism (An Excerpt from *Le Judaisme et ses Juifs*)." *Journal of Ethnographic Theory* 4.3 (2014): 335–40.

Force, James. *William Whiston, Honest Newtonian.* Cambridge: Cambridge University Press, 1985.

Frankfurter, David. "Jews or Not? Reconstructing the 'Other' in Rev 2:9 and 3:9." *HTR* 94.4 (2001): 403–25.

Frei, Hans W. *The Eclipse of Biblical Narrative: A Study in Eighteenth and Nineteenth Century Hermeneutics.* New Haven: Yale University Press, 1974.

Freudenthal, Gideon. *No Religion without Idolatry: Mendelssohn's Jewish Enlightenment.* Notre Dame, IN: University of Notre Dame Press, 2012.

Friedman, Jerome. "The Myth of Jewish Antiquity: New Christians and Christian-Hebraica in Early Modern Europe." Pages 35–55 in *Jewish Christians and Christian Jews: From the Renaissance to the Enlightenment.* Edited by Richard H. Popkin and Gordon M. Weiner. Dordrecht: Springer, 1994.

Frye, Northrop. *Fearful Symmetry: A Study of William Blake.* Princeton: Princeton University Press, 1947.

Funkenstein, Amos. *Theology and the Scientific Imagination from the Middle Ages to the Seventeenth Century.* Princeton: Princeton University Press, 1986.

Gadamer, Hans-Georg. *Truth and Method.* Translation revised by Joel Weinsheimer and Donald G. Marshall. New York: Continuum, 2004.

Gay, Peter. *The Enlightenment: An Interpretation. The Rise of Modern Paganism.* New York: Knopf, 1976.

Glaser, Eliane. *Judaism without Jews: Philosemitism and Christian Polemic in Early Modern England.* Basingstoke: Palgrave Macmillan, 2007.

Harnack, Adolf von. *Marcion: The Gospel of the Alien God.* Translated by John E. Steely and Lyle D. Bierma. Eugene, OR: Wipf & Stock, 1990.

Harrison, Peter. *The Bible, Protestantism, and the Rise of Natural Science.* Cambridge: Cambridge University Press, 1998.

Hanegraaff, Wouter. *Swedenborg, Oetinger, Kant: Three Perspectives on the Secrets of Heaven.* West Chester, PA: Swedenborg Foundation, 2007.

BIBLIOGRAPHY   169

Hegel, G. W. F. *Philosophy of Right*. Translated by S. W. Dyde. Kitchener, Ont.: Batoche, 2001.

Heinrichs, Michael. *Emanuel Swedenborg in Deutschland: Eine kritische Darstellung der Rezeption des schwedischen Visionärs im 18. und 19. Jahrhundert*. Frankfurt am Main: Lang, 1979.

Hooke, Robert. *Micrographia: Or Some Physiological Descriptions of Minute Bodies Made by Magnifying Glasses*. London: Martyn and Allestry, 1665.

Hudson, Wayne. *The English Deists: Studies in Early Enlightenment*. Brookfield, VT: Pickering & Chatto, 2009.

Huss, Boaz. "Translations of the Zohar: Historical Contexts and Ideological Frameworks." *Correspondences* 4 (2017): 81–128.

———. *The Zohar: Reception and Impact*. Translated by Yudith Nave. London: Liverpool University Press, 2016.

Idel, Moshe. "Kabbalistic Exegesis." Pages 456–66 in vol. 1.2 of *Hebrew Bible/Old Testament: A History of Its Interpretation*. Edited by Magne Saebø. Göttingen: Vandenhoeck & Ruprecht, 2000.

Israel, Jonathan. *Radical Enlightenment: Philosophy and the Making of Modernity, 1650–1750*. Oxford: Oxford University Press, 2001.

Jakapi, Roomet. "William Whiston, the Universal Deluge, and a Terrible Spectacle." *Folklore: Electronic Journal of Folklore* 31 (2005): 7–14.

Johnson, Gregory R., ed. *Kant on Swedenborg: Dreams of a Spirit-Seer and Other Writings*. Translated by Gregory R. Johnson and Glenn Alexander Magee. London: Swedenborg Foundation, 2002

Josephson-Storm, Jason Ānanda. *The Myth of Disenchantment: Magic, Modernity, and the Birth of the Human Sciences*. Chicago: University of Chicago Press, 2017.

Kant, Immanuel. *Anthropology from a Pragmatic Point of View*. Translated by Mary J. Gregor, The Hague: Nijhoff, 1974.

———. *The Conflict of the Faculties*. Translated by Mary J. Gregor. Lincoln: University of Nebraska Press, 1992.

———. "Conjectural Beginning of Human History." Pages 24–36 in *Toward Perpetual Peace and Other Writings on Politics, Peace, and History*. Edited by Pauline Kleingeld. Translated by David L. Colclasure. New Haven: Yale University Press, 2006.

———. *Dreams of a Spirit Seer*. Translated by John Manolesco. New York: Vantage, 1969.

———. *Lectures on Metaphysics*. Translated by Karl Ameriks and Steve Naragon. Cambridge: Cambridge University Press, 2001.

170 JEWISH ALLEGORY IN EIGHTEENTH-CENTURY CHRISTIAN IMAGINATION

———. "On the Common Saying: 'This May Be True in Theory, but It Does Not Apply in Practice." Pages 61–92 in *Kant: Political Writings*. Edited by Hans Reiss. Translated by H. B. Nisbet. Cambridge: Cambridge University Press, 1991.

———. *Religion and Rational Theology*. Translated and edited by Allen W. Wood and George Di Giovanni. Cambridge: Cambridge University Press, 1998.

———. *Religion within the Limits of Reason Alone*. Translated by Theodore M. Greene and Hoyt H. Hudson. Chicago: Open Court, 1934.

———. *Träume eines Geistersehers, erläutert durch Träume der Metaphysik*. Leipzig: Reclam jun, 1880.

Kelley, Theresa M. *Reinventing Allegory*. Cambridge: Cambridge University Press, 2010.

Kemper, Johan. *Avodat ha-Qodesh*. MS Uppsala University Library, Heb. 26.

———. *Beriah ha-Tikon*, MS Uppsala University Library, Heb. 25

———. *Even Gilyon Matityahu*, MS Uppsala University Library, Heb. 32.

———. *Maṭeh Mosheh o Maḳel Ya'aḳov*. MS Uppsala University Library, Heb. 24.

———. *Unterthäniger Bericht An einen Hoch-Edlen und Hoch-Weisen Rath zu Schweinfurth von der wunderlichen Güte Gottes, welche Er, der Allerhöchste erwiesen mir armen Menschen, Mosi Aaron, einem durch Gottes Gnad bekehrten Rabbi, auß Crackau gebürtig, Nechst Angehengter demüthigen Bitt Ihm die heilige Tauff wiederfahren zu lassen*. Schweinfurt: Drechsler, 1696.

Klepper, Deeana Copeland. *The Insight of Unbelievers: Nicholas of Lyra and Christian Reading of Jewish Text in the Later Middle Ages*. Philadelphia: University of Pennsylvania Press, 2007.

———. "Literal versus Carnal: George of Siena's Christian Reading of Jewish Exegesis." Pages 196–213 in *Jewish Biblical Interpretation and Cultural Exchange: Comparative Exegesis in Context*. Edited by Natalie Dormann and David Stern. Philadelphia: University of Pennsylvania Press, 2008.

Knaller, Susanne. "A Theory of Allegory beyond Walter Benjamin and Paul de Man." *Germanic Review* 77.2 (2002): 83–101.

Kozyra, Wojciech. "Kant on the Jews and their Religion." *Diametros* 17.65 (2020): 32–55.

Kuntz, Marion Leathers. *Guillaume Postel, Prophet of the Restitution of All Things: His Life and Thought*. London: Nijhoff, 1981.

BIBLIOGRAPHY

Langmuir, Gavin I. *Toward a Definition of Antisemitism*. Berkeley: University of California Press, 1990.

Lazier, Benjamin. *God Interrupted: Heresy and the European Imagination Between the World Wars*. Princeton: Princeton University Press, 2010.

Legaspi, Michael C. *The Death of Scripture and the Rise of Biblical Studies*. Oxford: Oxford University Press, 2010.

Lessing, Gotthold Ephraim. "The Education of the Human Race." Pages 195–217 in *Literary and Philosophical Essays: French, German and Italian*. Translated by F. W. Robertson. New York: Collier, 1910.

———. *Philosophical and Theological Writings*. Edited and translated by H. B. Nisbet. Cambridge: Cambridge University Press, 2005.

Leland, John. *A View of the Principal Deistical Writers That Have Appeared in England in the Last and Present Century*. London: Dod, 1754.

Levenson, Jon. *The Hebrew Bible, the Old Testament, and Historical Criticism: Jews and Christians in Biblical Studies*. Louisville: Westminster John Knox, 1993.

Levine, Amy-Jill. *The Misunderstood Jew: The Church and the Scandal of the Jewish Jesus*. New York: HarperCollins, 2006.

Levine, Hillel. "Paradise Not Surrendered: Jewish Reactions to Copernicus and the Growth of Modern Science." Pages 203–25 in *Epistemology, Methodology and the Social Sciences*. Edited by R. S. Cohen and M. W. Wartofsky. Dordrecht: Reidel, 1983.

Librett, Jeffrey S. *The Rhetoric of Cultural Dialogue: Jews and Germans from Moses Mendelssohn to Richard Wagner and Beyond*. Stanford: Stanford University Press, 2000.

Liebes, Yehuda. "Christian Influences on the Zohar." Pages 139–161 in *Studies in the Zohar*. Translated by Arnold Schwartz, Stephanie Nakache, and Penina Peli. Albany: State University of New York Press, 1993.

Lindroth, Sten. "Emanuel Swedenborg (1688–1772)." Pages 50–58 in *Swedish Men of Science, 1650–1950*. Edited and introduced by Sten Lindroth. Stockholm: Swedish Institute, 1952.

Lowth, Robert. *Lectures on the Sacred Poetry of the Hebrews*. Translated by G. Gregory. London: Tegg, 1839.

Lucci, Diego. "Judaism and the Jews in the British Deists Attacks on Revealed Religion." *Hebraic Political Studies* 3.2 (2008): 177–214.

———. *Scripture and Deism: The Biblical Criticism of the Eighteenth Century British Deists*. Bern: Lang, 2008.

Mack, Michael. *German Idealism and the Jew: The Inner Anti-Semitism of Philosophy and German Jewish Responses*. Chicago: University of Chicago Press, 2003.

———. "Law, Charity and Taboo or Kant's Reversal of St. Paul's Spirit-Letter Opposition and its Theological Implications." *Modern Theology* 16.4 (2000): 417–41.

Martens, Peter W. "Revisiting the Allegory/Typology Distinction: The Case of Origen." *JECS* 16.3 (2008): 283–317.

Mendelssohn, Moses. *Jerusalem: Or on Religious Power and Judaism*. Translated by Allan Arkush. Lebanon, NH: Brandeis University Press, 1983.

———. *Moses Mendelssohn: Selections from His Writings*. Edited and translated by Eva Jose. New York: Viking, 1975.

———. *Moses Mendelssohn: Writings on Judaism, Christianity, and the Bible*. Edited by Michah Gottlieb. Translated by Curtis Bowman, Elias Sacks, and Allan Arkush. Lebanon, NH: Brandeis University Press, 2011.

Mendes-Flohr, Paul. "Gnostic Anxieties: Jewish Intellectuals and Weimar Neo-Marcionism." *Modern Theology* 35.1 (2019): 71–80.

McGinn, Bernard. "Cabalists and Christians: Reflections on Cabala in Medieval and Renaissance Thought." Pages 11–34 in *Jewish Christians and Christian Jews: From the Renaissance to the Enlightenment*. Edited by Richard H. Popkin and Gordon M. Weiner. Dordrecht: Springer, 1994.

Möhler, Johann Adam. *Symbolism: Exposition of the Doctrinal Differences between Catholics and Protestants as Evidenced by Their Symbolical Writings*. Translated by James Burton Robertson. New York: Crossroad, 1997.

Morris, Max. "Swedenborg im Faust." *Euphorion* 6 (1899): 491–501.

Newton, Isaac. *Prolegomena ad lexici prophetici partem secundam in quibus agitur De forma sanctuarij Iudaici*. Ms. 434. Translated by Michael Silverthorne. The Newton Project. December 2013. https://tinyurl.com/SBL6706a.

Nirenberg, David. *Anti-Judaism: The Western Tradition*. New York: Norton, 2013.

Ocker, Christopher. *Biblical Poetics before Humanism and Reformation*. Cambridge: Cambridge University Press, 2002.

O'Higgins, James. *Anthony Collins: The Man and His Works*. The Hague: Nijhoff, 2012.

BIBLIOGRAPHY 173

Poole, William. *The World Makers: Scientists of the Restoration and the Search for the Origins of the Earth*. Oxfordshire: International Academic Publishers, 2010.

Price, Enoch S. "The Curricula in Swedenborg's Student Years." Published serially in *The New Philosophy* 34–38 (1931–1935).

Raine, Kathleen. *Blake and the New Age*. London: Allen & Unwin, 1979.

Rauer, Constantin. *Wahn und Wahrheit: Kants Auseinandersetzung mit dem Irrationalen*. Berlin: Akademie Verlag, 2007.

Ravven, Heidi. "Maimonides' Non-Kantian Moral Psychology: Maimonides and Kant on the Garden of Eden and the Genealogy of Morals." *Journal of Jewish Thought and Philosophy* 20.2 (2012): 199–216.

Reichert, Klaus. "Christian Kabbalah in the Seventeenth Century." Pages 127–47 in *The Christian Kabbalah: Jewish Mystical Books and Their Christian Interpreters*. Edited by Joseph Dan. Cambridge: Harvard University Press, 1997.

Resnick, Irevn. "The Falsification of Scripture and Medieval Christian and Jewish Polemics." *Medieval Encounters* 2.3 (1995): 344–80.

Robinson, Henry Crabb. "Extracts from the Diary, Letters, and Reminiscences of Henry Crabb Robinson." Pages 251–306 in *William Blake* by Arthur Symons. New York: Dutton, 1907.

Roche, Michel de la. *Memoirs of Literature*. London: R. Knaplock, 1722.

Rose, Paul Lawrence. *German Question/Jewish Question: Revolutionary Antisemitism in Germany from Kant to Wagner*. Princeton: Princeton University Press, 2014.

Rowland, Christopher. *Blake and the Bible*. New Haven: Yale University Press, 2010.

Ruderman, David B. *Connecting the Covenants: Judaism and the Search for Christian Identity in Eighteenth-Century England*. Philadelphia: University of Pennsylvania Press, 2007.

———. *Jewish Enlightenment in an English Key: Anglo-Jewry's Construction of Modern Jewish Thought*. Princeton: Princeton University Press, 2001.

———. *Jewish Thought and Scientific Discovery in Early Modern Europe*. New Haven: Yale University Press, 1995.

Sacks, Elias. *Moses Mendelssohn's Living Script: Philosophy, Practice, History, Judaism*. Bloomington, IN: Indiana University Press, 2016.

Sadik, Shalom. "When Maimonideans and Kabbalists Convert to Christianity." *JSQ* 24.2 (2017): 145–67.

174　JEWISH ALLEGORY IN EIGHTEENTH-CENTURY CHRISTIAN IMAGINATION

Schmidt-Biggemann, Wilhelm. "Epochs and Eras." Pages 369–408 in *Philosophia Perennis: Historical Outlines of Western Spirituality in Ancient, Medieval and Early Modern Thought*. Dordrecht: Springer, 2004.

Schoeps, Hans Joachim. *Barocke Juden, Christen, Judenchristen*. Bern: Francke, 1965.

———. "Philosemitism in the Baroque Period." *JQR* 47 (1956): 139–44.

———. *Philosemitismus im Barock: Religions und Geistesgeschichtliche Untersuchungen*. Tübingen: Mohr, 1952.

Scholem, Gershom. "The Beginnings of the Christian Kabbalah." Translated by Debra Prager. Pages 17–51 in *The Christian Kabbalah: Jewish Mystical Books and Their Christian Interpreters*. Edited by Joseph Dan. Cambridge: Harvard University Press, 1997.

———. "Redemption through Sin." Pages 78–141 in *The Messianic Idea in Judaism and Other Essays on Jewish Spirituality*. New York: Schocken, 1995.

———. *Sabbatai Sevi: The Mystical Messiah*. Translated by R. J. Zwi Werblowsky. Princeton: Princeton University Press, 1976.

Seidman, Naomi. *Faithful Renderings: Jewish-Christian Difference and the Politics of Translation*. Chicago: University of Chicago Press, 2006.

Shabetai, Karen. "The Question of Blake's Hostility toward the Jews." *English Literary History* 63.1 (1996): 139–52.

Shear, Adam. "William Whiston's Judeo-Christianity: Millenarianism and Christian Zionism in Early Enlightenment England." Pages 93–110 in *Philosemitism in History*. Edited by Jonathan Karp and Adam Sutcliffe. Cambridge: Cambridge University Press, 2011.

Sheehan, Jonathan. *The Enlightenment Bible: Translation, Scholarship, Culture*. Princeton: Princeton University Press, 2005.

Shell, Susan Meld. "Kant and the Jewish Question." *Hebraic Political Studies* 2.1 (2007): 101–36.

Sigstedt, Cyriel Sigrid Ljungberg Odhner. *The Swedenborg Epic: The Life and Works of Emanuel Swedenborg*. New York: Bookman, 1952.

Snobelen, Stephen. "'God of Gods, and Lord of Lords': The Theology of Isaac Newton's General Scholium to the Principia." *Osiris* 16 (2001): 169–208.

Sorkin, David. *The Religious Enlightenment: Protestants, Jews, and Catholics from London to Vienna*. Princeton: Princeton University Press, 2001.

Spector, Sheila. *Wonders Divine: The Development of Blake's Kabbalistic Myth*. Lewisburg, PA: Bucknell University Press, 2001.

BIBLIOGRAPHY

Stanton, Elizabeth Caddy, "Comments on Genesis." Pages 14–67 in *The Woman's Bible*. New York: European, 1895.

Stengel, Friedemann. *Enlightenment All the Way to Heaven: Emanuel Swedenborg in the Context of Eighteenth-Century Theology and Philosophy*. Translated by Suzanne Schwarz Zuber. West Chester, PA: Swedenborg Foundation, 2023.

Stroumsa, Guy. *A New Science: The Discovery of Religion in the Age of Reason*. Cambridge: Harvard University Press, 2010.

Stuckrad, Kocku von. "Christian Kabbalah and Anti-Jewish Polemics: Pico in Context." Pages 1–23 in *Polemical Encounters: Esoteric Discourse and Its Others*. Edited by Olav Hammer and Kocku von Stuckrad. Leiden: Brill, 2007.

Sugirtharajah, R. S. *Asian Biblical Hermeneutics and Postcolonialism: Contesting the Interpretations*. New York: Orbis, 1998.

Sutcliffe, Adam. *Judaism and Enlightenment*. Cambridge: Cambridge University Press, 2003.

Swedenborg, Emanuel. *Arcana Caelestia: Principally a Revelation of the Inner or Spiritual Meaning of Genesis and Exodus*. Translated by John Elliott. London: Swedenborg Society, 1983–1999.

———. *Divine Love and Wisdom*. Translated by John C. Ager. West Chester, PA: Swedenborg Foundation, 1995.

———. *Heaven and Its Wonders and Hell*. Translated by John C. Ager. West Chester, PA: Swedenborg Foundation, 2009.

———. *Letters and Memorials of Swedenborg*. Edited and translated by Alfred Acton. Bryn Athyn, PA: Swedenborg Scientific Association, 1955.

———. *The Spiritual Diary*. Translated by Johann Friedrich Immanuel Tafel, John Henry Smithson, and George Bush. New York: Bush, 1846–1850.

Swinden, Tobias. *An Enquiry into the Nature and Place of Hell*. London: Bowyer, 1714.

Tafel, Rudolph Leonhard, ed. *Documents concerning the Life and Character of Emanuel Swedenborg*. London: Swedenborg Society, 1875.

Tambling, Jeremy. *Allegory*. New York: Routledge, 2009.

Tannenbaum, Leslie. *Biblical Tradition in Blake's Early Prophecies: The Great Code of Art*. Princeton: Princeton University Press, 1982.

Toland, John. *Christianity Not Mysterious*. London: Buckley, 1696.

Wamsley, Rachel. "Characters against Type: Conversion, Mise-en-Page, and Counter-Exegesis in a Seventeenth Century Purim Play." *Lias* 44.1 (2017): 59–88.

176 JEWISH ALLEGORY IN EIGHTEENTH-CENTURY CHRISTIAN IMAGINATION

Warburton, William. *The Divine Legation of Moses Demonstrated: On the Principles of a Religious Deist, from the Omission of the Doctrine of a Future State of Reward and Punishment in the Jewish Dispensation.* London: Gyles, 1738–1741.

Weiss, Judith. "Guillaume Postel's 'Idea of the Zohar.'" *Aries: Journal for the Study of Western Esotericism* 19.2 (2019): 248–63.

Whiston, William. *The Accomplishment of Scripture Prophecies: Being Eight Sermons Preach'd at the Cathedral Church of St. Paul in the year MDC-CVII.* Cambridge: Cambridge University Press 1708.

———. *Astronomical Principles of Religion, Natural and Reveal'd: In Nine Parts.* London: Senex and Taylor, 1717.

———. *An Essay towards Restoring the True Text of the Old Testament, and for Vindicating the Citations Made Thence in the New Testament.* London, Senex, 1722.

———. *The Literal Accomplishment of Scripture Prophecies: Being a Full Answer to a Late Discourse, of the Grounds and Reasons of the Christian Religion.* London: Senex and Taylor, 1724.

———. *A New Theory of the Earth, from its Original, to the Consummation of All Things, Where the Creation of the World in Six Days, the Universal Deluge, and the General Conflagration, as Laid Down in the Holy Scriptures, Are Shewn to Be Perfectly Agreeable to Reason and Philosophy.* London: Boyle, 1755.

———. *A Supplement to Mr. Whiston's Late Essay, towards Restoring the True Text of the Old Testament: Proving, That the Canticles Is Not a Sacred Book of the Old Testament; nor Was Originally Esteemed as Such, Either by the Jewish or the Christian Church.* London: Senex, 1723.

Whitman, Jon. "From the Textual to the Temporal: Early Christian 'Allegory' and Early Romantic 'Symbol.'" *New Literary History* 22 (1991): 161–76.

———. *Interpretation and Allegory: Antiquity to the Modern Period.* Leiden: Brill, 2000.

Williams, Megan Hale. "Lessons from Jerome's Jewish Teachers: Exegesis and Cultural Interaction in Late Antique Palestine." Pages 66–86 in *Jewish Biblical Interpretation and Cultural Exchange: Comparative Exegesis in Context.* Edited by Natalie Dormann and David Stern. Philadelphia: University of Pennsylvania Press, 2008.

Wistrich, Robert S. *A Lethal Obsession: Anti-Semitism from Antiquity to the Global Jihad.* New York: Random House, 2010.

Wolfson, Elliot. "Messianism in the Christian Kabbalah of Johann Kemper." Pages 139–87 in *Millenarianism and Messianism in the Early Modern European Culture: Jewish Messianism in the Early Modern World*. Edited by M. D. Goldish and R. H. Popkin. New York: Springer, 2001.

Wotton, William. *Miscellaneous Discourses Relating to the Traditions and the Usages of the Scribes and Pharisees in Our Blessed Savior Jesus Christ's Time*. London: Bowyer, 1718.

Yeats, W. B. *Essays and Introductions*. New York: Collier, 1961.

Zank, Michael, and Hartwig Wiedebach. "The Kant-Maimonides Constellation." *Journal of Jewish Thought and Philosophy* 20.2 (2012): 135–45.

Zhang, Longxi. *Allegoresis: Reading Canonical Literature East and West*. Ithaca, NY: Cornell University Press, 2005.

Zimmermann, Rolf Christian. "Goethes Verhältnis zur Naturmystik." Pages 333–63 in *Hermetische Tradition im wissenschaftlichen Fortschritt*. Edited by Antoine Faivre and Rolf Christian Zimmermann. Berlin: Schmidt, 1979.

ANCIENT SOURCES INDEX

Hebrew Bible

Genesis

1	7
1:26	66
3	98
28	65
30:9–11	10
44:18	79

Exodus

4	65
7	65

Numbers

21	65

2 Kings

15:20	59

Isaiah

7:14	30

Jeremiah

23:36	77

Ezekiel

37:4–5	81

Zechariah

8:19	95

Psalms

59	125
118:22	65

Ruth

2:12	64

New Testament

Matthew

1:22–23	30
8:26	64
21:42	65–66

Luke

2:30–32	56

John

1:1	57
11:35	153

2 Corinthians

3:4	81

Galatians

4:21–31	12

Revelation

2:9	148
3:9	148
14:4–6	142
14:10–11	24

Babylonian Talmud

Shabbat

116a	63

180 ANCIENT SOURCES INDEX

Sanhedrin
  39b   63
  97a   86

Modern Authors Index

Auerbach, Eric — 11, 84–85
Axinn, Sidney — 127
Baldwin, James — ix
Beiser, Frederick — 108, 118–19
Benz, Ernst — 107
Berman, David — 42–44
Berti, Silvia — 42–43
Bloom, Harold — 127, 132, 146
Böhme, Gernot — 105–6, 128
Böhme, Hartmut — 105–6, 128
Burnett, Stephen — 6
Carlebach, Elisheva — 51–52
Coudert, Allison P. — 57
Daniélou, Jean-Guenolé-Marie — 11
Dawson, John David — 11
de Man, Paul — 13, 135
Force, James — 25, 27
Frei, Hans — 8–9, 11, 42–43
Friedman, Jerome — 58–59
Frye, Northrop — 11, 13, 135–37, 141
Gay, Peter — 23
Hanegraaff, Wouter — 106–7
Harrison, Peter — 7–9, 12
Hudson, Wayne — 23, 42
Huss, Boaz — 55, 69
Idel, Moshe — 13
Israel, Jonathan — 23, 75
Johnson, Gregory — 109
Kelley, Theresa M — 136, 138–39
Klepper, Deeana Copeland — 2, 7
Knaller, Susanne — 13
Legaspi, Michael — 5
Lucci, Diego — 21–3
Mack, Michael — 120–24, 126, 128
Martens, Peter W. — 11

McGinn, Bernard — 55, 57
Nirenberg, David — 17
Ocker, Christopher — 5–6
O'Higgins, James — 42–43
Rose, Paul Lawrence — 123–24
Rowland, Christopher — 137, 146
Ruderman, David — x, 44–45, 75
Schoeps, Hans Joachim — 58, 60, 65
Seidman, Naomi — 6, 80, 82–85
Shabetai, Karen — 147–48, 150
Shear, Adam — 31–32
Sheehan, Jonathan — 5–6, 23
Shell, Susan Meld — 121–23
Spector, Sheila — 146
Stengel, Friedemann — 106, 115–16, 126, 129
Stroumsa, Guy — 5
Sutcliffe, Adam — 6, 31, 60, 160
Tambling, Jeremy — 135, 139
Tannenbaum, Leslie — 137–38
von Stuckrad, Kocku — 146
Wamsley, Rachel — 52–53
Whitman, Jon — 10–13, 138–39
Williams, Megan Hale — 3
Zhang, Longxi — 13
Zornberg, Avivah Gottlieb — x

Subject Index

Abraham, biblical figure
  in Blake's poetry, 131, 142, 147
  marking an era, 85, 124, 142
  sacrifice of Isaac, 99, 36, 124
  typological interpretation, 36, 68, 124, 147
Adam, biblical figure
  allegory for human development, 88–89, 98–99, 102
  and ancient wisdom, 57
  in Blake's poetry, 132, 142, 146
  feminist interpretation, 162
  Kadmon, 146
  marking an era, 85
allegory
  allegoric mode (Blake), 139–45, 149–55
  ambivalence, 1, 6, 10, 19, 45, 56, 97–98, 127, 133, 136–38, 158–60
  association with Jews and Judaism, 1–6, 14, 21–45, 67–68, 73–74, 124–25, 145–55, 157–63
  as conversion, 15, 36, 47–70, 159
  early Christian, 12, 31, 39, 124–25
  demise of, 6–13, 19, 24–31
  Greek, 11–13
  and memory, 139–40
  versus moral sense (Kant), 98–101
  neoclassical, 139
  rehabilitation of, 12–13, 61, 135–38
  versus symbol. *See* symbol
  versus typology. *See* typology
  versus vision (Blake), 10, 18, 131–35, 138–39

angels
  in Blake's poetry, 14345, 151
  compared to Adam, 88
  speech of, 105–6, 114, 117, 128–29
  Swedenborg's visions, 103, 105–6, 114, 117, 143
  as witness or guard, 24, 141
anti-Judaism, 2–6, 14, 17–19, 29–30, 39–41, 54–55, 67–68, 119–30, 145–55
anti-Semitism, 17–18
apocalypse
  final age, 26, 52, 58, 85–90
  judgment day, 102
  See also Revelation, book of
Arianism, 26, 31
Augustine, 2, 27, 99–100, 104, 137
Bahir (book), 55
Barry, James, 139
Bede, the Venerable, 85–86
Benjamin, Walter, 13
Benzelius, Eric, 48, 104,
Blake, William, 10–11, 18–19, 105, 131–55, 158–59
  Book of Urizen, The, 152–55
  Everlasting Gospel, The, 142–43, 152
  Jerusalem: The Emanation of the Giant Albion, 141–42, 146–47
  Song of Los, The, 141
  Marriage of Heaven and Hell, The, 143–45, 147–48, 151–52
  Vision of the Last Judgement, A, 131–32, 139, 147
Buber, Martin, 148–49, 162
Burnet, Thomas
  Telluris Theoria Sacra, 27–28

-182-

SUBJECT INDEX

Buxtorf, Johannes, the Younger, 3
Buxtorf, Johannes, 3–4, 31
  Lexicon chaldaicum, talmudicum et rabbinicum, 3
  Synagoga Judaica, 31
Canticles. *See* Song of Songs
cantillation, 81–82
Catholic converts and kabbalah, 58–59
Cavendish, Margaret, 4
Chandler, Edward, 37–39
Chandler, Samuel, 39–40
Charles XI of Sweden, 59–60
Coleridge, Samuel Taylor, 10–11, 133
Collins, Anthony, 14, 24, 32–45
  Discourse in Freethinking, 32
  Discourse of the Grounds and Reasons of the Christian Religion, A, 32–45
  Scheme of Literal Prophecy Considered, The, 38
Collins, William, 139
conversion, 47–72, 121
  and allegory, 15, 48–53, 69–70, 159
  in the Bible and Talmud, 63–64
  Christian efforts to convert Jews, 32, 40, 49–52, 53–54, 58–60, 71–72, 121, 147, 159
  and kabbalah, 54–59
  and messianism, 32, 49–52
  narratives, 49–53, 69–70
  and translation, 6, 65, 82
creation, story of, interpretation, 7–8, 26–28, 57, 66, 88, 99, 153–54, 161–62
Cranz, August Friedrich, 71–72, 90
Cudworth, Ralph, 27, 91
Curteis, Thomas, 39
David, biblical figure, 63–64
deism, 1, 8, 19–24, 27, 37, 40, 42, 133, 137–38, 147, 149–50, 154, 158
demiurge, 148–49, 154
  Urizen, 19, 133, 149, 152–55
  See also Marcionism
derush, 77, 105
Descartes, René, 22, 59, 114
Dietrick, Ellen Battelle, 161–62
Djurberg, Daniel, 61

Documentary Hypothesis, 161–62
Ecclesiastes, book of, 77–80
Eden, garden of, 57, 98–99, 132, 141
Egypt
  allegory for science, 140, 154
  association with allegory, 31, 41
  biblical, 41, 79, 140, 154
  as idolatrous, 31, 40
  See also hieroglyphics
epistemology, 9, 22, 74, 97, 103, 106–119, 128
Esther, book of, 52–53
externality
  external sense of Bible, ix–x, 17, 94, 104
  hell the external of heaven, 143
  of language, 78, 106
  Jewish, x, 2–3, 18, 104, 119–21, 129
  and memory, 116
  See also literalism
Feder, Johann Georg Heinrich, 112
fourfold sense (Christian *quadriga*), 55, 58
Galatians. *See* Paul
gematria, 58, 64–65
Greek
  allegory, 11, 13, 134
  biblical language, 57, 63, 142
Grotius, Hugo, 22
Harnack, Adolf von, 148, 159
Haskalah, 73–75. *See also Maskilim*
Hebrew
  Hebraism, Christian, ix, 1–2, 6, 8–9, 19, 24, 31, 44, 52–61, 68, 104–5, 128–30, 162
  theories of, 16, 22, 30, 40–42, 49, 77–83, 91–92
  wordplay, 29–30, 34–37, 49, 58, 63, 65–66. *See also* kabbalah
Hegel, Georg Wilhelm Friedrich, 89–90
hell
  in Blake, 142–45, 148, 151
  permanence of, 86
  scientific theories of, 24–25
  in Swedenborg, 105, 143–44

184 SUBJECT INDEX

Helmont, Francis Mercurius van, 59
Herder, Johann Gottfried, 110, 112, 115
Heunisch, Johann Friedrich, 50–51
hieroglyphics, 8, 71–72, 91–92
Hooke, Robert, 4
Hugh of St. Victor, 8
Ibn Ezra, Abraham ben Meir, 60, 80
inner/internal sense of scripture
    Christian interpretations of, ix, 58, 99,
      111, 116–17, 128, 144
    Jewish interpretations of, 72, 82, 87,
      94
    See also externality; spiritual sense
Isaac, biblical figure, 64
    figure for Jesus, 36, 68, 124
    sacrifice of, 36, 124–25
Jacob, biblical figure
    figure for Jesus, 68
    rod of, 49
    stone pillow, 65–66
Jerome, 2–3, 10, 104–5
Joachim of Fiore, 85–86
Joseph, biblical figure, 79
Judah, biblical figure, 79
Judah ben Bezalel Loew of Prague, 76
Justin Martyr, 66
kabbalah,
    "Antikabbalah" (Kant), 18, 97, 115,
      126–27
    Christian ideas about Jewish kabba-
      lah, 3–5, 34–36, 126–27
    Christian kabbalah, 9, 15, 19, 47–70,
      104–5, 145–46
    in Judaism, 13
    See also Zohar; Hebrew: wordplay
Kabbalah Denudata, 56–57
Kant, Immanuel, 17–19, 89–90, 97–130,
    133, 149, 154, 158–59
    *Anthropology from a Pragmatic Point
    of View*, 110–11, 123
    Lectures on Metaphysics, 100
    *De mundi sensibilis atque intelligibilis
    forma et principiis* (*On the Form
    and Principles of the Sensible and
    Intelligible Worlds*), 118

Kant, Immanuel (*cont*.)
    *Mutmaßlicher Anfang der Menschen-
    geschichte* (*Conjectural Beginning of
    Human History*), 98–99
    *Religion innerhalb der Grenzen der
    bloßen Vernunft, Die* (*Religion
    within the Limits of Reason Alone*),
    89–90, 100, 120–21, 125–26
    Streit der Fakultaten, Der (*The Conflict
    of the Faculties*), 97, 99–102, 124
    Träume eines Geistersehers (*Dreams
    of a Spirit Seer*), 102, 111–19, 122,
    126
kashrut, 31, 47–48
Kemper, Johan, 15, 47–70, 104, 130, 159
    Maṭeh Mosheh o Maḳel Yaʿaḳov (*Liq-
    qute ha-Zohar*), 47–49, 61–62, 67
    Meʾirat Einayim (*Even Gilyon Matit-
    yahu*), 62–67
    Purim play translation, 52
    Unterthäniger Bericht, 49–53, 69
kenosis, 127
Knobloch, Charlotte von, 109, 116
Knorr von Rosenroth, Christian, 56, 59
Leibniz, Gottfried Wilhelm, 22, 57, 91,
    93, 107–8, 126
Lessing, Gotthold Ephraim, 16, 76, 82,
    86–87, 95
literalism
    biblical, 17, 24–38, 80–81, 99–101,
      110–11, 128
    in Chinese literature, 13
    Christians as literalists trope, x, 1–9,
      25, 39, 45, 68, 72, 84, 96, 157–58,
      161
    Jews as literalists trope, x, 1–4, 20–21,
      41, 56, 68, 101, 104–5, 129, 157
    and science, 6–8, 14, 24–29, 37, 104
    See also externality
Locke, John, 22, 42–43, 57, 158
    Reasonableness of Christianity, 158
Lowth, Robert, 41–42, 137
    *Lectures on the Sacred Poetry of the
    Hebrews*, 41–42
Luther, Martin, 2, 10, 35, 80, 104, 152

SUBJECT INDEX

185

Marcionism, neo-Marcionism, 19, 133, 146, 148–49, 152, 154, 159, 162. *See also* demiurge
Maskilim, 76–77, 96, 122–23. *See also* Haskalah
Matthew, gospel, interpretation, 62–66
Mendelssohn, Moses, 15–17, 71–98, 112, 115–16, 121–22, 157
  "Biur Megilat Kohelet," 77–80
  Jerusalem, 72–73, 87–88, 90–96
  Sefer Netivot ha-Shalom (*Bi-ur*), 80–85, 88–89
miracles, biblical, 22, 27–28
Maimonides, Moses, 60, 76, 98–99
manuscript corruption, accusation against Jews, 14, 26, 29–33, 80, 161–62
Masoretic Text
  accusations against, 26, 29–30
  defense of, 73, 80–81
Messiah, messianism
  Christian, 27, 29–32, 36, 47, 56, 62, 64–66, 69, 85–86
  Jewish, 50, 74, 95
  Jewish, Christian ideas concerning, 38, 40, 50–52, 65, 69, 124
  prophetic texts interpreted, 27, 29–32, 36, 38, 43, 49
  See also Apocalypse; conversion
Metatron, 47, 68
Mishnah, Christian reading of the, 5, 34, 44
Modena, Leon, 5
Möhler, Johann Adam, 104–5
More, Henry, 27, 59
Moses, biblical figure
  in Blake's poetry, 131
  compared to Homer, 5, 90
  figure for Jesus, 64–65, 68
  Oral Torah, 81, 92
  receiver of Torah, 81, 92–93, 95, 116
  staff of, 49, 64–65
  veiled face, 71–72, 95
mysticism
  and allegory, 8, 10, 14, 29, 31, 33, 41–42, 101–2

mysticism (*cont.*)
  associated with Judaism, 1–5, 18, 34–37, 39, 41–42, 97–98
  excluded from metaphysics (Kant), 115–19, 122–23, 126–28
  of Joachim of Fiore, 85–86
  mystical interpretations, 1–2, 34–37, 41–42, 65–69, 85–86, 101–2
  of Swedenborg, 17, 103–7
  of Blake, 133–34
  See also kabbalah
Nathan of Gaza, 65, 69
Neoplatonism, 9, 60
Newton, Isaac, 7, 9, 14, 22, 25–27, 57, 108
Norrelius, Anders, 48, 54, 62, 68
Norrmannus, Laurentius, 60–61
Ockley, Simon, 5, 44
Oetinger, Friedrich Christoph, 112, 115
Old Testament
  God of vengeance trope, 19, 80, 90, 148–55, 159
  and infancy of humanity, 85–90
  negatively characterized, 40–41, 101–2, 119–20, 126–27, 129, 145, 148–55, 159
  New Testament integrity, 22, 26–41, 44–45, 48–49, 52–53, 57, 62, 64, 85–86, 101, 151, 158, 160
  study and interpretation of, 7, 22, 26, 60, 63, 103, 125, 127, 129
  and the Swedish monarchy, 59–60
Oppenheim, Moritz Daniel, 82
Oral Torah
  Christian interpretation of, 55–56, 62, 68
  in Mendelssohn, 92
Origen, 2, 10–11
Paine, Thomas, 149–51, 154
parables, 3, 68
partsufim, 65, 67
Passover, allegorical interpretation of, 41, 47
Paul
  comparison to Blake, 137
  Galatians' use of allegory, 2, 12, 160

186 SUBJECT INDEX

Paul (cont.)
as master of Jewish allegory, 36, 39
See also *kenosis*; spirit-letter opposition
Pentecost, Kant's interpretation of, 124–25
peshat, 55, 65–66, 68, 77–81, 105
Pfefferkorn, Johannes, 54
pharaoh, biblical figure, 79
Philo, 31, 105
philosemitism, 15, 32, 54–61
Pico della Mirandola, Giovanni, 54, 57–58, 146
Postel, Guillaume, 54–57, 62
primitivism
concerning early Christianity, 4, 26, 58
concerning Old Testament religion, 16, 120–21, 130
concerning paganism, 90, 137, 142, 144–45
concerning the Zohar and kabbalah, 5, 15, 54–59, 61
prophecy
of Blake, 137–38, 152–54
biblical, interpretation of, 7, 22, 26–38, 42, 49, 64, 158–59
false, 21, 50, 52
versus priesthood (Blake), 145
Protestantism
converts, 58–59
and kabbalah, 15, 59–61
literalism, 7–8, 58, 84
Reformation, 7–8
sola scriptura, 7
See also Martin Luther
Purim, play, 52–53
Rashi, 60, 65–66, 80
Ray, John, 8
remez, 64–66, 77
resurrection, 100–102, 125
Reuchlin, Johann, 54–55, 57
Revelation, book of, 37, 86, 131–32, 142, 148
Roche, Michel de la, 34–35
Rosenzweig, Franz, 148–49, 162

Ruth, biblical figure, 63–64
Sabbatianism, 65, 69
Schelling, Friedrich, 107
science
and biblical literalism, 3, 7–9, 14, 24–32, 45, 157
in Blake's poetry, 132–37
and Christian truth claims, 1, 7, 45, 59, 103, 107–8, 124, 158–61
Egypt as figure for science, 140, 154
and Judaism, 74–76
metaphysics, 17, 60, 75, 97–130, 158
scientific revolution, 6–9
Swedenborg, 103–4, 107–8
See also epistemology
Sefer Yetzirah, 55
sefirot, 55, 57
Septuagint, 26, 30
Shabbetai Tzvi, 50, 52, 65
Shimon bar Yochai, 55–56, 64
sod, 55, 65–66, 68, 77, 105
sola scriptura. See Protestantism
Song of Songs, 13, 30–31, 63
soul
immortality of, 79, 86, 100, 103–4, 108, 110, 113, 119
soul-body connection compared to scripture, 17, 93–94, 102–4, 117, 123
Spencer, John, 91
Spinoza, Baruch, 22, 27, 73, 76, 94–95, 121
spirits, communication with, 103, 110–19, 127–29
spiritual sense, 2, 6, 8, 17, 36, 67, 97, 103, 119, 158
spirit-letter opposition, 2, 81–82, 84, 95, 126
See also inner/internal sense
Surenhuis, Willem, 34–36, 42, 59
Swedenborg, Emanuel, ix–xi, 17–18, 97–130, 140, 143–44, 154
Arcana Coelestia (*Secrets of Heaven*), 102–5, 108, 111–16, 119, 126, 129, 140, 144
Divine Love and Wisdom, 140

SUBJECT INDEX

187

Swedenborg, Emanuel (cont.)
   Heaven and Its Wonders and Hell, 129,
     140, 143–45
   Spiritual Diary, 129
Swinden, Tobias, 24–25
symbolism
   versus allegory, 10–12, 84–85, 133–35
   Jewish, 16, 91–92, 130
   Kant, 110–11, 114, 117
   Newton, 25–26
tabernacle, 141
Talmud
   Christian views on, 3–4, 26, 29–30,
     34, 54
   Jewish study of, 76, 122
   in Kemper, 15, 47–53, 62–64, 66–69,
     159
Toland, John, 4, 43, 158
   Christianity Not Mysterious, 4, 158
Trinity, 7, 57, 66–67, 100, 102
typology
   biblical figures, 36, 65, 68, 88, 102
   in Blake's poetry, 138, 143
   demise/rejection of, 8, 14, 22, 29, 39,
     44, 124–25, 158–59
   developmental model of history, 16,
     85–86
   of Jewish-Christian relationship, 56,
     90, 101
   Kemper's self-identity, 49, 53
   versus allegory, 11
   See also Old Testament: New Testa-
     ment integrity
university
   Cambridge University, Whiston and
     Newton, 14, 25–26
   Kant's lectures, 100, 109–111, 119
   University of Cologne, Pfefferkorn, 54
   Uppsala University, 15, 47–49, 53–54,
     59–62, 69, 104
Wagenseil, Christof, 52
Warburton, William, 40–41, 91, 137
   Divine Legation of Moses, The, 40–41
Wellhausen, Julius. *See* Documentary
   Hypothesis

Whiston, William, 7, 14, 24–38, 44–45,
   73, 104, 128, 158, 161
   *Accomplishment of Scripture Prophe-
     cies, The*, 14
   *Astronomical Principles of Religion,
     Natural and Reveal'd*, 24
   *Essay towards Restoring the True Text
     of the Old Testament, An*, 28, 30
   *Literal Accomplishment of Scripture
     Prophecies, The*, 25, 30
   New Theory of the Earth, A, 28
Wolff, Christian, 107–8, 126
Woman's Bible, 161–62
Wotton, William, 5, 44
Yeats, William Butler, 131, 133–35, 137
Yiddish, 16, 52, 83
Zohar
   Christian kabbalah, 54–57
   Christian interest in, 5, 61, 69, 160
   Kember's commentary, 15, 47–50, 54,
     61–67
   Torah as unveiling maiden, 93
   See also kabbalah

Printed in the USA
CPSIA information can be obtained
at www.ICGtesting.com
LVHW041914070624
782645LV00002B/30